LA
unconventional

LA
unconventional

the men and women who did LA their way

by Cecilia Rasmussen

foreword by Kevin Starr, California State Librarian

"For my father, Francis McNamara,
and to the memory of my mother,
Ruth McNamara."

Los Angeles Times

Book Development Manager: Carla Lazzareschi
Contributing Writer: Amy Dawes
Copy Editor: Pat Connell
Design: Jeanine Colini Design Associates

ISBN 1-883792-23-1
Copyright © Los Angeles Times 1998
Published by the Los Angeles Times
Times Miror Square

First printing October 1998

Printed in the U.S.A.

Contents

Foreword

by Kevin Starr

Journalism is in a hurry. Day by day, week by week, year by year, newspapers subsume and preserve the multitudinous pageant of our time. In the files of our metropolitan newspapers are stored millions of telling details that would otherwise be lost to history.

Cecilia Rasmussen of the *Los Angeles Times* belongs to a distinctive branch of the journalistic profession: those who have mastered the files, otherwise known as the morgue. It is a special calling. The majority of us, first of all, would find ourselves overwhelmingly intimidated by the sheer bulk of the material accumulated, in the case of the *Los Angeles Times* across a sesquicentennial of reporting. And the majority of us, as well, would most likely have trouble making sense of it all: the millions of clips, the thousands of feet of microfilm, and new, the digital record of a great city and a great region pursuing its cumulative existence.

Professionally, Rasmussen has mastered the art of retrieving the past and making it relevant. For years, her solid background research has supported hundreds of in-depth *Los Angeles Times* articles. In the course of these investigations, moreover, Rasmussen found herself not only doing editorial research as a matter of information and statistics, she found herself in day-to-day contact with the living, breathing past as preserved in the clips. That encounter, in time, transformed her into an historian. Over the past decade and more the *Los Angeles Times* has to the delight of its readership run numerous historical columns by Rasmussen, each of them skillfully written and based on solid research. Cumulatively, these columns have touched upon just about every phase of Southern California life, from the Native American era to the recent past. In researching and writing these columns, Rasmussen has achieved a gallery of pointillist-realist portraits and images of people, places and events which, while presented in increments, constitutes an engaging chronicle of Southern California across three centuries of human existence.

Despite the diversity of her interests, Rasmussen again and again has returned to one intriguing theme amid the many articles she has written. That theme is the City of Los Angeles and, even more specific, the colorful and emblematic people who, for better and for worse, have added the story of their lives to the total and panoramic story of the City of Angels. And now, in *L.A. Unconventional: The Men and Women Who Did L.A. Their Way*, Rasmussen has brought these columns—and many others besides—into one fun-filled (and sometimes horrifying!) book.

Among other things, *L.A. Unconventional* will soon take its place alongside an increasing number of books about Los Angeles appearing over the past two decades: proof positive that historians have come more and more to recognize Los Angeles as a preeminent American (indeed world) city whose story, warts and all, must be told.

But while it is one of many books, *L.A. Unconventional* will also from the start, I predict, create its own space. Why is this? Because Rasmussen has gone back to the files and extricated the story of these types of people—bohemians, eccentrics, the off-beat, the bizarre, the marginal, even the criminal—whom history frequently forgets. In so many instances, the stories of such marginal figures, the unconventional who "did it their way" can recover for us the texture and patina of the past which are otherwise lost to statistics and social science.

It is almost a cliché to say that Los Angeles has had more than its share of eccentrics. Once and for all, Rasmussen proves that point. As delightful as her portraits are to read, however, they also contain within themselves fragments of a larger meaning. I have always believed that cities have DNA codes: clusters of traits from the founding time which remain throughout subsequent history. From the first, Boston was always an academic center, even in the 1630s; and New York was always eclectic, inclusive and aggressively commercial. In California, the San Francisco of the 1850s and the San Francisco of the 1990s share a persistent DNA code of classic urbanism and high self-regard.

As *L.A. Unconventional* suggests through its many well-written portraits, the City of Angels has always been a place for mavericks, eccentrics, outsiders. True, that tolerance for the unusual has sometimes made, say, the Los Angeles of the 1920s and 1930s into an American Gothic carnival. But on a deeper level, that tolerance has also across two centuries made welcome in the City of Angels those who, for positive or negative reasons, did not fit in elsewhere and were seeking a second chance. Rasmussen has written more than an interesting book. Within the format of popular history, she has added another chapter, another interpretation, to our ongoing understanding of the City of Angels.

Fearless Females

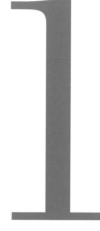

1

Doctor Dorsey, Medicine Woman

She was plagued by sexism, slowed by early poverty and ravaged by tuberculosis. But Rebecca Lee Dorsey persevered to become a pioneer: the first woman physician to practice in Los Angeles, and the first female gland specialist, or endocrinologist, in the world.

Rebecca Lee Dorsey, at age 80 in 1941. Courtesy of *Herald Examiner* Collection: LA Public Library.

Throughout a medical career that spanned almost seven decades, according to her unpublished memoirs, Dorsey delivered 5,000 babies, among them future California governor and chief justice of the Supreme Court Earl Warren. Authoritative medical libraries, including UCLA's Biomedical Library, say their collections contain nothing that contradicts Dorsey's claim to have:

- delivered the first baby born in a Los Angeles hospital.
- administered the city's first diphtheria vaccination.
- performed the area's first successful appendectomy and kidney removal.
- founded L.A.'s first nursing school.
- administered the first injection of adrenaline to prevent heart failure.

Born in Maryland two years before the Civil War, Dorsey was propelled through a difficult childhood by her stubbornness and appetite for learning. The war ravaged her father's fortune, and tuberculosis took her mother and several of her siblings. While baby-sitting for a neighbor's handicapped children, she decided their condition could have been prevented by the right doctor. She claims she determined then and there to become one. She was not yet five years old.

At seven, she persuaded a local storekeeper to send away for the medical school catalogues she loved to pore through. With no schooling provided by her financially strapped father, she ran away from home and "hired out for wages," a shocking move for a girl of genteel birth. From farm labor and housework she saved enough to educate herself, and when the time came, she won a scholarship to Wellesley College—the first female ever to do so.

No sooner had she graduated from Wellesley and entered Boston University School of Medicine than she began coughing up blood—the onset of the dreaded TB. Undaunted, she stuck with her studies and concealed her repeated cycles of fever, sweats and drastic weight loss.

Meanwhile, she had fallen in love with a law student, William Heard. But he was also stricken with TB, and his parents opposed a marriage. Heard headed to California and tried to persuade Dorsey to come, believing the dry and sunny climate would save their lives.

Dorsey believed the answer was in Berlin, where German physician Robert Koch had isolated the TB bacterium. With a loan from a U.S. senator and his wife who had befriended her, the newly graduated doctor traveled to Europe in 1883.

Between her letters of introduction and her boldness, she managed to become one of the first few people treated with Koch's serum. Another was chemist Paul Ehrlich, who would later develop a "magic bullet" treatment for syphilis. Both he and Dorsey recovered their health, and they became friends.

In Europe, Dorsey found herself exposed to world-class medical knowledge. She stayed on the continent for three years, studying with future Nobel Prize winners and some of the founders of modern medicine. In Paris in 1885, it was she who steadied Louis Pasteur's arm as he injected a small boy with a new serum for rabies. The boy recovered. (Later, in Los Angeles, Dorsey would amaze local officials when she used a serum to cure a series of rabid dogs that were terrorizing the city.)

She returned to the U.S., brimming with ideas. The senator wanted her to practice in Washington, but his wife feared that her progress would be slowed in so conventional a place. She argued, "You had better go to Los Angeles, where everything is still new and you will be accepted more readily."

In L.A., Dorsey reunited with Heard, who had recovered from TB. Both had busy careers, and Heard's soon took him out to Palm Springs, where he was appointed a judge of the Superior Court, the youngest man on the bench in Southern California. But his heart had been fatally weakened during his illness. Before they could announce their engagement, he died as Dorsey sat beside his hospital bed. She called him in her memoirs "the only man I ever loved," and she never married, though she did adopt a daughter. She called her Little Rebecca "the greatest source of comfort and happiness in my long life."

Dorsey's specialized knowledge of glands and hormones had made her

"You had better go to Los Angeles, where everything is still new and you will be accepted more readily."

the world's first female endocrinologist. But in L.A., she quickly learned that the less said about her work as it touched on the prevention of mental and physical birth defects by prenatal care, the better.

"For 40 years, I had to do my endocrinological work in secret," she said. "Madness was still taken to be the work of God, and anybody who said he would do anything to prevent it in children would have been run out of town."

In those days, nobody talked about ACTH, cortisone or adrenaline. "They did not know that much of such [birth defect] trouble originates in a lack of hormones in the placenta," Dorsey told a *Times* reporter in the 1950s.

She didn't let much of anything get between her and her patients. In 1886, as a raging smallpox epidemic was running its course, she hit the streets, going door to door to vaccinate people.

Dorsey made house calls every Wednesday morning in a red-wheeled buggy, heading west on Pico Boulevard toward Hollywood. Through binoculars, she searched over the orange trees for a flag flying upside down, which signified that one of her patients needed her services.

Children then were routinely stricken with measles, mumps and diphtheria. In an 1893 diphtheria epidemic, many doctors tried a new vaccine, but most did not know the correct dosage, and patients died. The vaccine was so distrusted that some doctors still threw cold

water into a child's face to get him to cough up diseased mucous membrane.

Dorsey, who had studied proper vaccine dosages, was called to save a dying boy. The boy's father was so anxious that he had to be tied down as Dorsey administered the city's first successful diphtheria inoculation. The boy's life was saved.

Not long afterward, she made headlines when she successfully removed a little girl's inflamed appendix, at a time when an appendectomy was almost as risky as appendicitis.

She was a mover and shaker at St. Vincent's Hospital, where she performed 90 percent of the surgeries. It was one of the rare hospitals to admit Latino, Chinese and black patients.

With trained nurses in great demand and short supply, Dorsey recruited 10 women and gave them free classes in first aid and basic nursing skills in the evenings, leading the way for the establishment of Los Angeles' first nursing school, at California Hospital in 1898. The next year, at St. Vincent's, she organized the city's first maternity ward.

Always politically minded, Dorsey eventually became a thorn in the side of the city council with her public health campaigns for better drinking water, food inspection and cleaner streets and playgrounds. When councilmen saw her coming, they literally shut the chamber doors.

Dorsey continued to practice medicine until the age of 95, when she suffered a broken hip in a fall. By the time she died a year later, in 1954, many of her celebrated causes and convictions had been vindicated.

Concealed Weapons, Arrested Ambitions

The Los Angeles Police Department was in its fourth decade before it was forced by city ordinance in 1910 to accept its first woman as a sworn officer. But while the hiring of Alice Stebbin Wells gave L.A. the distinction of having the first woman on a police force anywhere in the United States, the effect of Wells' breakthrough was not immediate.

It would take another 60-plus years before L.A.'s women in blue were finally issued holsters for the guns they had been carrying in their purses, and badges that called them police officers instead of policewomen.

Los Angeles had a force of 250 officers when Wells, a Pentecostal minister from the Midwest whose church work in the city had made her aware of the number of women and children involved in police cases, decided in 1910 that the rights and welfare of her charges would be better served if there were women on the police force. She took her petition to the mayor, the police commissioner and the city council, which passed an ordinance creating her unique position.

"How could you make an arrest?" she was asked by the authorities she petitioned for support. "I don't want to make arrests; I want to keep people from being arrested, especially young people," she answered.

Wells' appointment was of great interest to the media, generating interviews across the U.S. and in Europe and spurring the hiring of women officers in cities across the country.

But in L.A., they hardly knew what to do with her. She was accepted onto the force, but not into the fraternity. On her first day, the chief of police called her into his office. "Well, you wanted the job and apparently know what you want to do. Go ahead and do it!" he growled.

She got no uniform and no training. But she was issued a first-aid book and a badge and assigned to go after her juveniles, enforcing laws on loitering at dance halls, skating rinks, penny arcades and picture shows. Her office consisted of a spare courtroom that she had to vacate whenever a judge needed it, and the meetings she held there were often interrupted by scurrying rats.

But still, Wells made progress. She was deemed an asset to the department, and within 18 months, another female officer had been hired. Demands for speaking engagements poured in from other cities, and Wells took many lecture trips—at the forfeit of her salary—to promote her ideas on youth protection and preventing juvenile crime.

In 1915, only five years after she began her job, Wells organized the International Association of Police Women, and served as its president for five years. By 1916, policewomen were serving in at least 20 states and in such cities as New York, Chicago, Boston, Detroit, Washington, D.C., San Francisco, Toronto and London, which had followed L.A.'s example.

Meanwhile, a juvenile crime prevention program called the City Mother's Bureau had been organized in the LAPD. It was headed by one of the department's four female officers, Aletha Gilbert, whose job was to counsel children and elicit confessions—sympathetically—from young criminals. Not until 1963 was the City Mother's Bureau disbanded, its duties taken over by new social welfare agencies.

In 1916, shortly before officers began enlisting for World War I, Georgia Ann Robinson, 37, set aside her civic work to volunteer for the LAPD. Three years later, she became the city's first black policewoman when she was hired as a jail matron.

In 1925, five years after women across the nation got the vote, Police Chief R. Lee Heath decided it was time to expand training for the city's policewomen. He wanted them to become "quick on the draw and to shoot straight"—not an easy task

Women police officers receive instruction in the use of their service revolvers in 1925 after the chief said he wanted them to learn to become "quick on the draw and to shoot straight." The officers were required to carry the .45-caliber weapons in their purses.

On her first day, the chief of police called her into his office. "Well, you wanted the job and apparently know what you want to do. Go ahead and do it!" he growled.

when their department-issue .45-caliber revolvers were tucked inside their purses, as ordered.

Out on the shooting range, "jail matrons" whose job was to monitor female suspects had to compete with policewomen from the juvenile crime prevention department.

When the gun smoke cleared, Stella Wallen had scored 75 out of 100, and the competition became an annual event.

In 1937, Mable "Dee" Stevens—wearing the white nurse-style uniform the department ordered for its 39 policewomen—won the competition. When her scores were compared with those of the top male contestants, Mable Stevens had outpointed them too and was declared an arms expert.

As World War II pulled men out of the force, five women aviators, among them the legendary Bobbie Trout, were issued badges and hired

"for the duration" as aerial policewomen—bringing the number of females sworn in to 39.

Trout used the Police Academy for target practice and won second place in a competition shoot. But the women's services were never requested in an emergency situation. As the war heightened, the females on the force went to the aid of their country in the Women's Air Reserves, and the aerial policewomen faded into memory.

As the war ended in 1945, the "policewoman sergeant" rank was created. A year later, 20 women posed for photos as the first all-female graduating class of the Police Academy.

In uniforms of skirts and high heels, with purses serving as holsters, policewomen were finally assigned to radio cars and night-watch foot beats.

But their new assignments were short-lived. After two officers (male and female) were caught out of uniform and in flagrante in a police car, acting Police Chief Joseph Reed decided this "unseemly and foolish" behavior would cease.

It did, because he took every policewoman—but no men—off patrol. It would be almost three decades before male and female officers were allowed to work together again.

In 1972, still unable to protect, only to serve, more than a dozen female officers traded their uniform skirts for hot pants and paraded before a table of judges by a hotel pool for the title of "Miss Fuzz." A newspaper story listed the winner's measurements and called the beauty pageant "an arresting sight." The contest was sponsored by the Los

Alice Stebbin Wells. Courtesy of LAPD Historical Society.

By 1916, policewomen were serving in at least 20 states and in such cities as New York, Chicago, Boston, Detroit, Washington, D.C., San Francisco, Toronto and London, which had followed L.A.'s example.

Angeles Police Protective League, both to humanize female officers, it said, and to promote a movie by the same name.

At the time, women in the LAPD could not be promoted beyond sergeant or take on "full duties" of street patrol. Police Chief Ed Davis said he didn't think the department needed them, and that he would hire a female police officer "when the Los Angeles Rams hire a female linebacker."

Within a year, at least one female officer had had enough.

Fanchon Blake, a veteran of 23 years' service, filed a 1973 class-action suit alleging discrimination. Seven years later, her action spawned two historic consent decrees. One ordered the LAPD to recruit more women and minorities for "full-duty" policing. The other lowered the women's height standard—which had been a prime obstacle—by two inches, to 5 feet, 6 inches. (It later became 5 feet.)

Even before the consent decrees, the city council had ordered Davis to open up higher ranks to women, and to hire more women. Davis

Alice Stebbin Wells in 1910. Courtesy of Marc Wanamaker/Bison Archives.

called his solution "unisex": All LAPD cops were henceforth referred to as "officers."

Patricia Berry was the first to take up Davis' offer; she graduated with four new female recruits. In 1975, Connie Speck became the first female lieutenant, scoring the highest of all 285 applicants. By 1980 she was the LAPD's first female captain.

In 1997, Betty Kelepecz became the LAPD's first woman commander.

As for officer Wells, who started it all, she remained active for 35 years, retiring at age 72. By the time she died at her Glendale home in 1957, she had lived to see her cause to its fulfillment. The Glendale Police Department had 24 sworn women officers, and the LAPD had 1,513.

A Saint for The City of Angels

She was a tiny woman with a colossal faith. Twice rejected by Roman Catholic religious orders because of her physical frailty, this birdlike woman's perseverance and heroic virtue ultimately led the church to elevate her to sainthood.

Mother Frances Xavier Cabrini—America's celebrated "saint of immigrants"—left a part of her legacy in Los Angeles, today the foremost destination among a new generation of newcomers to the United States.

An immigrant from Italy herself, Cabrini in 1946 became the first American citizen to be declared a saint by the Catholic Church. The order of nuns she founded, the Missionary Sisters of the Sacred Heart, once offered care and assistance to foreign-born Angelenos via an orphanage, school, sanitarium and one of the city's first day-care centers.

Those institutions have long since vanished. But one relic of the sainted nun's presence remains: a small, one-room chapel nestled in the Verdugo foothills and open to the public as a shrine in her memory.

Maria Francesca Cabrini was born in Italy in 1850, the youngest of 13 children. She was orphaned at the age of 13. She became a schoolteacher and was director of an orphanage by age 30. Twice she tried to become a nun, but each time the church rejected her, fearing that her chronic poor health and small size would make her a liability.

Undaunted, Cabrini remained a devout Catholic and set about establishing her own order of nuns, the Missionary Sisters.

Meanwhile, millions of poor, illiterate Italians were emigrating to America, where they struggled to get a foothold. A bishop asked Cabrini to undertake a mission to help them. She left Italy with five other nuns and arrived in New York in 1889 to begin the service to immigrants that would become her life's work.

"God's gypsy," as she was affectionately called, would cross the Atlantic Ocean between Italy and America 30 times in 35 years. In New York, she found a community of 40,000 Italian Catholics served by only 19 priests and five churches. She immediately organized a school and then a hospital, which stands today as Columbus Hospital. In the lore of the great city, it was said that "the little nun could walk unharmed in places where even the police dare not go."

She later predicted to her sisters: "One day we shall have to go to California, where we will do something for the glory of God."

Mother Cabrini arrived in Los Angeles in 1905—the 25th anniver-

Mother Frances Xavier Cabrini in 1903

sary of the founding of the Missionary Sisters. Venturing deep into the city's slums, she found growing numbers of homeless children and decided to build them an orphanage. Her face jutting from a tightly wrapped wimple beneath a straw hat, she set out every morning with her old horse and dilapidated buggy looking for used and discarded lumber.

The children begged to help, and she taught them how to straighten the rusty nails that would be used in their future home. Children who were too unhealthy to work were given a dose of an herbal concoction that Cabrini formulated herself.

The orphanage, dubbed Regina Coeli ("Queen of Heaven" in Latin), rose up north of downtown in Angelino Heights, on what is now Hill Street at Cesar Chavez and Grand avenues. It was next to the Mexican and Italian communities Cabrini served, on land formerly owned by department store founder J.W. Robinson, who called it Edgemont.

Rock by rock (about 2,000 of them), Cabrini built a three-sided shrine to the Virgin Mary next to the orphanage. There she spent hours day and night deep in personal prayer.

In 1908, a year before she became a naturalized citizen, she personally supervised the construction of two more buildings at the orphanage. She lived on the site in a small room with an iron bed and a battered roll-top desk for six months at a time while visiting Los Angeles.

But Mother Cabrini had another dream: to fight the scourge of tuberculosis by building a "preventorium" where young girls at risk for the disease could be taught while in isolation. In 1912, after studying local maps, she founded the institution on 475 acres in Burbank. There, on barren land of "sand and snakes," Cabrini envisioned lush vineyards and orchards like those in her Italian homeland.

In 1916, after she had planted olive trees and grapevines and added a school and chapel, the Knights of Columbus built her a one-room shrine to the Virgin Mary, complete with stained-glass windows in whose light she prayed daily.

A Seattle woman recovered from an illness doctors had told her was terminal. She said Mother Cabrini had appeared to her in a vision, and a few days later she was well.

The next year, in Chicago, she fell ill and died while hospitalized. Her remains were enshrined in New York in the chapel at Mother Cabrini High School.

But even after her death, good works continued in her name, and miracles were attributed to her spiritual presence by the faithful who prayed to her.

In Los Angeles in 1919, the Missionary Sisters of the Sacred Heart opened one of the city's first day-care centers—Mother Cabrini Day Home—at 1406 Mateo St. Up to 110 babies and small children were cared for while their immigrant mothers labored in fruit-packing plants and their fathers worked in factories.

The nuns began a movement for her canonization in 1946. "Especially toward immigrants . . . did she extend a friendly hand, a sheltering refuge, relief and help," noted Pope Pius XII.

Several miraculous healings were attributed to Cabrini as evidence of her saintliness. In 1921, a New York schoolboy regained his sight after having been blinded as a newborn when his eyes were accidentally washed with an acid solution instead of silver nitrate. Nuns who had prayed to Mother Cabrini believed she had taken their prayers to God. In a separate incident in 1925, a

Seattle woman recovered from an illness doctors had told her was terminal. She said Mother Cabrini had appeared to her in a vision, and a few days later she was well.

But by 1970, enrollment at her order's Los Angeles school had dropped, and both it and the orphanage were closed. The Missionary Sisters of the Sacred Heart were ordered to pack up and head for other cities. Months later, most of their buildings in both Los Angeles and Burbank were destroyed by the Sylmar earthquake. Only the shrines remained untouched.

The stone grotto Cabrini built in 1906 sat sheltering the homeless until 1997, when it was dismantled and taken to a retirement center in Sunland, where the rocks sit in a pile waiting to be rebuilt.

The tiny shrine called the "place of healing" was moved in 1974 to St. Francis Xavier Catholic Church in Burbank, where it still stands on the upper grounds, open to the public on the first Sunday of each month from noon to 3 p.m. Next to it, the Italian Catholic Federation has added a library to house some memorabilia.

Woodbury University now sits on 22 acres called Villa Cabrini, and students cross paths where Mother Cabrini often gave spiritual solace and guidance.

She left behind 67 clinics, hospitals and schools that she founded throughout the world, but her compassion and devotion to immigrants was her greatest contribution to the people of Los Angeles for almost 70 years.

Getting Out the Vote: The West Coast Crusade Of Caroline Severance

Caroline Severance, standing at left, is joined by other leaders in the suffrage movement, including Susan B. Anthony, seated at right. The photo was taken to commemorate the founding of the Friday Morning Club in 1891.

Of all the fabled 19th-century women on whose shoulders the suffrage movement can stand, perhaps none was more famous in her own time and place—nor more forgotten by historians—than Caroline Severance.

Abolitionist, socialist, outspoken agitator and quiet instigator, Severance achieved a string of "firsts" that included founding the first women's political club in Los Angeles; the city's first Unitarian Church, city library and juvenile court; and California's first kindergarten.

She came to adulthood at a time when the washtub, water pump and cooking stove were the center of most women's lives. She worked with all those things, married a successful banker and had five children.

But she also led a voter registration drive that made Angeleno women a surprisingly influential force in the post-Victorian era. Her efforts prompted the men of California to give women the vote in regional and state elections in 1911, nine years before nationwide suffrage was instituted in 1920.

And although she could not cast a ballot until she was 91, she could look back on a life of service to her community and her gender.

A natural leader, she constantly challenged those around her to expand their horizons. When she invited the wife of renowned black scientist Booker T. Washington to a club meeting, several members walked out. Later, she called them on it, asking why they invited Mexican women into their homes but not black women.

Her efforts prompted the men of California to give women the vote in regional and state elections in 1911, nine years before nationwide suffrage was instituted in 1920.

In turn-of-the-century Los Angeles, when women were excluded from politics and policymaking, they generally crusaded for equality through such genteel means as social clubs and church groups. But Severance, driven by a street-level sense of right and wrong reinforced by her strong spirituality, organized her band of crusaders and formed the nucleus of the Friday Morning Club, whose pursuits included political issues and women's rights.

For this, she was jeered in the streets and prayed for in the pulpit. A newspaper editorial ridiculed her, claiming that "virtue and intellect are incompatible in women."

Among her friends were women who, shockingly, wore bloomers and rode astride. Nothing stopped this remarkable pioneer woman of Irish-Dutch descent; she believed that all things were possible for women if they organized.

Caroline Seymour was born in

New York in 1820, the oldest of five children whose family believed strongly in education. At 20, after her grades earned her valedictorian honors from Miss Record's Female Seminary, she began teaching and married Theodoric Severance. Staunch abolitionists, they later moved to Boston and devoted themselves to many reform movements.

In 1852, she attended a life-changing event: a gathering of leaders of the suffrage movement in Syracuse, New York. "I was thrilled and spell-bound by their eloquence and enthusiasm," she later wrote, adding that from then on she channeled her energies toward the cause of "social and civic justice and peace."

In 1853, after writing a paper on women's rights, Severance gained the attention of the press and was invited to speak before the all-male Cleveland Mercantile Library Assn. and the Ohio state Senate. Refined women of the time did not speak in public, and the boldness of

The Friday Morning Club's first clubhouse, on Figueroa Street between 8th and 9th streets. It was torn down later to make way for the club's second meetinghouse, shown here, which today is home to the Variety Arts Center.

Severance's words—combined with the diplomatic graciousness of her delivery—was both outrageously untraditional and captivating, especially to men.

Her fame became such that she once filled in for an ailing Elizabeth Cady Stanton, one of the nation's leading suffragists, speaking to a crowd of several hundred. In 1868, Severance's reputation grew when she organized the world's first incorporated women's club in Boston. Unmindful of her plain exterior, simplicity of manner and disregard for fashion, the group elected her president and thrived under her leadership.

After arriving in Los Angeles in 1875, intending to raise oranges with their son, the Severances bought 10 acres along West Adams Boulevard and built their home, El Nido, or "the nest," where a decade later members of the Unitarian Church would first worship.

At age 55, Severance opened the door for the women's suffrage movement in Los Angeles.

She had already drafted an equal rights resolution, which Susan B. Anthony proposed to the U.S. Senate in 1878. Almost 20 years later, in 1896, women's statewide suffrage

---

Severance and her colleagues weren't tight-lipped Victorian women who only cared about proper social credentials; these women waged a hard-nosed struggle for social change with a no-nonsense spirit and ability to cope.

---

was placed on the California ballot, but the amendment failed. Undaunted, Severance continued the crusade. After 15 more years, in 1911, the same measure passed. Ahead of women in many other states, California women could vote.

So at 91, the grande dame of clubs, who had spent a lifetime goading and irritating in the name of social justice, was finally driven by carriage "in a queenly procession," according to newspaper accounts, to the county registrar's office. According to some records, she was among the city's first registered female voters. (Charlotte Carlin, a deputy clerk in the county probate department in Long Beach, was the first to register, according to Cal State Northridge librarian Virginia Elwood-Akers.)

Severance and her colleagues weren't tight-lipped Victorian women who only cared about proper social credentials; these women waged a hard-nosed struggle for social change with a no-nonsense spirit and ability to cope. They opened club doors for more than the tinkling of teacups and parlor chatter. They leveraged the club into an arena of power, establishing a model kindergarten, juvenile hall, mental health clinic, cooking classes for the daughters of working mothers and a book club that became the city's first traveling library, along with launching a drive for the preservation of landmarks.

Severance had twice failed to get such a club to thrive, but in 1891 she finally succeeded, with a determined band of 87 women who had "the time, wealth, brains and culture—plus the ability to use them to the last inch of value."

Borrowing techniques from its members' businessmen-spouses, the Friday Morning Club formed a cor-

poration and issued stock, becoming the first women's group to finance and build its own clubhouse. In 1899 the group purchased two lots at 9th and Figueroa streets and built a two-story, Mission-style clubhouse graced with arches and patios. A quarter-century later, a newer, five-story clubhouse would rise on the same spot with the club's staunch motto engraved over the entrance: "In Essentials Unity… In Nonessentials Liberty…In All Things Charity."

Shortly before her death in 1914, Severance was asked to describe the perfect man. Her reply: "The ideal man would use a Chinese paper hankie [an old term for what became paper tissue], accept women as equals, and not wear a hat because it created too much heat in his head."

Bulldozers razed the Severance family home in 1950, providing land for the John Tracy Clinic, a free nonprofit educational institution for deaf children founded by Louise Tracy, the wife of actor Spencer Tracy, and named for their son. The Moreton Bay fig tree and garden that Severance planted more than a century ago remain, along with a plaque marking the historical site that pays tribute to the "Mother of Clubs."

In 1977, escalating costs and a declining membership forced the Friday Morning Club to sell its cherished landmark building, where poet William Butler Yeats once read and novelist Hugh Walpole spoke. Today about 20 active members instead meet twice a month at the Wilshire Country Club. The Friday Morning Club's venerable home, an Italian Renaissance structure that is now the Variety Arts Center, stands alone on the Figueroa Street block.

Civil Rights Borne On Eagle's Wings

Not just along Central Avenue, but throughout the city, people knew Charlotta Bass. For more than 50 years, she defended and taught and shaped Los Angeles' growing black community.

The pioneering African American journalist, who became a labor activist and the Progressive Party's candidate for vice president of the United States, arrived in Los Angeles in 1910, destined to become the editor of the *California Eagle*, the West Coast's oldest black newspaper.

She was 36 years old and had traveled here from Rhode Island. The job she found—and it would lead to her real career—was as a papergirl, collecting and selling subscriptions to a small black newspaper, the *Advocate*, that had been founded by John J. Neimore in 1879.

Charlotta Spears was soon promoted to helping Neimore in the office for $5 a week. And within two years of arriving in Los Angeles, she found herself at the helm of the newspaper following Neimore's death.

Spears stood, too poor to bid, when the newspaper was put on the auction block after Neimore died. A neighbor, a secondhand-

Charlotta Bass, left, with her niece in front of the *California Eagle* offices in 1944. Courtesy of Vera Jackson.

store dealer, saw her anxiety. "If I buy it for you, do you think you can earn enough to [re]pay me?" he asked.

Spears said yes. The neighbor bought it with a $50 bid and handed over the deed. With assets consisting of printing presses and $10, Spears began her long career with vision, courage and perseverance—and $150 in overdue bills.

The same year, Spears changed the paper's name and her own. The *Advocate* became the *California Eagle*, and she became Charlotta Bass, marrying Joseph B. Bass, a founder of the *Topeka Plain Dealer*, who had been caught up in the urge to "go West." This new

team plunged right in, beginning their fearless campaign against segre-gation and discrimination in Los Angeles.

In 1914, Bass worked with the NAACP and other groups to try to halt the making of D.W. Griffith's film *The Birth of a Nation*, which

Late one evening, eight white-hooded men showed up at her office. They cut their visit short when she pulled a gun out of a desk drawer and aimed it at them.

glorifies the Ku Klux Klan. Though filming went ahead, they did manage to persuade Griffith to cut some offensive scenes.

As World War I was raging two years later, Bass launched her own fight—this time for fairer voting rights.

In the November 1916 election, she noticed a tab on the right-hand corner of each ballot with instructions that said, "Tear off if the voter is a Negro." Black election board members raised objections, and no such tabs appeared again on Los Angeles ballots.

Racism showed itself on many fronts, and in 1925, after the *Eagle* printed a letter exposing KKK plans to take over Watts, the Knights of the White Camellia sued the paper for libel.

More than two months later—on June 25, in a crowded courtroom—the *California Eagle*, circulation about 12,000, beat the Klan and the libel charge. Soon Bass began getting anonymous, insulting phone calls. And late one evening, eight white-hooded men showed up at her office. They cut their visit short when she pulled a gun out of a desk drawer and aimed it at them.

By 1938, the *Eagle* was extending its reach, taking its message to the airwaves on a newspaper of the air. Its columns about sports, drama and opinion were heard six nights a week on station KGFJ.

On the eve of World War II, Bass and the *Eagle* began a campaign against restrictive housing covenants, part of the common "Jim Crow laws," and supported black families trying to move into all-white areas. Among them were Henry and Texanna Laws, who in 1936 had bought a house on 92nd Street in

On the eve of World War II, Bass and the Eagle began a campaign against restrictive housing covenants, part of the common "Jim Crow laws," and supported black families trying to move into all-white areas.

Watts, then a mostly white and Latino community.

When the Lawses decided they wanted to live in their own house, they found that the law said they could own it but not live in it. They took the matter to court. After eight years, the case reached the California Supreme Court, which upheld the couple's position—and the *California Eagle*'s. After the U.S. Supreme Court ruled on a similar case, restrictive real estate covenants became unconstitutional.

Bass was in her sixties one winter day in 1941 when she heard a report of bonfires, KKK leafleting and mock lynchings at Fremont High School. She went there to cover the incident and found herself counseling the angry students.

"Negroes just can't go to school with white people anymore. They can't mix," one student told her.

"Oh, I don't know," answered the woman who was walking picket lines to protest segregation in the aircraft industry. "I just can't make myself believe that you would object to my child going to this school or even living next door to you. I believe we would learn to like each other if we ever really became acquainted."

When police tried to stop their discussion, a white student protested, "We like this woman; she is giving us good advice." But police ordered the group to disperse.

Later, Bass reported in her memoirs, the students responsible for inciting the riot were forced to sign statements saying that in the future, they would recognize the rights of Negro students to attend their school.

By 1951, Bass had sold the *Eagle* to pursue new challenges.

She had already served as the first African American on the Los Angeles County grand jury, and she lost her first political campaign, a city council race, in 1945.

For 40 years, Bass had supported the Republican Party in her newspaper, but after World War II her thinking changed, and she joined the new Progressive Party. She ran for Congress in 1950 but lost to future Los Angeles mayor Sam Yorty. That same year, she was labeled a communist by some for traveling to a peace conference in Czechoslovakia.

She was 78 when she made her last run at politics, as the Progressive candidate for vice president—the first black female candidate for the office—on the ticket with presidential candidate Vincent Hallinan.

The *Eagle* folded in 1964, a year after the man who bought it from Bass became a judge. The newspaper's last home, on Central Avenue, is now an appliance store.

And the woman who made the paper's reputation died in 1969. She was 95.

Golden Age Survivor: China's Amelia Earhart

Katherine Sui Fun Cheung. Courtesy of Katherine Cheung collection.

Katherine Sui Fun Cheung stepped onto the world's stage and into its heart in 1932, as the first licensed Asian American aviator in the nation.

She was a barnstorming mother whose dreams reached greater heights when she began competing in air races and performing vertigo-inducing aerobatics for crowds at county fairs across the country.

Very few women then sought careers in such male-dominated professions, and aviation was a dangerous and new one at that. Cheung's success opened a window on a world in which the sky was, literally, the limit.

Speaking in her Thousand Oaks home in the spring of 1998, Cheung displayed the same feisty spirit she must have had at 28, when she was seated in her Fleet biplane.

"I wanted to fly, so that's what I did," the 93-year-old said with a twinkle in her eye. She is one of the few living reminders of the long-ago Golden Age of Aviation. "I always thought very positive. I never thought there was anything that couldn't be done."

Born in 1904 in Guangdong Province in China, Cheung began to spread her wings at age 17, when she headed for Los Angeles and an education in music at USC.

Her family soon followed her, and a few years later, her father, a produce buyer, taught her how to drive a car at Dycer airfield, located at 136th Street and Western Avenue. The car was fine, but it was the planes that transfixed her as she watched them take off and land. Her love affair with aviation had begun.

She dropped out of USC after three years and married her father's partner, George Young.

Reluctant to surrender her own identity, she kept her family name. Her nontraditional, supportive husband endorsed her decision. And later, when she donned pants and an aviator helmet, he didn't bat an eye.

For a time, she devoted herself to her husband and, later, her two daughters. But her interest in flying persisted. In 1932 she took to the skies for the first time when her pilot cousin offered to take her for a spin. She was hooked. Flying was as absorbing and exciting as music had been—but even more so. She impulsively signed up for lessons at $5 an hour with the Chinese Aeronautical Assn.

Accompanied by flight instructor Bert Ekstein, Cheung was always eager to climb into the cockpit and prove herself. After 12 1/2 hours, she soloed for the first time. Winning her wings soon thereafter, she soared into a new age, becoming the first Chinese woman in the nation to legally fly a plane, at a time when only about 200—or 1 percent—of licensed American pilots were women.

That began Cheung's solo career of aerobatics. With stunts like loop-to-loop, barrel rolls and inverted flying, she thrilled and terrified thousands of spectators at county fairs along the coast. Once she even flew an open-cockpit plane upside down with her two children strapped inside—but they nearly slipped from under their belts, and the experience scared her so much that she never repeated it.

Though Cheung set no speed or endurance records, she regularly entered competitive air races. In 1934 various members of the Chinese community, including actress Anna May Wong, chipped in to buy her a 125-horsepower Fleet biplane for $2,000.

The following year, Amelia Earhart's four-year-old international Ninety Nines club for women pilots welcomed Cheung into the group, and through it, she met such trailblazers as Charles Lindbergh, Roscoe Turner and Pancho Barnes. She flew thereafter with dozens of

---

Cheung was always eager to climb into the cockpit and prove herself. After 12 1/2 hours, she soloed for the first time. Winning her wings soon thereafter, she soared into a new age, becoming the first Chinese woman in the nation to legally fly a plane.

---

remarkable women, including Earhart, in a Glendale-to-San Diego race.

In 1936 she entered the Ruth Chatterton Derby from Los Angeles to Cleveland. Every contestant except Cheung was flying a new, high-powered plane supplied by manufacturers. Undaunted, she climbed aboard her little Fleet plane and took off, barely making it over the Rocky Mountains. Seven days later, not the least bit embarrassed, she landed in Cleveland, coming in next to last.

Flying to U.S. cities with large Chinese populations, she gave speeches that made flying seem less dangerous and more possible for others. "I don't see any reason why a Chinese woman can't be as good a pilot as anyone else," she would tell her audiences. "We drive automobiles—why not fly planes?"

In July 1937, while Cheung was still grief-stricken over the disappearance of her friend Earhart somewhere in the Pacific, the Japanese invaded her homeland in the horrifying genocide remembered as the Battle of Marco Polo Bridge.

In Asia, it was the start of hostilities that would escalate into World War II. China was desperate to boost its air force, and Chinese Americans were soon hoisting Cheung onto their shoulders, proclaiming her a heroine and role model while contributing $7,000 to buy a Ryan ST-A plane so she could fly to her homeland and teach Chinese volunteers how to fly.

But it wasn't to be. In a twist of fate, the same cousin who took her up on her first flight may have saved her life—tragically.

Members of the Ninety Nine's club, an early women's aviation group, meet in Los Angeles in the late 1930s. Katherine Sui Fun Cheung is standing second from left, immediately behind Amelia Earhart. Courtesy of Security Pacific Collection: LA Public Library.

Once she even flew an open-cockpit plane upside down with her two children strapped inside—but they nearly slipped from under their belts, and the experience scared her so much that she never repeated it.

Just as a group of Chinese American women was presenting Cheung with her new Ryan airplane at Dycer airfield—by then at Western Avenue and 94th Street—Cheung's cousin ran by, hopped into the plane and took off as a prank, literally stealing it from under her nose. Within moments, everyone watched as the plane crashed, killing him.

It was never determined whether the fault lay with the pilot or the plane, but many believed that Cheung would have suffered the same fiery end.

Unwilling to let his daughter continue to tempt fate, Cheung's father, on his deathbed, made her promise that she would never fly again. She did promise, but was back up in the air shortly after his death.

Soon after, she hung up her wings at age 38, after almost a decade of flying. Three things—Earhart's disappearance, her cousin's death and the promise to her father—haunted her.

Cheung is listed in the Smithsonian's National Air & Space Museum as the nation's first female Asian aviator. The Beijing Air Force Aviation Museum calls her "China's Amelia Earhart" and displays items recording many of her accomplishments.

Faded newspaper clippings, pictures and forgotten mementos of Cheung's life fill two small scrapbooks in her home. As for her memories, she still carries them in her heart and talks about them at the senior center where she plays bingo and dances up a storm—though not quite a barnstorm.

High Times Served At the Happy Bottom

One of the most unforgettable characters who ever barrel-rolled through the aviation world in Southern California was the legendary flyer and dude ranch owner Pancho Barnes.

Pancho Barnes

A tough-talking woman in a man's world, she turned her back on the conventions of her stuffy, privileged upbringing and set out on a lifelong quest for adventure, bringing excitement and high times to crowds of other people along the way.

"Imagination rules the world, and you've got to keep thinking of new things to do," she told one of her four husbands. As a woman born at the turn of the century, there were limits to the things she could do, but they were limits that she spent a lifetime defying.

She was born into a wealthy San Marino family, the granddaughter of inventor and entrepreneur Thaddeus S.C. Lowe, for whom Mt. Lowe above Pasadena is named.

After a childhood of ballet and finishing school, she entered an arranged marriage with an Episcopal minister, the Rev. Rankin C. Barnes. But she quickly grew bored and, on a whim, disguised herself as a man and joined the crew of a banana boat headed for Mexico. She was given the nickname "Pancho" on that adventure, and took it as her new identity.

Upon her return, she took her first flying lesson in 1928, and thereafter signified her rejection of her marriage, and high society in general, by buzzing her husband's Pasadena church during his Sunday sermons. A salty talker whose foul mouth could make other ladies blanch, she once said flying made her feel as excited as "a sex maniac in a whorehouse with a credit card."

She went on to become a renowned stunt pilot, flying in numerous movies, including Howard Hughes' *Hell's Angels,* and she organized the Motion Picture Pilots Association to win better conditions for movie aviators. She was a regular on the air race circuit and in 1930 stole away Amelia Earhart's airspeed record when she peaked at 196.19 mph.

Rarely seen in anything other than jodhpurs and a flight jacket, Pancho was described by one female detractor as having "a face like a mud fence." But despite her masculine ways, it was men she preferred, both as companions and lovers. She wed numerous times after she and Barnes were legally divorced in 1942; the marriage that took, to ranch foreman Eugene (Mac) McKendry, lasted 15 years.

And she knew what men liked. In 1947 she opened her dude ranch, The Happy Bottom Riding Club, and it became immensely popular with airmen from nearby Edwards Air Force Base (then called Muroc Army Air Base).

Built on 380 acres east of Rosamond in the Antelope Valley, the ranch featured a landing strip often used by celebrities, two bars, a dance hall and a motel. A swimming pool, restaurant, rodeo corral and civilian pilot training school were also on the property.

Barnes worked hard to make the club an oasis for servicemen. Her most popular move was hiring women to dance with the airmen. Despite posted rules for the conduct of hostesses, the atmosphere was loose, congenial and spontaneous. Former patrons remember impromptu underwater ballets that hostesses performed in the club's pool—in the nude. During its prime in the late 1940s and early 1950s, the ranch drew as many as 500 guests for its Wednesday-night dances.

A "Notice of Non-Responsibility" was posted at the club that read: "We're not responsible for the bustling and hustling that may go on here. Lots of people bustle, and some hustle. . . . But that's their business, and a very old one."

But when the Air Force decided it wanted to expand its base onto Pancho's land, it also decided that activities at the popular flyboy hangout were indeed its business. It charged Barnes with running a brothel and said she was guilty of undermining the morals of the men on the base.

But the Air Force could not prove its allegations. Barnes filed a $1-million suit against the Air Force, claiming it had insulted her by calling her a madam. A prolonged and expensive legal battle followed. Before it could be settled, a mysterious explosion in one of the club's main buildings set off a fire that destroyed most of the property.

The Air Force eventually settled with Pancho and awarded her almost

> ## A salty talker whose foul mouth could make other ladies blanch, she once said flying made her feel as excited as "a sex maniac in a whorehouse with a credit card."

half a million for her land, but it was the end of the club. Most of the money was spent on legal expenses, according to her husband, McKendry.

Still, the hundreds of ex-flyers and patrons who began gathering at Edwards in 1980 for the annual Pancho Barnes Memorial Barbecue remember the ranch and its owner as providing what one called "one hell of a good time."

Luminaries like Gen. Jimmy Doolittle and ace pilot Chuck Yeager were the club's first official members when Barnes made it private in an attempt to control membership. Doolittle is credited with coming up with its name after a long ride on a fresh horse. He said the ride gave him "a happy bottom."

In a now famous incident, Yeager and his wife Glennis took a couple of Pancho's horses out for a nighttime ride. Yeager fell from his horse and cracked two ribs. Only a select few, including Pancho, knew that Yeager's side was still smarting the following Tuesday, when he became the first pilot to break the sound barrier on October 14, 1947.

From then on, Pancho offered a free steak dinner to any pilot who could equal Yeager's feat and reach Mach 1.

When she and McKendry wed after seven years of living together,

Pancho, left, with Amelia Earhart following an air race in the early 1930s.

Pancho surrounded by her flyboy friends, including famed test pilot Chuck Yeager on her immediate left. Courtesy of Edwards Air Force Museum.

Pancho offered a free steak dinner to any pilot who could equal Chuck Yeager's feat and reach Mach 1.

they turned the event into a gala bacchanal. Pancho wore a dress for the first time in years, and Yeager gave the bride away before a crowd of 1,500 tipsy airmen and guests.

In the end, though, the couple's happy playground was reduced to ashes. Pancho and McKendry moved to a ranch in nearby Cantil

and tried to start a club again, but it never caught on. They eventually divorced.

Pancho moved to a ranch in Boron, where she devoted herself to a few dozen dogs and other animals. She battled cancer and underwent a double mastectomy. "It wore her out," McKendry remembers. In 1975 she was found dead in her small house. Some of the dogs, who'd been without water in the week since she'd passed away, had also succumbed. For a woman who'd spent her life at the center of a jolly crowd, it seemed a lonely end.

But she was not forgotten. Her former crowd held a memorial service a

week later, at the annual barnstormers' reunion in Lancaster. Jimmy Doolittle delivered the eulogy. A bust of Pancho was erected at Lancaster's Fox Field. A museum at Edwards includes relics from her life. A CBS-TV movie about Pancho aired in 1988. And the annual memorial barbecues, where a band plays on the foundation of what was once the club and old flyboys reminisce about the irrepressible spirit who once brought them together, attract more revelers each year.

Bricks, Mortar— And No Glass Ceiling

In 1927, when women had barely gained the right to vote, Mary Louise Schmidt believed she was capable of reaching great heights.

So she went as high as the law then allowed—12 stories, the altitude of the impressive Architects Building, which rose on the southeast corner of 5th and Figueroa streets under the supervision of one pregnant, determined entrepreneur.

Three times Schmidt had tried to round up enough architects to form the building's core group of tenants while at the same time corralling the financing, and twice the plan had collapsed. This time, construction proceeded—with a remarkable 90 percent of the space leased before the building was complete. Schmidt wanted to stimulate business by bringing architects, contractors and suppliers into the same convenient location, and at last the plan had become a reality.

It was a tribute to the perseverance and vision of the woman who, early on, became one of the most prominent movers and shakers in Los Angeles' male-dominated architecture and construction industries.

One of her 15 grandchildren— Keith A. McAllister, then at Amherst College—later wrote in a college essay, "Grammy built things—houses, businesses, a family—and more lastingly, the impression that anything might be possible. She created her own world, . . . where imagination seemed only the beginning. It was a powerful spell."

Schmidt had come into the world privileged, the daughter of a successful German American who ran a grocery importing business in Mexico. "Business is a matter of ideas," he taught her. "If one works, you run with it. If it fails, you go on to the next one."

Beautiful and charming, Mary Louise was hounded by suitors but had goals beyond marriage. "I want to make a million dollars," she often told her brother.

The Mexican Revolution sent her family back to California in reduced circumstances, but they were still able to enroll her at Smith, the upper-crust women's college in Massachusetts. But after the freedom she'd enjoyed in Mexico, Mary Louise found the school's rules and regulations appalling. After less than a year, she returned to L.A., convinced she could make her way without benefit of a degree.

She had a vast belief in action and a wide streak of confidence in herself. After taking a stenography course, she landed her first job in the office of Arthur Kelly, architect, and soon persuaded the young men in the drafting room to teach her how to draw. Kelly quickly put her in charge of an annual architectural show he was organizing, and she made a great success of it. She had a gift for persuasion and managed to convince the architects that each had the best space in the exhibit.

Schmidt had always been fascinated by architecture and would study the progress of buildings under construction, sketching the ones she liked. She designed and built a small house for her family,

Mary Louise Schmidt's Building Center on 3rd Street and Fairfax Avenue. Courtesy of Rosemary Silvey.

Mary Louise Schmidt. Courtesy of Rosemary Silvey.

Schmidt had come into the world privileged, the daughter of a successful German American who ran a grocery importing business in Mexico. "Business is a matter of ideas," he taught her. "If one works, you run with it. If it fails, you go on to the next one."

but thereafter, her activities were entrepreneurial. She never became a licensed architect.

Rather, she was a saleswoman with an intuitive knack for figuring out how to get an edge in business. Operating on the hunch that architects wanted a convenient way to find and choose building materials, she became the link between architects and the building materials industry. She opened the world's first building materials exhibit in the Metropolitan Building at 5th and Broadway. Manufacturers paid high rent for space (enough for Schmidt to gross the then-considerable sum of $600 a week), while architects paid nothing.

Her younger sister Florence, who worked for her at the exhibit, had writing skills, and Schmidt helped her get a job at the *Times*, writing the widely read Construction Primer column. Thereafter, Schmidt's endeavors got plenty of publicity in the *Times* under her sister's byline.

In 1921 she married a struggling Los Angeles attorney, Byron Dick Seaver, and began a family that would include four children. She continued to use her own name in business and kept on launching new projects.

After she launched and established the Architects Building in 1927, Schmidt went on to other projects. New ideas about the American house were evolving, and new materials and methods were being introduced. In 1936 Schmidt successfully launched her new idea: the California House and Garden Show.

In a lot on Wilshire Boulevard, six model houses were built by five architectural firms (Richard Neutra, Paul Williams, John Buyers, Arthur Kelly and Risley & Gould). The styles were Modern, French Classic, New Orleans Modern, English, and California Ranch, respectively. Landscape architects and interior designers donated their plans, and manufacturers provided free materials and $10 a month for upkeep.

Movie celebrities helped host the openings, and, helped by some of sister Flo's publicity, the exhibit was a great success, visited by 70,000 Angelenos its first year. But Wall Street wasn't cooperating. Two years after it opened, the California House and Garden Show succumbed to the Great Depression. The houses were raffled off, and the winners moved them off the leased property.

Schmidt had another idea. She had seen architects turned off by the calls of pushy salesmen who offered only one line of building materials. She decided to hire young women who would bring samples of an array of materials and type specifications for free.

Competitors howled, but that was too bad. Schmidt launched her business, which she called Architects and Engineers Service, putting her name and connections behind it and getting manufacturers to foot all the costs. She hired only women who were recent college graduates, and held them to strict standards of propriety. The service was a hit, and Schmidt's girls were in great demand. Soon a San Francisco office had to be opened, and then one in New York's Rockefeller Plaza. Then there were Seattle, Portland and Phoenix branches. Schmidt herself traveled from one to the other as supervisor.

Schmidt's final business venture came in 1957, when the 67-year-old grandmother realized another dream by opening the Building Center at 3rd and Fairfax (oilman Earl Gilmore had leased her the property). A one-story building in a garden setting, it became a meeting place for manufacturers and architects, decorators and landscape architects for almost two decades. With her typical entrepreneurial flair, Schmidt boosted attendance by offering low-cost buffet lunches and holding elaborate annual parties with Mexican food and music. She never did amass a million dollars, but by the time she died in 1974, her wealth and accomplishments were undisputed.

Our Gal Aggie: Tenacious Typist's Remarkable Rise

From the 1930s through the 1960s, there was almost nobody in city life who didn't know Aggie Underwood, one of the most colorful, commanding and demanding executives of Los Angeles' six competing daily newspapers.

Aggie Underwood, on the job at the *Los Angeles Herald-Express* in the late 1940s. Courtesy of the George Underwood Collection.

The first city editor of a major metropolitan newspaper anywhere in the country, Agness Underwood was notorious for knowing the private phone numbers, middle names and carefully guarded secrets of everyone from police chiefs to gangsters to movie stars.

She led the crew of the *Los Angeles Herald-Express* with a combination of toughness, professional know-how and sentimentality. At home, the mother of two cooked her special spaghetti not only for her kids, but for visitors who ranged from mobster Mickey Cohen to film heartthrob Errol Flynn. At work, when the temperature inside the old building reached 100 degrees, she ordered up cold beers for the entire news crew.

Named city editor of the *Herald-Express* in 1947, she would stand at her desk looking out over the crew like a galley slave master, shouting out orders or encouragement in a voice that, someone once said, "would seduce only a foghorn."

As testimony to her unparalleled position, the rival paper, the *Los Angeles Times*, named her its first Woman of the Year in the professional journalism category.

But for all the prominence and authority she acquired, Aggie didn't get an easy start in life. Neither the times she lived in nor her rough-and-tumble childhood hinted at the success that was to come.

She was born in San Francisco four years before the 1906 earthquake. Orphaned at 6, she was raised mainly in foster homes. Life was hard, and Aggie learned to fight back. To protect her little sister from an abusive foster mother, she poured a bottle of catsup over the woman's head. At age 16 she moved to Hollywood to live with an aunt, but came home one day after work to find her clothes wrapped in newspaper on the front porch and her aunt gone.

Aggie was living at a Salvation Army home and working as a waitress for $11 a week when she met Harry Underwood, a soda jerk, whom she married in 1920.

The couple had two children and struggled financially. In 1926, tired of adhering to a no-frills budget, Aggie went to work as a switchboard operator at the *Los Angeles Record*, the smallest of the city's dailies.

There she began to get the idea that she could do better at newsgathering than some of the men whose calls she was routing.

By looking over reporters' shoulders and practicing her four-finger typing for more than a year, she was ready for the city's biggest crime story of 1927—the grisly kidnapping-murder of a 9-year-old girl. The city editor dictated the story to Underwood because she could type fast—and she was hooked. After landing several exclusive crime interviews, the switchboard operator was put on the payroll as a reporter.

For nearly eight years, she bucked male reporters and scooped the rival

By looking over reporters' shoulders and practicing her four-finger typing for more than a year, she was ready for the city's biggest crime story of 1927—the grisly kidnapping-murder of a 9-year-old girl.

Herald Express. In 1935 the *Herald* hired her as its police and court reporter, with a $2 raise to $27 a week.

It was a time when women journalists were not admitted to the National Press Club, and female journalists were openly called "broads" by their hard-drinking colleagues. Still, newspapers competed fiercely for crime scoops and juicy gossip, and Aggie took to the competitive atmosphere with brio.

One of the first stories she covered was the still mysterious death of actress and comedienne Thelma Todd, whose body had been found in her parked car at her Malibu restaurant. After observing Todd's autopsy at the morgue, Underwood looked around at the bodies of dead men covered by white sheets and quipped: "Can you imagine what any of these guys would have given to be under a sheet with Thelma Todd?"

Aggie prided herself on christening murder cases with catchy names. In a moment of inspiration—and calculation—she dropped a white carnation on the body of a waitress who had been stabbed to death,

just to give the story a name: "The White Carnation Murder." When she told her photographer to take a picture of her creation, a cop objected—and Underwood smacked him with her purse.

Later she scored a scoop with her interview of a yacht tragedy survivor who had cannibalized her shipmates. She developed an enormous variety of friends and sources, including Cohen, who called her every time he landed in jail to give her an exclusive, and phoned when he was hungry for one of her spaghetti dinners.

Her command of the news business became so apparent that in 1947 she was named the first female city editor of the *Herald-Express*. Television was in its infancy, and the newspaper business in L.A. was at its peak. To scoop its rivals, the *Herald-Express* produced up to eight editions a day, and Underwood tried to make each one newsier and more entertaining than the last.

The journalism she served up was brewed for working-class tastes. Aggie loved a good crime story, and she expected her reporters to be no less aggressive or inventive than she was.

She was a handsome woman with a firm jaw and strong, clear eyes that could see through a reporter's lame excuses. Few had the temerity to lie to her. When things got too quiet in the city room, she fired off blanks from a pistol she stored in her desk drawer. A baseball bat also sat nearby to keep overzealous Hollywood press agents in line.

At a time when women journalists were scarcely recognized,

At home, the mother of two cooked her special spaghetti not only for her kids, but for visitors who ranged from mobster Mickey Cohen to film heartthrob Errol Flynn.

Underwood won scores of awards, ranging from Most Outstanding Woman in Journalism from the National Federation of Press Women to the rival *Times*' first Woman of the Year award. She was named in the first edition of *Who's Who of American Women* in 1959, and Ralph Edwards featured her on his national TV show "This Is Your Life."

E ven with all the recognition that finally came, she remained bitter at her early treatment by her bosses at William Randolph Hearst's newspapers. "I can't recall one Hearst executive ever saying 'nice work' over a story I'd covered . . . or even buying me an ice cream cone on my birthday. So help me."

In 1964, two years after the *Herald-Express* merged with the *Examiner*, the *Her-Ex* gang moved into the *Examiner* building at 11th Street and Broadway, and Underwood was kicked upstairs as assistant managing editor.

The lobby of the former *Herald Examiner* offices at 11th Street and South Broadway, as it was in 1981. The Mission Revival-style building was constructed in 1912 for publisher William Randolph Hearst. The architect was Hearst favorite, Julia Morgan. Courtesy of Bruce Boehner.

But for a woman who habitually returned early from vacations to get back to work, the inactivity was too much. For four years she wandered around like a "half-assed executive," she said. So after 33 years of service and increasing circulation for the Hearst papers, she retired. At her retirement party in 1968, the Hollywood Palladium was overflowing. Telegrams came in from mayors, senators, governors and President Lyndon B. Johnson. Bob Hope emceed.

Retirement didn't quiet her. In 1981 she filed a $110-million defamation suit against the publisher of *The Last Mafioso*, claiming she had been falsely portrayed in the book as having helped Cohen steal $1 million. A judge dismissed the suit, saying the statements were "mere opinions." Three years later a state appeals court granted a rehearing, but Underwood died in 1984 before the case was resolved. She was 81.

She said of her trade, "A good story is a good story. And you fill the holes with putty if you can't make it hold together."

A onetime employee of hers, the late *Times* columnist Jack Smith, elaborated. "Aggie always reminded me of an old rhyme that used to be painted on the wall of a doughnut shop at 8th and Olympic: 'As o'er life's road you roll / Keep your eye upon the doughnut, and not upon the hole.' "

Short-Lived Blooms On the Football Field

In an era when women athletes have made enormous strides in such sports as tennis, golf and basketball, it's difficult to remember how marginalized women's sports were as recently as 1973.

That was the year tennis star Billie Jean King won some respect for women by trouncing her strutting male challenger, 55-year-old Bobby Riggs, in a contest that drew unprecedented media attention.

In that condescending atmosphere, it's all the more remarkable that L.A.'s first women's pro football team—the L.A. Dandelions—sprang up and bloomed even as briefly as it did.

But when a Downey electrician named Bob Matthews advertised a chance for women to compete in a national league, these maverick spirits came out to play, bucking social pressures and general skepticism for the chance to don a yellow jersey with green numbers and try to make their hometown proud.

One was Gail Werbin, 27, a former member of the U.S. swim team who held a master's degree in cinematography from USC. "I always thought that If I had been a man, I would have played football," said Werbin, who was 5 foot 8 and 140 pounds. "And then lo and behold, I didn't have to be."

The team drafted 31 players, who ranged in age from 19 to 34. There was a business owner, a secretary, an auto mechanic, a housewife.

They had one thing in common: They loved to play sports, including football.

They ranged in size from 5 foot 11 and 215 pounds to 5 foot 1 and 118 pounds. Most had grown up playing football with their brothers or in high school "powder puff" games. Chances at a career in pro sports were slim to none.

"I always wanted to play pro ball of any kind," said Vicki Garcia, a 5-foot-5, 165-pound native of Lincoln Heights, who became the quarterback. "I started playing football in my neighborhood when I was nine."

The players kept their day jobs but turned out for long hours of training at various high schools, including Hollywood and Fairfax, charging through tackling drills and lung-burning distance runs. The prize would be a chance to compete

The Los Angeles Dandelions train by running laps at Fairfax High School in 1974.

in the nascent Women's Football League, which had already fielded teams in Dallas, Detroit, Columbus, Ft. Worth and Toledo.

The brother of the owner of the Dallas team, Bob Matthews persuaded five other men to form an owner's group for the Dandelions and put up $50,000 to join the league. The team's coach was Bob Edwards, a former college football player who taught at Los Angeles City College.

The men's theory was that women's tackle football would provide a profitable new form of family entertainment. That was a miscalculation, and over the league's three-year life span the Dandelions considered it cause for celebration when they drew enough fans to pay the cost of renting the stadium and hiring officials.

The team's first game turned out to be something of an omen. On July 22, 1973, the Dandelions took the field at Long Beach Veterans Stadium and lost, 16-12, to the Dallas Bluebonnets. A local television crew turned up to cover the opener but spent most of its time filming voluptuous actress and professional spotlight-stealer Edy Williams, who turned up wearing her signature attire—bikini top and hot pants.

The Dandelions went on to finish the short season at an encouraging 2-1, but drew dauntingly small crowds of 500 to 2,000 to their Sunday games. "An idea whose time has not come," said a *Times* sportswriter after the season ended with a $12,000 loss for the owners.

But the team kept training as if they were on the verge of filling the Coliseum, even as they continued working at other jobs. That was mandatory, since salaries in the league topped out at $25 a game.

Dandelion halfback Charlotte Raff watches the action during a 1973 game against the Bluebonnets.

Linebacker Barbara Patton, who once cracked the helmet of an opponent with a hit, would later see her son, linebacker Marcus Patton, receive a $2-million bonus when he signed with the Washington Redskins.

Despite the discouraging atmosphere, the Dandelions were soon joined by another L.A. team, the California Earthquakes (known briefly as the California Mustangs), whose home field was Citrus Junior College in Glendora. The Earthquakes held workouts at La Salle in Pasadena—an all-boys high school at the time, which nonetheless boasted on its marquee that it was the "Home of California Earthquakes Women's Pro Football."

Both teams opened their locker rooms to male reporters, but none had the temerity to enter. Sportswriters who did cover the team focused on the novelty angle,

asking about things like what kind of chest protection they required on the field. ("Heavily padded bras," admitted Matthews.)

Off the field, the players battled the stereotypes and stigmas that still attach themselves to women's athletics.

"It gets boring having to explain that you're not a freak, or crazy," said halfback Sue Davidson, a 21-year-old P.E. major at Long Beach State who joined the team because she "wanted to learn a new sport."

Then, as now, particular prejudice was directed at lesbian athletes, and the Dandelions were at pains to declare their heterosexual orientation. "People blow it out of proportion because they're already looking for it; they want to label you," said Davidson.

But in the end, what people didn't want to do was watch women's football.

In 1974, when the Dandelions defeated the California Mustangs 20-0 in a home-team showdown at the Santa Ana Bowl, 1,500 fans showed up. The owners needed to sell 4,000 tickets just to break even. That same weekend, the Rams played before a crowd of 70,000.

After three years, the owners threw in the towel, and the women's brief opportunity for gridiron glory was over. But the league persisted in many of the other cities that had teams.

"A dandelion is a pretty spring flower that you cannot kill," Matthews' wife had told him when she suggested the name for the team.

And though the players may not have realized it, they helped sow the seeds for a women's sport movement that would one day blossom beyond all expectations.

Past Imperfect

A Genuine Lady-Killer

By 1936, Los Angeles had become acquainted with a fair number of wicked wives and homicidal husbands. But for sheer viciousness and utter lack of conscience, none of these miscreants compared with "Rattlesnake" James, an arrogant, smooth-talking Southerner who earned his nickname from the method of attempted murder that finally led to his capture.

Robert S. James, a.k.a. "Rattlesnake" James

His real name was Major Raymond Lisenba, but on the run from trouble, he took to calling himself Robert S. James. His most notorious crime—and long overdue arrest—came during his fifth marriage, when he used two rattlesnakes to poison his pregnant wife and then, when she didn't die fast enough from the snakebites, drowned her in the bathtub.

Although this was the murder that put James' neck at the end of a hanging rope at San Quentin, testimony at his trial uncovered details of four previous marriages—and the heinous acts that had ended them. And so it was not without ample evidence that the newspapers took to calling him a "genuine lady-killer."

Born in 1895, the redheaded boy was an Alabama share-cropper's son who was yanked from school and sent to work in the cotton fields at the age of eight. His sister's husband intervened and sent the boy to barber school. Though competent with a shave and a haircut, the youth found himself always far more interested in women.

After his first two marriages ended in divorce, he escaped to North Dakota and changed his surname to James.

Despite his beady eyes, greased-back hair and sallow complexion, James held an inexplicable appeal to women and often kept several mistresses at once, regardless of his marital status. But it took a lot of money to impress so many ladies. So James turned to a means of support far more lucrative than barbering: life insurance fraud.

In 1932 he opened his own barbershop and married wife no. 3, a beautiful blonde named Winona Wallace, whom he persuaded to buy life insurance that would pay him $14,000 in case of her accidental death.

On their Colorado honeymoon, he hit his wife on the head with a hammer, then sent her down a cliff in their car. He reported the tragedy to the toll-road operator, claiming that his wife had lost control of the car and gone over the edge, while he

---

Despite his beady eyes, greased-back hair and sallow complexion, James held an inexplicable appeal to women and often kept several mistresses at once, regardless of his marital status. But it took a lot of money to impress so many ladies. So James turned to a means of support far more lucrative than barbering: life insurance fraud.

Witness Charles Hope lies on table during 1936 trial as prosecutor Russell Parsons thrusts Hope's foot into a box to demonstrate how murder defendant Robert James, right, put his wife's foot into contact with two rattlesnakes.

had survived by jumping from the moving vehicle. However, when the two of them ran to the scene, they found Winona injured but alive, spared from a fatal plunge by a protruding boulder some 150 yards down the cliff.

His wife recovered and, fortunately for James, had no memory of the incident. But James, growing annoyed at Winona's good health, lifted her out of her sickbed at home and drowned her in the bathtub. The death was judged accidental, and James collected the insurance money. (These details didn't surface until James' "rattlesnake" trial, when investigators interviewed the toll-road operator, who remembered being suspicious of James' story because his shoes were not muddy and there were no footprints in the soft dirt of the hillside.)

The newly flush widower then headed home to Alabama, where he seduced his 18-year-old niece, the daughter of the man who had set him up in barber school, and swept her away to Los Angeles, where he set up a barbershop at 8th and Olive streets.

Convinced that he could pull off another scam, he married again, keeping his niece on the side. But when wife No. 4 refused to take the physical required for the life insurance policy James wanted to take out on his latest prey, he had the marriage annulled.

It didn't take long for James to turn his sights on a 25-year-old strawberry blonde named Mary Busch, whom he had hired to give manicures in his shop. Within weeks of dumping wife No. 4, James put Mary into a $10,000 life insurance policy and made her wife No. 5.

The couple moved into a secluded new home on Verdugo Boulevard in La Cañada, and Mary became preg-

30

nant. And then, a few months later, James came home from work with two friends and "found" his young, pregnant wife drowned in the fishpond, facedown in six inches of water.

James confidently tried to redeem his insurance policy on Mary. But an insurance investigator discovered that the barber had been married five times and that his third wife had also died by drowning, and tipped the police.

They bugged James' house in hopes of overhearing a confession, but all they heard was James' amorous activities, most often with his niece. Finally he was caught in the act with the young girl and arrested.

The day the incest headlines hit, police were tipped that a fry cook named Charles Hope had a story to tell about James.

Under pressure, the cook said James had paid him $100 to help him procure two angry rattlesnakes named Lethal and Lightning. Their job was to poison Mary.

How? Hope testified at James' trial that the barbaric barber had persuaded his wife to have an abortion. But noting that the procedure was illegal, James told her he must tape her mouth and eyes shut to protect the doctor's identity. As an anesthetic, she was made to chug a pint of whiskey.

James strapped his wife to the kitchen table. Then Hope arrived with Lethal and Lightning in a box. James lifted his trusting wife's leg

Officials measure venom emitted by one of the rattlesnakes that authorities claimed James used to poison his wife.

The barbaric barber had persuaded his wife to have an abortion. But noting that the procedure was illegal, James told her he must tape her mouth and eyes shut to protect the doctor's identity. As an anesthetic, she was made to chug a pint of whiskey. James strapped his wife to the kitchen table. Then . . .

and thrust it into the box. The snakes bit her three times.

Her leg swelled to double its normal size, and she writhed in agony. Hours into this torture, James became impatient. So, as he had with wife No. 3, he drowned Mary in the bathtub. Then he carried her off to the fishpond to make it appear that she had tripped and plunged in headfirst.

During the police investigation and ensuing five-week murder trial, investigators turned up details of James' previous evildoing under a precedent that made such evidence admissible at the time under California law. The results, according to police investigator Eugene Williams, "demonstrated that James had engaged upon a career of marrying, insuring and murdering women."

What's more, he was about to do it again. Just before his arrest, James had become engaged to yet another woman, and was advising her about acquiring life insurance.

Columnist Walter Winchell dropped by the courtroom; so did actor Peter Lorre, who studied James' impassive face and beady eyes as research for the psychotic killer roles he often played.

James, who was found guilty of Mary Busch's murder, kept himself alive for several years on Death Row with appeals. His luck ran out in 1942, when he became the last man to be hanged in California, which thereafter adopted the gas chamber.

Traveling Man Seeks Wealthy Women For Short-Term Matrimony

If the standards of perseverance and industry were ever to be applied to the act of wife murder, surely the quiet, bespectacled man the newspapers dubbed James "Bluebeard" Watson would become the pacesetter. After all, when the final count was made, Watson had managed to murder at least a third of his 22 wives, all in a misguided quest for fortune.

From the turn of the century until 1920, Watson, a soft-spoken, mild-mannered Southerner, eluded law enforcement officials from Washington State to Idaho to Los Angeles, leaving a bloodstained trail of dead women who had responded to his newspaper proposals of marriage.

Even in those days, long before the era of online seduction and abduction via the Internet, there was peril as well as companionship to be found among the personal ads.

Advising the ladies to keep their replies confidential, Watson, a compulsive liar, described himself variously as a banker, a federal agent or a traveling salesman, and promised a home, money and trips around the world to his prospective brides.

Hundreds wrote him and vied to be chosen. But it was the rich, emotional women whom Watson tended to marry, the ones who needed comfort and a little help spending their money.

Far from being a suave swinger, Watson had made his way with few advantages in life. Orphaned and abused during childhood, he'd had little education. Nor was he handsome—his appearance was described as "gnome-like" by a reporter.

But he wined and dined scores of women and endeared himself to the children of the wealthy widows.

Had he not been so compulsive, he might have kept his freedom

James "Bluebeard" Watson

much longer than he did. But Watson could not keep himself from marrying nearly as fast as the opportunity arose.

At one time, using several aliases, he was married to three women at once—and they all lived in the same town.

But in 1920, while two other women were making plans to wed him, Watson was arrested in Los Angeles. In his possession was a list of yet 60 more marriage prospects.

The con had begun to unravel while he was living in Hollywood, when one of his brides became suspicious of his sudden out-of-town business trips and reported him to authorities.

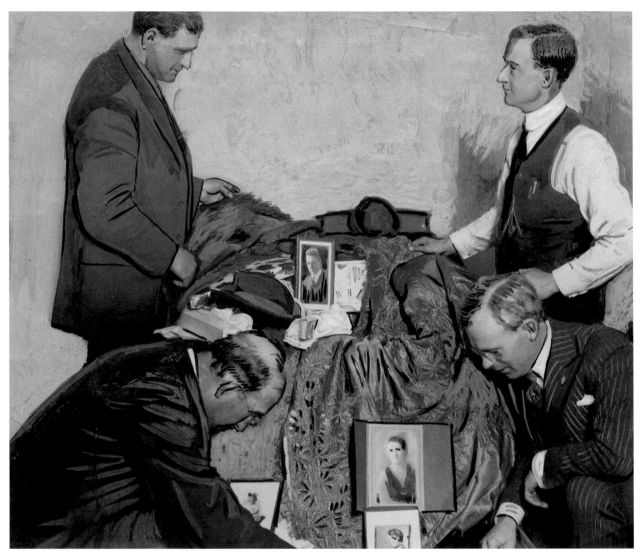

Investigators examine evidence in the 1920 case, including pictures, love letters and marriage licenses belonging to James Watson.

Kathryn Wombacher, a Spokane, Washington, dressmaker, had married a man in 1919 who called himself Walter Andrew and said he worked as a federal agent. Soon after, he was hitting Wombacher up for thousands of dollars in loans.

He moved on to Los Angeles, with Wombacher close on his heels. She unexpectedly joined him and set up house with him in Hollywood. Then he left town on a second business trip, supposedly to investigate a diamond smuggling ring. A locked black bag, constantly in his possession, had aroused her curiosity. She hired the Nick Harris Detective Agency to follow him.

Her husband, whose real name was Watson, did not go far. Less than a mile away, he walked into another house and didn't leave until morning.

Private eye J.B. Armstrong called for backup, and he and a sheriff's deputy were soon breaking into the house, where they picked the lock on the black bag. Scores of tokens from Watson's crimes fell out, including savings bonds, marriage licenses, love letters, pictures, telegrams, storage receipts, bankbooks, safe deposit keys, women's jewelry, wedding rings and property deeds.

When Watson returned, they arrested him. He took his capture hard. Although in handcuffs, he managed to extract a small pocketknife and cut his throat. While in the hospital, he attempted to slash his wrists.

As Watson recuperated, law enforcement officers pieced everything together, and national publicity about the case got Watson's other wives to identify themselves. Some were too embarrassed to press charges, but all of the remaining dozen filed for annulments and divorces.

For weeks, Los Angeles County Dist. Atty. Thomas Lee Woolwine, suspecting that murder was involved, interrogated Watson in an effort to elicit a confession. Finally Watson confessed that he had indeed killed seven of his wives, and there were possibly three more whose whereabouts he couldn't account for.

Newspapers dubbed him "Bluebeard," after a folktale about a man who married and murdered a string of women, and went to town with his story.

Though he never mounted a defense of insanity, Watson maintained that something outside of his own person had driven him into this heinous pattern of murder.

"Something just told me to go and marry them, and yet something told me not to," Watson told Woolwine. "Yet I would go do it, and it seemed all at once an impulse came over me to go someplace and make away with [kill] them. It seemed like I had done something I was ordered to."

According to Watson, he was a friendless orphan who had endured beatings with a baseball bat throughout his childhood. He said he didn't know his real name or when he was born.

When the mutilated bodies of two of his wives, Nina Lee Deloney and Elizabeth Pryor, were found, some observers dubbed him an American

Alice M. Ludvigson, one of Watson's wives who died in an "accidental" drowning.

Had he not been so compulsive, he might have kept his freedom much longer than he did. But Watson could not keep himself from marrying nearly as fast as the opportunity arose.

Bertha A. Goodnick, another Watson wife, another "accident" victim.

"Jack the Ripper." He confessed that his methods of killing had included strangling, drowning and beating his victims with a hammer or hatchet.

Watson led a posse to a shallow grave in El Centro where he had buried his last victim, and told the group where it could find another. But he couldn't remember what he had done with the rest of the bodies. In a public outcry, Angelenos demanded that he hang, but instead, he was sentenced to life in prison.

While at San Quentin, Watson managed to keep his saga very much in the public eye when he fed stories to a Los Angeles newspaper about Mason jars full of life insurance money that he had allegedly buried in the desert.

The newspaper printed stories and maps based on Watson's accounts of his buried treasure, and the public was soon scurrying over hill and dale trying to dig up the blood money, which had supposedly been converted into $50,000 worth of Liberty Bonds.

No money was ever found.

Meanwhile, Watson became a model prisoner, even helping out guards. When fellow inmate Edwin Booth, a successful Depression-era writer until he ran afoul of the law, tried to escape by knotting sheets together, Watson happened along and cut the makeshift rope. Booth fell a bruising one and a half stories, his escape foiled.

Watson died of pneumonia at 61 and now lies in San Quentin's Boot Hill Cemetery, in a grave marked only with his prison number.

Boy Toy in the Attic

Not for nothing was the term "femme fatale" coined by fiction writers of the era. These women used their wiles to seduce both lovers and juries, rarely paying the price for the crimes they were tried for. The men who had aided them were far more likely to be found guilty.

Even in the cutthroat climate of the 1920s and '30s, when L.A. newspapers spun routine crime stories into sensations in a battle for readership, the outrageous conduct of one Dolly Oesterreich in the infamous "Bat Man" case was enough to feed the city's front pages for eight years.

Walburga "Dolly" Oesterreich was a young woman of prodigious sexual appetites who went to great lengths to see that they were satisfied. She landed in court on charges of conspiracy to murder after her lover allegedly shot her husband to death. When reporters learned that the accused trigger man had been a virtual sex slave for Dolly, awaiting her call while hidden away in the cavelike attic of her house, they dubbed it the "Bat Man" trial.

Newspapers described Dolly as "comely" and a "naughty vamp." Her eyes and her appetites would bring a long line of men into her life—and send one to his death.

She had been a Milwaukee housewife, married to a dour, hard-drinking apron manufacturer named Fred Oesterreich. But the housewife, and

the house, had a secret: Her lover, Otto Sanhuber, a small, quiet youth who had worked for Oesterreich as a sewing machine repairman, lived for 10 years in the attic over the apron manufacturer's bed, hidden there by Dolly.

When the Oesterreiches moved to Los Angeles, Sanhuber came along and took up residence in the attic of a house above Sunset Boulevard.

One summer night, when he heard the Oesterreiches quarreling, Sanhuber came out of his hideaway and shot Fred Oesterreich to death.

The investigations and trial were to last eight years and end in a mistrial. Dolly Oesterreich was never

---

She had been a Milwaukee housewife, married to a dour, hard-drinking apron manufacturer named Fred Oesterreich. But the housewife, and the house, had a secret: Her lover lived for 10 years in the attic.

---

retried on charges of conspiracy to commit murder. However, her "sex slave," Sanhuber, was convicted.

Their bizarre arrangement began in 1913, when Dolly Oesterreich, 26, called her husband at the apron factory to complain that her sewing machine did not work. Her husband sent Sanhuber, then 17, to fix it. Dolly Oesterreich, who had noticed Sanhuber at the factory, greeted him in a silk robe, stockings, heavy perfume and nothing else. It was the beginning of a decade-long affair.

In 1918, when the Oesterreiches moved to Lafayette Park Place in Los Angeles, Sanhuber quietly moved in right over them. At night, he read mysteries by candlelight and wrote stories of adventure and lust. By day he made love to Dolly Oesterreich, helped her keep house and made bathtub gin.

On August 22, 1922, the Oesterreiches returned home arguing. As the fight grew louder, Sanhuber hurried down from the attic to protect Dolly, carrying two .25-caliber guns. When Oesterreich recognized Sanhuber, he flew into a rage. They struggled, the guns went off and Oesterreich was shot.

Thinking fast, Sanhuber locked Dolly in a closet, then hurried upstairs to his hideaway before police arrived, summoned by a neighbor who heard the shots.

She told police that a burglar had shot her husband, taken his expensive watch, locked her up and fled.

Jurors visit the Lafayette Park Place home where the Oesterreich's lived and Dolly kept her lover, Otto Sanhuber, aloft. The home has since been converted into an apartment building. One unit is the attic where Otto lived hidden for 10 years.

Their bizarre arrangement began in 1913, when Dolly Oesterreich, 26, called her husband at the apron factory to complain that her sewing machine did not work. Her husband sent Sanhuber, then 17, to fix it.

But the detective became suspicious. Fred Oesterreich was a wealthy man, and the detective considered that motive for murder, but he had no evidence.

Dolly moved to a house nearby, and Sanhuber stayed in that attic too, writing on a typewriter he bought with proceeds from the sale of his stories and with the nickels and dimes—never anything larger—bestowed on him by Dolly.

Freed from her marriage, she became fond of her estate attorney, Herman S. Shapiro. She gave him a diamond watch, which he recognized as the one that the supposed burglar had stolen the night her husband was slain. She explained that she had found it later under a window seat cushion.

While Sanhuber wrote and Shapiro spent long hours in court, Oesterreich took up with a businessman named Roy H. Klumb. She begged him for a favor: She had a gun that looked just like the one that had killed her husband. And she worried that the police might find it and suspect her of murder. Would

Dolly Oesterreich is questioned by Chief Investigator Blayney Matthews of the Los Angeles County District Attorney's Office in 1935.

At night, he read mysteries by candlelight and wrote stories of adventure and lust. By day he made love to Dolly Oesterreich, helped her keep house and made bathtub gin.

he get rid of it for her? Dutifully, Klumb threw the gun into the La Brea Tar Pits.

She told the same story to a neighbor, who buried the second gun in his yard.

When Oesterreich broke off with Klumb, he told police about the gun and the tar pits. On July 12, 1923, 11 months after the murder, police found the gun near the oozing tar, and Oesterreich was arrested.

The day the headlines hit, the neighbor walked into the police station with the second gun.

But both were too rusted to determine whether they had fired the fatal bullets.

From jail, Oesterreich pleaded with Shapiro to buy groceries for Sanhuber and to tap on the ceiling of the bedroom closet to let him know he should come out.

Sanhuber, starved for conversation, began telling the attorney lurid tales about his 10 years with Dolly. Shapiro issued an ultimatum, and Sanhuber left the state.

After Oesterreich was released on bail, Shapiro moved in with her—but not into the attic. The charges against her were eventually dropped.

But in 1930, after seven stormy years with Oesterreich, Shapiro moved out and came clean. He told authorities what he knew.

A second warrant was issued for Oesterreich's arrest; she was charged with conspiracy, and Sanhuber was charged with murder.

The jury found Sanhuber guilty of manslaughter, in spite of his defense that he had been enslaved by Dolly. But by the time they reached a verdict, the statute of limitations had

run out, and Sanhuber, by then 43, walked free.

At Oesterreich's conspiracy trial, famed attorney Jerry Giesler won a hung jury, and Oesterreich was free.

In 1961 she died at age 75, less than two weeks after marrying her second husband and 30-year companion, Ray Bert Hedrick.

In 1995, Dolly's misdeeds inspired a movie made for HBO called "The Man in the Attic." With Anne Archer in the lead role and Neil Patrick Harris (of TV's "Doogie Howser, M.D.") as her teenage sex slave, it was promoted as "based on a true story."

The house where Fred Oesterreich was shot to death still stands at 858 Lafayette Park Place. It has now been divided into six apartments, one of those being the attic.

Bewitching Beauty Lures Chain of Fools

Many yearn for it, but beauty can be a curse, if you believe long-ago murder suspect Madalynne Obenchain, who blamed her chain of troubles on her dark-eyed good looks.

When her second trial ended in a hung jury, she told reporters she intended to spend the rest of her days "in a leper colony," in hopes of destroying the loveliness that had led so many to grief.

For 16 months, Angelenos had devoured newspaper accounts of the five trials surrounding the triangle of love and obsession centered on the alluring young woman.

So unyielding was her hold on her men that her spurned ex-husband paid for her defense—and was promptly dubbed by prosecutors as "the Human Doormat."

The trouble began on the evening of Aug. 5, 1921, when J. Belton Kennedy, an insurance broker, was found shot to death on the stairs of his cabin on Beverly Glen Boulevard, in a then-rustic neighborhood near the Los Angeles Country Club.

Obenchain, 28, Kennedy's girlfriend, was charged with first-degree murder. So, too, was Arthur Courtney Burch, her old college sweetheart, accused of pulling the trigger.

But Madalynne's ex-husband, Chicago attorney Ralph Obenchain, came to her rescue, spending thousands of dollars to finance trials that

all ended with hung juries. Madalynne and her alleged conspirator were freed.

The *Times* commented acidly that Madalynne Obenchain "puts men gently aside when she tires of them and they yield with a smile of pain. When she wants them again, they throw aside careers, freedom—everything, in answer to her nod."

The object of all this attention was born Madalynne Donna Connor in 1893 in Superior, Wisconsin. At Northwestern University, she met her future husband, law student Ralph Obenchain. At the same time, she captured the heart of Arthur Burch, a college track athlete with protruding ears and thick glasses.

Both men were madly in love with her and wanted to marry her. But her father saved her from having to choose by dying in 1914 and leaving her $50,000.

After a three-year travel and shopping spree, Madalynne came to her mother's home in Los Angeles and met Kennedy, who worked at his wealthy father's insurance company.

Kennedy's relentlessly possessive mother did everything in her power to discourage their relationship. She even intercepted her son's mail and phone calls.

Madalynne Obenchain

Nonetheless, Kennedy proposed, and Madalynne accepted, but two years later, the young man still hadn't managed to get himself to the altar. Their plans stalled, the frustrated Madalynne decided to take Obenchain up on his earlier offer of marriage and wed him in 1919.

But four days after the marriage, she was seeing Kennedy again. Once more he made promises he would never keep. But this time, Madalynne really believed that Kennedy was altar-bound. Her extremely understanding husband—with the generosity that helped earn him his nickname—allowed her to divorce him and gave her $80 a month in alimony and blank checks as needed.

When Madalynne realized that her affair with Kennedy was hopeless—that she had been deceived again by her mama's boy—she apparently went into a rage and wired Burch, her old college admirer, in Chicago.

Burch hopped on the next train to Los Angeles to aid the woman he called his "goddess."

According to accounts of the trial, Burch waited in the bushes outside Kennedy's cabin. As Kennedy and Madalynne came up the stairs, Kennedy bent to retrieve a lucky penny Madalynne said she had left under a rock—and Burch blew off the back of his head with a shotgun. A witness testified that she heard a man yell "I got him!" The gun stock was later found washed up on the beach.

After the *Los Angeles Examiner* paid him $4,500—a common practice for Hearst-owned newspapers at the time—Burch confessed to plotting the murder with Madalynne. But his attorney maintained that the confession was worthless.

Madalynne's first trial, in 1922, created a sensation.

Her ex-husband, the hapless Obenchain, came rushing to her defense, leaving his job. He even tried to remarry her in jail, but a judge refused to permit the ceremony.

At Christmas she received more than 100 gifts of flowers, perfume and a $1,000 bill, all delivered to her cell, all from admirers.

In what would surely have caused a mistrial had it come to light in time, a smitten juror at whom she winked in court sent her "food delicacies."

But the trial ended in a hung jury. And the mystery persisted of why the slain Kennedy had been the one lover who ultimately could resist Madalynne's charms.

So unyielding was her hold on her men that her spurned ex-husband paid for her defense—and was promptly dubbed by prosecutors as "the Human Doormat."

The answer would soon emerge, sparked by a strange relationship that Madalynne—who found it impossible to pass a day without male attention—began by passing tender love notes in prison to a fellow inmate, Paul Roman, a convicted robber who had supposedly eyed her from afar.

She wrote, "Tonight I have a little pale pink rose near me—the rose will be your soft warm lips, dear Paul," and "Your nearness as I try to sleep seems like a caress." He wrote, "What you need is a lot of attention, and I'm the guy to give it to you."

Ever energetic on her own behalf, Madalynne made a loan to Roman and got him to promise to testify that before he was incarcerated, he had heard two men on a street corner plotting to kill Kennedy.

But in a bizarre twist, it emerged that Roman had already played far more of a role in Madalynne's troubles than she ever suspected.

In the second trial, a costume shop owner testified that Roman and Kennedy had been customers who often rented women's clothing that they themselves would wear to parties. Even Madalynne was stunned.

A few weeks before Kennedy's murder, the shop owner testified, she heard him say that his "friend"

Madalynne Obenchain, center, is escorted from court by authorities.

had threatened to beat him up if he ever married. She identified the friend as Paul Roman. Suddenly Kennedy's inability to succumb completely to Madalynne could be seen in a whole new light.

All five trials—two for Madalynne and three for Burch—ended in hung juries. Legal experts interviewed at the time theorized that the male jurors who voted for acquittal in Madalynne's trial were all in love with her. In addition, it was learned that one of the jurors had spoken with the defendant's ex-husband for more than an hour during the trial.

Afterward, Madalynne made her dramatic vow to reporters about exiling herself to a leper colony. But she chose a more comfortable existence, settling in Eagle Rock.

When the loyal Burch died in 1944, he willed his $1,500 estate to his "lifelong friend," Madalynne Obenchain.

Railroaded at the Station? Trunk Murders Still Mystify

In the sensation-hungry headlines of Depression-era L.A., Winnie Ruth Judd was a star, the so-called "Velvet Tigress" or "trunk murderess" who had killed her best friends, cut up their bodies and shipped them off to Central Station. Railroad officials discovered her grisly deed when they saw blood leaking from the overripe trunks and, thinking they contained smuggled venison, ordered them broken open.

Investigators inspect trunks in which the bodies were shipped to Central Station.

But had she really done it, all by herself and out of simple jealousy, as prosecuters alleged when she was sentenced to hang? Or was she a feeble-minded victim of circumstances who killed in self-defense and was pushed into a cover-up by her big-shot boyfriend, who feared a scandal, promised to come to her aid and then abandoned her to take the rap?

Even some 60 years later, with Winnie Ruth Judd a genteel old lady living comfortably in Northern California, her guilt is still debated.

But one thing is certain: The saga of Judd, a tiny, sweet-faced young woman with red hair, heartrending blue eyes and a family history of mental illness, galvanized the public like few others during the 1930s. And her story remained alive for decades, after she avoided the gallows by pleading insanity and then escaped from an asylum no fewer than seven times.

Virtually from the moment a porter discovered the two trunks leaking blood at L.A.'s Central Station in October 1931, reporters and photographers recorded every twist and turn in the bizarre case.

Judd was born a Methodist minister's daughter in 1905 in Illinois. She came to Los Angeles to attend

Winnie Ruth Judd is surrounded as she surrenders to authorities.

The saga of Judd, a tiny, sweet-faced young woman with red hair, heartrending blue eyes and a family history of mental illness, galvanized the public like few others during the 1930s. And her story remained alive for decades.

nursing school, but quit at 18 to wed Dr. William Judd, a widower more than 20 years her senior. By the late 1920s, Winnie had become ill with tuberculosis.

She moved to Phoenix for treatment, while her husband remained in Santa Monica. Instead of entering a sanitarium, she took up residence with female roommates—Helwig Samuelson, 25, who also suffered from tuberculosis, and 27-year-old Agnes Anne LeRoi, who worked as an X-ray technician.

The new friends set up a lively lifestyle, enjoying Prohibition hooch and the company of the free-spending men they partied with. But when Judd and LeRoi ended up dating the same man—rich, married playboy businessman Jack Halloran—Judd moved out.

On the sultry night of October 16, 1931, when her beau didn't call, Judd went to her former apartment to find him.

She didn't. But, according to prosecutors, Judd killed LeRoi and Samuelson out of jealousy, then shot herself in the hand so she could claim self-defense.

Judd's version was different. She said she and LeRoi argued loudly. Samuelson, hearing the dispute, appeared with a .25-caliber pistol Judd had left behind when she moved out. Defending LeRoi, Samuelson shot Judd in the left hand. As the two struggled, the gun went off twice, killing Samuelson. Then, Judd claimed, LeRoi beat Judd with an ironing board until

Judd had to shoot her to stop her. The gunshot wound, along with 147 bruises on her petite frame, lent credence to Judd's story.

But she never told it until it was too late.

At her trial for LeRoi's murder, she kept silent to protect Halloran, hoping he would come forward and tell how he had reassured her that he "would take care of" things with the help of a doctor friend—the same doctor friend, she later claimed, who had cut up the bodies at Halloran's behest in a cover-up that would save his name.

But Halloran never appeared, and self-defense never came up at her trial. Her attorneys argued that she was not guilty by reason of insanity—she had a family history of mental illness—but she was convicted of murder anyway.

The most anyone heard her say was when she was sentenced: "Those girls weren't murdered!" she screamed at the judge. "You're trying to hang me, and I won't have it!" Her husband slapped her face to quiet her, and then held her in his arms.

Judd went to Death Row. But details about Halloran had emerged in a subsequent grand jury hearing. A new picture of Winnie Judd emerged: a woman mentally incapable of making the right decision who had been pressured into the cover-up by her cowardly cad of a lover. Thousands wrote asking the governor of Arizona to show mercy, including Eleanor Roosevelt and Henry Ford. New lawyers worked for free, filing appeals to overturn her sentence. With nine days left to live,

Judd was granted a sanity hearing, and psychiatrists ruled her insane.

(When Halloran's name was mentioned at the hearing, she jumped to her feet and said: "That damn Jack Halloran, I would like to take his head and break it against the ceiling and splatter his brains like a dish of oatmeal.")

Confined at Arizona State Mental Hospital, she managed to escape seven times, often walking great distances across wilderness to freedom. In 1962, the escapee made it to Concord, California, where she remained for six years, working as a housemaid and companion to a wealthy blind woman, Ethel Blemer.

Upon her discovery and arrest in 1969, she was defended by no less a lawyer than Melvin "King of Torts" Belli, who offered to take her into his own home as a housekeeper.

Governor Ronald Reagan sent her back to Arizona. She was paroled in 1971 on the condition that she live in California. She returned to the Blemer home. When Ethel Blemer died in 1983, Winnie sued for part of her estate, claiming that other members of the family had used her as an "indentured servant" for all those years. She wound up winning a hefty cash settlement along with a lifetime monthly income of $1,250.

Since then, by all accounts, she has lived quietly, hosting tea parties and gathering many new friends.

When Halloran's name was mentioned at the hearing, she jumped to her feet and said: "That damn Jack Halloran, I would like to take his head and break it against the ceiling and splatter his brains like a dish of oatmeal."

Seated in the courtroom during her 1931 murder trial. Dr. W. C. Judd is standing directly behind his wife, Winnie Ruth.

Tigress Mauls, Says It's for "Mother Love"

Persuading love-struck men to carry out killings was all right for some women, but Clara Phillips' style was far more direct.

Clara Phillips, center, steps off ship flanked by her sister, Etta May Jackson, at left, and Mrs. Eugene Biscailuz, wife of the Los Angeles County undersheriff, who brought Phillips back from Honduras after a jailbreak in 1923.

Dubbed "Tiger Woman" by the press, she merely went after her husband's gorgeous young lover with a claw hammer, leaving her brains strewn over the summer grass.

She then went straight home, still clad in her blood-dappled clothes, threw her arms around her man and said, triumphantly:

"Darling, I have killed the one you love most in this world. Now I'm going to cook you the best supper you ever had."

Alas, Phillips' method left jurors with no one to blame but her, and she was ultimately convicted in the grisly murder of her husband's paramour, a beautiful 21-year-old widow named Alberta Meadows.

During the early part of the Roaring '20s, when oil wells were springing up across Los Angeles, Phillips' husband, Armour, was beginning a career as an aggressive, persuasive oil stock salesman. Charming and handsome, he bought expensive suits and a big house—all on credit—for his 23-year-old wife, whom he had married when she was still a teenager.

As his credit began to dwindle and other problems arose, he started turning his attentions to a seductive bank clerk, the aforementioned Meadows.

Phillips, a former hoofer with a fine figure and a toothpaste-ad smile, began spending her days surreptitiously following her husband. She soon found out whom her husband had been seeing and decided what to do about it.

She stopped by a dime store and bought the hammer.

The next day, July 12, 1922, she told a friend, former chorus girl Peggy Caffee, of her pain and outrage over her husband's infidelities. The women decided to drown their woes in bathtub gin at a Long Beach speakeasy before catching a cab back to Los Angeles.

By then a bit unsteady on their feet, the two waited outside the bank at 9th and Main streets for Meadows to finish work.

When Meadows saw them, she recognized Clara, who coolly asked Meadows if she would drive them to the house of Clara's sister in Montecito Heights, then a new subdivision below a hilltop in northeast Los Angeles.

At the end of Montecito Drive, then a winding dirt road, Meadows stopped the car when Clara accused her of having intimate relations with Armour. When Meadows denied it, Clara punched her hard, knocking her out of the car.

Fleeing down the hill, Meadows fell when the heel of her shoe broke. Phillips caught her, hoisted the hammer and brought it straight down into Meadows' face, over and over again.

Then Phillips attacked her with the claw end of the hammer. A police detective would later say that it looked as if the victim had been mauled by a tiger. Thanks to the newspapers, that description of Clara Phillips' handiwork would stick.

When a hysterical Caffee had finished vomiting in the grass, Phillips dropped her off at her house, then casually drove home in Meadows' new Ford.

Her husband panicked as she drove up in his girlfriend's car. Calmly, she told him what she had done. He insisted that she flee.

With her husband following in his car, they drove to Pomona, abandoned Meadows' car, returned to Los Angeles and spent the night at a downtown hotel. Armour Phillips

She then went straight home, still clad in her blood-dappled clothes, threw her arms around her man and said, triumphantly: "Darling, I have killed the one you love most in this world. Now I'm going to cook you the best supper you ever had."

Clara Phillips, center, walks out of Tehachapi prison after serving 12 years for murdering her husband's mistress.

Authorities inspect the automobile of Alberta Meadows, whom Phillips murdered after ordering the young woman to drive her to a remote hillside northeast of L.A.

then put his wife on a train heading toward Arizona.

But then he had second thoughts. Hoping to save his own neck, he turned her in. She was arrested in a raid on the train.

But even in adversity, the former showgirl did not shrink from the spotlight. According to a newspaper account, the fugitive with the dimples and broad smile wore a tight-fitting tailored suit that "showed off her stunning figure to advantage, and posed for a crowd of photographers as she got off the train at Union Station."

Her trial created a sensation and won her new admirers. Letters, candy and flowers from men who had seen her photo in the papers were delivered to her cell.

Armour Phillips went further into debt, borrowing heavily to pay for his wife's defense. But a jury found her guilty.

"The three women [jurors] wanted to see her hang but compromised on second-degree murder," said the jury foreman. Supposedly, her smile had softened the hearts of male jurors.

As she walked from the courtroom back to her cell after the judge sentenced her to 10 years to life in prison, a besotted spectator whispered to her that he would set her free. Her attorney overheard and laughed at the notion.

But the stranger proved to be a former gun runner who knew a thing or two about jailbreaks. A few days later, Phillips escaped. A hacksaw had been smuggled into her cell.

She might have spent the rest of her days in Honduras, where her escape route led. But a reporter—none other than the future famous attorney Morris Lavine, who at that time was working as a news hound for the *Los Angeles Examiner*—learned of her whereabouts and tipped the authorities. Undersheriff Eugene Biscailuz brought her back in handcuffs.

During Phillips' 12 years in prison, she found religion, organized a seven-piece orchestra, trained as a dental technician and, in a low period, slashed her wrists in a suicide attempt.

In a 1931 jailhouse interview, Phillips said, "I don't know whether I killed Alberta Meadows or not, but if I did, I did it for mother love.

"I fought with Alberta on the top of Montecito Drive to protect the only love I have ever known. I did what any mother in the world would do if she saw her baby being taken from her.

"Armour L. Phillips is my baby. He has been my only baby. He is my very life, and when I realized he was being taken from me, I fought, fought, fought—so that I might always have him."

The public was entranced. Upon her release in 1935, hundreds of supporters gathered at the prison and shouted, "Tiger Woman! Tiger Woman!"

But despite her vows of undying love, Phillips divorced her "baby" in 1938. For a time, she lived in San Diego, caring for her ill mother. Then she petitioned for permission to move to Texas. And there she vanished from public view.

Women Went Wild For Woo Woo Boy

More than 50 years before schoolteacher Mary Kay Letourneau shocked the nation by becoming the lover of a 13-year-old student in Seattle, a string of other women were making headlines by dallying with a certain underage Casanova in Los Angeles.

Elaine Ludlum, 21, nuzzles with husband Sonny Wisecarver, age 14, during a courtroom break.

Sonny "Woo Woo" Wisecarver became part of the national folklore in the 1940s after he nabbed his first bride—a 21-year-old mother of two—when he was just 14.

But in those days, the courts held the youth just as responsible as his adult lovers. Charges of statutory rape never came up. The public, seeking distraction from the grim events of World War II, was more titillated than outraged by Sonny's romantic prowess. His deeds became the stuff of Bob Hope jokes and, eventually, a movie.

Sonny's heyday came at a time when women were gaining new independence in wartime jobs and a Japanese invasion of Southern California—by sea or by air—was a common fear. Angelenos needed a diversion, and that's just what they got, 33 days before D-day.

On May 4, 1944, the story of Ellsworth "Sonny" Wisecarver, a lean, lanky Los Angeles teenager who eloped with Elaine Ludlum, a 21-year-old mother of two, made front-page headlines. A year later, Sonny's legend grew when he unrepentantly ran off with another woman, a glamorous 25-year-old mother of two who was married to a much-decorated soldier.

The press dubbed Sonny the "Compton Casanova," the "Love Bandit" and the "L.A. Lothario."

But *Life* magazine came up with the nickname that stuck: "The Woo Woo Boy, the world's greatest lover."

In later years, some called him "America's first liberated man." Comedian Alan Sherman, writing satirically about the sexual revolution, said it began with Sonny Wisecarver.

The clean-cut youth—who in fact came from Willowbrook, but that didn't go with "Casanova" as well as nearby Compton did—wasn't exactly the passive party suggested by the early headline "Mother of Two Faces Charge of Stealing Neighbor's Son, 14."

It was he who had wooed and won Ludlum, and the two ran off in the car of her live-in boyfriend, James Monfredi. Sonny and Ludlum were married in Arizona, where he presented the preacher with a forged note from his mother purporting that he was of legal age. "Age makes no difference. Sonny acts old for 14. We like the same foods, the same music and everything. We just click, that's all," Ludlum later said.

When they found out, Sonny's working-class parents objected, and one week into the Colorado honeymoon, the marriage was annulled.

Ludlum was legally freed of "malice, fraud or force" charges by a judge and sentenced to three years' probation. She was ordered to go to a church of her own choosing at least once a month to obtain "moral training." She was also ordered to repay the county $194.66 for the cost of transporting the couple back from Colorado, where police found them.

Sonny was sent to live with an aunt in Northern California and ordered to stay away from his former wife. Ludlum said she still loved him, that "his kisses make my heart stand still," and she'd be waiting for him when he turned 18.

But Sonny soon lost interest in Ludlum and in school, and he moved back to L.A., getting a job at a fish cannery. Within 18 months he was at it again, running off this time with a soldier's wife named Eleanor Deveny. She, too, had two toddlers and called Sonny "the kind of a guy every girl dreams about but seldom finds."

The authorities were unmoved. A judge ruled Sonny incorrigible and sent him to a youth camp. Deveny was sentenced to three years' probation for contributing to the delinquency of a minor and was fined $250. A judge urged her to come to her senses. "Your husband still loves you...and is willing to forgive

> "Age makes no difference. Sonny acts old for 14. We like the same foods, the same music and everything. We just click, that's all."

and hopes that you can have a chance to atone for your wrongdoings," said Superior Court Judge Edward R. Brand.

Sonny made big news after the war, too.

In 1946 he escaped from the youth camp. "Wisecarver Still at Large" screamed the headlines, practically warning men to get their wives off the street.

While Sonny was on the lam, Hollywood producers approached his parents hoping to make a movie about him, with Eddie Albert as Sonny. But the elder Wisecarvers wanted nothing to do with it.

In 1947, at age 17, while working as a busboy at a Las Vegas hotel, Sonny got married again. This time the bride was theater usherette Betty Reber, who, surprisingly to Sonny's public, was also 17.

After honeymooning for a year in a $40-a-month trailer in Las Vegas, Sonny tired of running from the law and turned himself in. Three months later and after several psychiatric exams, the California Youth Authority released Sonny into the arms of his teenage wife, who would stay with him on and off for 22 years.

The adult Sonny drifted through life, spending time in and out of jail for misdeeds including breaking parole, traffic violations, trespassing and selling pornographic material in a bookstore. He got married for a third time when he was 40, to a woman half his age. Twelve years later, she left him.

It wasn't until the late 1970s that Sonny once again gained notoriety,

The girls ogle Sonny Wisecarver outside the courtroom where his 21-year-old bride, Elaine, was being tried for child stealing.

The adult Sonny drifted through life, spending time in and out of jail for misdeeds including breaking parole, traffic violations, trespassing and selling pornographic material in a bookstore. He got married for a third time when he was 40, to a woman half his age. Twelve years later, she left him.

when a novice screenwriting team bought the rights to his story for $500, plus 7% of whatever they made on the 1987 film "In the Mood," starring Patrick Dempsey. Sonny made a cameo appearance, playing a mailman who delivered one line when asked what he thought of the Woo Woo Boy: "I think he's a pervert and quite possibly a Communist too."

Sonny seemed quite proud that his youthful amours had inspired a film. He even brought his 11-year-old son Michael to the set to bear witness.

Cast and crew described the adult Sonny as modest, a good guy who deserved better than he got in life. But few could forget that well before he was old enough to drive a car, Sonny was getting quite a lot.

"He's just the grandest guy I ever met," his first wife had enthused to the press. "He doesn't drink or use profanity, and he has respect for a woman. That's a combination that's hard to find these days, you know."

Mobster Moves in; Brentwood Goes Ballistic

The winding, tree-lined lanes of affluent Brentwood can hardly be described as mean streets. But over the years, this leafy Westside enclave has harbored more than its share of sensational crimes and notorious residents.

Long before the bodies of Nicole Brown Simpson and Ronald Lyle Goldman were found outside her Bundy Drive condo, and decades before two wealthy Jewish brothers gunned down their parents on Yom Kippur in the so-called Ninja murders, the neighborhood was well known as the residence of the colorful gangster Mickey Cohen.

At 5 feet, 5 inches, the physically unimpressive but highly quotable Cohen was beloved by Los Angeles' crime-obsessed press, which dubbed him "Public Nuisance No. 1."

The nickname took hold in 1950 after some of his neighbors, including actor Dean Jagger and actress Linda Darnell, branded Cohen an "intolerable nuisance" after an attempt on his life shattered every window in the area. Gangland rivals had tossed a bomb into his house at

Johnny Stompanato, left, and Mickey Cohen on way to 1949 inquest into attack on them outside Sunset Strip nightclub.

513 Moreno Avenue, near the Brentwood Country Club. The explosion was heard 10 miles away. Cohen escaped, alerted by a recently installed radar alarm system, but the 30 sticks of dynamite left a crater 20 feet wide and six feet deep where his bed had been.

Mickey was born Meyer Harris Cohen in New York in 1913, the son of a widowed Russian immigrant with six children. The family soon moved to Boyle Heights on Los Angeles' Eastside, then the largest Jewish community west of Chicago. While Fanny Cohen struggled to raise her brood by running a small grocery store near their home, 8-year-old Mickey sold the *Los Angeles Record* newspaper for two cents at 7th and Broadway. It was his last fling at respectability.

Within a short time he was running a dice game in the alley behind the newspaper's office.

Mickey soon graduated from back-alley craps to professional boxing, bootlegging and full-service racketeering. Along the way, he became a famous big tipper and fashion plate, wearing snap-brim fedoras and flashy suits. Also the owner of a haberdashery, Cohen literally tossed his suits away rather than send them to the cleaners.

Cohen's success drew the attention of rival gangster Jack Dragna, who battled him for control of the city's bookmaking operation. By 1947, East Coast mobsters were also vying for a piece of the action, offering to "protect" Mickey for a hefty cut of his estimated monthly income of $80,000.

Cohen declined their offer, and the violence that ensued over control of the city's gambling and loan-

At 5 feet, 5 inches, the physically unimpressive but highly quotable Cohen was beloved by Los Angeles' crime-obsessed press, which dubbed him "Public Nuisance No. 1."

sharking rackets came to be called the "Sunset Wars."

One of that struggle's more notable skirmishes occurred in 1948, when three gunmen, including Jimmy "The Weasel" Frattiano, walked into Cohen's haberdashery—a front for bookmaking on Sunset Boulevard—and started blasting away. One of Cohen's bodyguards was killed, but Cohen, who had stepped into the bathroom to wash his hands (something he did about 50 times a day), escaped unhurt.

On July 19, 1949, Cohen and a few friends (including bodyguard Johnny Stompanato, who would later become Lana Turner's boyfriend) emerged from a post-midnight supper at Sherry's, a Sunset Strip nightclub, and were greeted with a hail of gunfire. Cohen and three "associates" were hit. One died eight days later, but Cohen and the others survived.

Cohen's attorney, Samuel L. Rummel, known in the press as the "mob's mouthpiece," was slain by a blast from a sawed-off shotgun outside his home in Laurel Canyon the following year. Word on the street was that Cohen had ordered the

hit, believing that Rummel had betrayed him.

The mob couldn't take Cohen off the streets, but the Feds did. In 1962 he was sentenced to 15 years in prison after a second conviction for income tax evasion. There, another inmate clubbed Cohen several times with a lead pipe, leaving him partially paralyzed.

"It was some lunatic. Never knew him, never saw him. Can you imagine them putting some lunatic in there with normal people?" Cohen said in an interview. He sued the government for $10 million over the attack. Remarkably, he won, and was awarded more than $100,000. The Internal Revenue Service promptly seized the money for back taxes.

After his parole in 1972, Cohen appeared on talk shows and published a book, *Mickey Cohen, in My Own Words*. Its tiny profits were also confiscated by the IRS.

Cohen continued his friendship with the city's reporters, although he often complained about the way he and his associates were portrayed. "If I see a guy a couple of times or go out socially with him, all of a sudden he becomes my 'henchman,'" he said. "What the hell is a henchman, anyway?"

Los Angeles' premier gangster, a man who never drank or smoked and had evaded countless violent attempts on his life, died of stomach cancer in 1976. He was 62.

Badges and Brothels: From Cozy to Cagey

Brenda Allen, '40s era empress of vice.

They don't call it the world's oldest profession for nothing. Long before there was a Hollywood, or a Hollywood madam who could make studio heads tremble with the information in her "little black book," the business of prostitution was alive and well in Los Angeles.

And in contrast to the 1990s, when call girl ringleader and pediatrician's daughter Heidi Fleiss was sent to prison for pandering and tax evasion, the madams of an earlier era often enjoyed the protection and even the patronage of the city's top officials.

Back in the horse-and-buggy era, a stylish and fun-loving redhead named Pearl Morton was the uncontested queen of the brothel owners. Where the Hall of Justice now stands downtown, at the corner of Spring and Temple streets, Morton operated her lively sporting establishment with the full knowledge of the law.

Her landlord was Deputy Sheriff Juan Murrieta (for whom Murrieta Hot Springs in Riverside County is named). Her operations were in direct sight of the police station and the old County Courthouse, a red sandstone building across the street.

Men never had to call ahead for a date; they just dropped in, often in city or federal uniforms.

Their "hostess" was L.A.'s bawdiest madam. She was so fondly remembered that 40 years after her heyday, when the movie "Gone With the Wind" was released, those who had known Morton said Ona Munson, who played Belle Watling, the madam who often kept Rhett Butler company, was made up to look exactly like her, down to her dyed red hair.

Morton ran the most lavish, the most lucrative and perhaps the most genteel prostitution business in Los Angeles. Her parlor featured overstuffed chairs, massive chandeliers, full-length mirrors in magnificently carved, gilt-edged frames, thick red carpets, huge oil paintings of naked fat ladies and two Steinway pianos.

Her attitude of "charity for all and malice toward none" was legendary. She was a soft touch for local charities and anyone with a sad story, and when she went out in public, she always dressed respectably, her profession hinted at only by her rosewater perfume.

Angelus Hospital founder Charles William Bryson, a doctor known also as "Diamond Tooth Charlie," dropped by weekly in a carriage pulled by two white horses to check Pearl's girls for occupational hazards.

Her clientele included railroad executives, lawyers, mayors and senators who came from as far away as Sacramento, Washington and New York. U.S. Sen. Stephen White became a frequent visitor, and famed L.A. attorney Earl Rogers would stay for weeks at a time during his lamentable drinking binges. He often sent Morton a gift of books at Christmastime.

In such an open climate, Pearl and her strumpets hardly felt the need to hang their heads in public—they would often get gussied up in their finest, with plumed hats, to take the air in an open carriage. Up behind the women sat an elderly Irish herald in a green coat, blowing a trumpet to announce their arrival and bring in business.

But in 1909, a reform movement called the "Crusade Against Vice" took hold, spelling the beginning of the end for Pearl Morton. Mayor Arthur C. Harper resigned from office amid charges that he was taking payoffs from gambling casinos. Reformers also claimed that he was often found inebriated in Morton's brothel.

"Parlor houses and cribs were padlocked. . . . The girls were scattered throughout the rooming houses of Los Angeles. Poker games were silent. A haze of holiness heavy as a Pittsburgh pall settled upon the disgruntled pioneers."

Those were the words of Alfred Cohn and Joe Chisholm, who wrote "L.A.—The Chemically Pure" in 1913. They blamed the blotting out

Morton ran the most lavish, the most lucrative and perhaps the most genteel prostitution business in Los Angeles. Her parlor featured overstuffed chairs, massive chandeliers, full-length mirrors in magnificently carved, gilt-edged frames, thick red carpets, huge oil paintings of naked fat ladies and two Steinway pianos.

of public sin on the invasion of "Midwest Puritans into the land of the Padres and the Dons."

Morton skipped town and headed north for the more welcoming climate of San Francisco. She soon became known as the "Queen of the Underworld" at the Uptown Tenderloin establishment on Mason Street—at least until 1917, when the Red Light Abatement Act destroyed all the parlors, including hers.

But as the Prohibition era gave rise to the scofflaw spirit of the Jazz Age, prostitution and its attendant vices came roaring back into Los Angeles. Often the compliance of the cops came with it.

The film industry emerged in Hollywood, ushering in an era of big spending and decadent living during the so-called "golden age" of the 1920s and 1930s. But the madam of

Lee Francis treated vice officers to champagne and caviar.

the moment could usually count on the cops she paid off to give her enough "pre-raid" warning to clear out any big-name customers.

The renowned brothel operator Lee Francis always had French champagne chilled and dishes of Russian caviar waiting for the vice squad when it arrived. After going through the motions—and finding no one to arrest—the officers would sit down and enjoy her hospitality.

But when Francis' luck ran out and she spent 30 days in jail on a

Ann Forrester, dubbed the "Black Widow."

Allen, a redheaded "party girl," reigned as the bawdy empress of L.A. vice, serving millionaires and movie stars alike. She delighted in boasting that she had never spent a day in jail. There was a reason: She had improved on her predecessors' notion of safe sex by taking a Hollywood vice cop, LAPD Sgt. Elmer V. Jackson, as her lover and business partner.

morals charge, an aggressive comer named Ann Forrester, soon dubbed the "Black Widow" by the police, stepped in to seize the opening. Ever since, a parade of Hollywood madams has kept the town lively and the vice squad in business.

By the late 1930s, the "Black Widow's" lavish prostitution business was raking in $5,000 a week while she set Hollywood atwitter with talk of files containing the identities of male customers. But Forrester, too, was eventually con-

victed of pandering and went to jail. At her trial, the famous reform mayor Fletcher Bowron unsuccessfully pleaded for a lenient sentence because "her information was of great value in determining the identity of those Police Department members whose honesty was questionable."

In 1940, while the "Black Widow" sat in jail, her protégée, Brenda Allen, began spinning her own web.

For the next decade, Allen, a redheaded "party girl," reigned as the bawdy empress of L.A. vice, serving millionaires and movie stars alike. She delighted in boasting that she had never spent a day in jail. There was a reason: She had improved on her predecessors' notion of safe sex by taking a Hollywood vice cop, LAPD Sgt. Elmer V. Jackson, as her lover and business partner.

But in 1948, Allen was indicted after an LAPD telephone tap recorded an all-too-chummy business chat between the bordello queen and her badge-bearing partner. Her arrest shook Hollywood, which instantly began to buzz with rumors about a little black box containing the names of 250 celebrity clients, including entertainment industry figures, politicians and gangsters.

The sting embarrassed the Los Angeles Police Department even more. The key players in Allen's operation included not only Jackson, but other vice cops who'd been paid to protect prostitutes. Police Chief Clemence B. Horrall was forced into early retirement by the scandal. He was eventually replaced by the hard-nosed William H. Parker, who came in with a mandate from City Hall to clean things up.

During the scandal, it emerged that Allen's real name was Marie Mitchell. She had been a teenage streetwalker working a seedy stretch of 6th Street between Union and Alvarado when she was "discovered" by Forrester, who took her into a pricey brothel. But when the "Black Widow" ran afoul of the law, the young Mitchell didn't hesitate to betray her mentor, testifying that her former boss had lured her into this "shameful business."

But it was a business that Allen was born for. At her peak, she had 114 party girls working for her, taking in $9,000 a day from customers who paid from $20 to $100 for a go-round with one of "Brenda's girls." Allen took 50% off the top and spent a third of her income to pay off cops, doctors, lawyers and bail bondsmen.

Heidi Fleiss, Hollywood's latest, but undoubtedly not the last, madam.

Allen rented large, ornate party houses above the Sunset Strip. After each of her 19 arrests, she packed things up and moved to another house on the next street.

Allen's downfall came in a roundabout way. On the night of February 21, 1947, she and Jackson were necking in his car in front of her apartment at 9th and Fedora streets when a robber stuck a machine gun through Jackson's open window. Jackson, pretending to reach for his wallet, pulled out a pistol instead and killed the stickup man. The getaway driver sped off. When police arrived, Jackson maintained that Allen was a stenographer for the LAPD.

A year later, a newspaper reporter stumbled across information that the woman who'd been with Jackson

Elizabeth Adams, the "Beverly Hills Madam," became an underground celebrity in the 1970s and 1980s. She took the business international, dispatching a bevy of beautiful young women to Saudi princes and millionaire businessmen. Her average cash flow grew to $100,000 a month.

that night was the head of a prostitution ring.

Subsequent headlines led to a grand jury investigation. Allen was quick to turn on her man. While Jackson denied any wrongdoing, Allen testified that she gave him $50 a week to protect each woman she employed, as well as paying other sums to other vice squad members.

Allen's successor was Barrie Benson, 29, who in 1951 conducted business in a gaudy 13-room Moorish castle on Schuyler Road north of the Sunset Strip. It was a favorite hangout for gangland figures, including Sam Farkas, bodyguard to mobster Mickey Cohen. Benson's business went under soon after Police Chief Parker took command.

Elizabeth Adams, the "Beverly Hills Madam," became an underground celebrity in the 1970s and 1980s. She took the business international, dispatching a bevy of

beautiful young women to Saudi princes and millionaire businessmen. Her average cash flow grew to $100,000 a month. Acting as a police informant by passing along "pillow talk," Adams managed to keep the cops at bay for 20 years.

When Adams' business went under in 1988, her rival—a twenty-something party girl and former Adams protégée—picked up where Adams left off, stealing her business, books, girls and guys.

But the cops weren't as kind to Heidi Fleiss as they'd been to some of her predecessors. After they busted her ring of expensive call girls in 1993, the very officers who had arrested her went after her in court for making disparaging remarks about their personal lives to the media. The cops got Heidi not only for pandering but for slandering, and she was ordered to pay $343,000 in damages.

Never quite able to understand how the party could have ended so badly, Fleiss, who had grown up the privileged daughter of a Los Angeles pediatrician, capitalized on her post-arrest notoriety with a short-lived line of lingerie. In 1997 she began serving a 37-month federal prison term for tax evasion and money laundering, along with a concurrent 18-month state sentence for pandering.

Meanwhile, somewhere in Hollywood, the beat, no doubt, goes on.

Life With Col. Griffith No Picnic In the Park

One of the city's most generous early benefactors was Col. Griffith Jenkins Griffith, whose gift of parkland became L.A's largest oasis and whose name is everywhere—Griffith Park, Griffith Observatory, Griffith Park Drive and Griffith Park Boulevard.

Col. Griffith Jenkins Griffith

But the colonel's name was once prominent for entirely different reasons: At the turn of the century, he was at the center of one of the most bizarre and hair-raising domestic scandals of the age.

A Welsh-born immigrant who made his fortune in mining, Griffith was a man who demonstrated luxurious tastes and civic generosity. He also displayed an unquenchable thirst for alcohol and a violent temper, a combination that very nearly became his undoing.

In 1882, when the city was new and growing, the colonel, who acquired his title in the California National Guard, bought 4,071 acres of Rancho Los Feliz for $50,000.

Four years later, he presented the city with a Christmas gift of the 3,015 acres of hills, green valleys, streams and meadows that today is Griffith Park.

Some cynically declared that the donation was a tax dodge; others believed it came from the goodness of his heart. Either way, the gift was offered with Griffith's injunction: "Public parks are a safety valve of great cities…and should be accessible and attractive, where neither race, creed nor color should be excluded."

Griffith's wife, Mary Agnes Christina Mesmer, was a descendant of the Verdugo family, who received the king of Spain's first land grant in the region, the 36,000-acre Rancho San Rafael—which made her a landowner, too. The colonel asked her to deed him a piece of her land as collateral in a business deal. Being an obedient wife, she did. But later, when she asked for it back, Griffith blew his top.

His reputation as a man of temper was cemented by what happened next during a vacation with his wife at the Arcadia Hotel, an elaborate four-story seaside resort overlooking Santa Monica Bay.

On a late summer afternoon in 1903, the Griffiths took a leisurely walk on the beach. Mrs. Griffith returned to their room, the Presidential Suite. A short time later, Griffith appeared with blood-

A Welsh-born immigrant who made his fortune in mining, Griffith was a man who demonstrated luxurious tastes and civic generosity. He also displayed an unquenchable thirst for alcohol and a violent temper.

shot eyes, handed his wife her prayer book and ordered her to kneel as he took out his pistol and cocked it.

The Protestant Griffith accused his wife of being "in league with the Pope and the church to poison him so she could turn all his money over to the Catholics," according to the *Griffith Park Quarterly*. He told her to close her eyes and swear she had been a faithful wife. She said, "Darling, you know I have." She begged for her life. Their 12-year-old son, she sobbed, needed his mother.

Griffith, very drunk, was unmoved by her claim of faithfulness and her plea of motherhood.

As Mrs. Griffith opened her eyes and saw the pistol barrel only inches from her head, she jerked her head. The gun went off, the bullet piercing her left eye.

Screaming in terror, she jumped through the open window and tumbled two stories to the roof of the veranda below, breaking an arm when she landed.

She dragged herself through a window into a room. Screaming for help, she found a towel to hold over the eye, which was gushing blood.

The hotel manager answered her call for help, but Griffith was on his heels. "Please don't let him come in," his wife wailed. "He shot me! He's crazy!" Griffith calmly denied it and insisted that his wife had accidentally shot herself.

The manager summoned the sheriff.

Griffith's attorney, the legendary Earl Rogers, was himself familiar with the effects of prolonged drinking. He tried to "prove that Mrs. Griffith had too much religion, and the colonel too much champagne," wrote a *Los Angeles Times* reporter. Rogers argued that Griffith was a victim of "alcohol insanity." The colonel was convicted of attempted murder, but he drew only a two-year sentence. A year later, he left San Quentin a new man—sane, sober and still very rich.

He soon made further gifts, willing even more land and a substantial trust fund for the upkeep of the park and for building an observatory and theater.

A Catholic whose religion forbade divorce, Mrs. Griffith stayed with her husband in their 17-room mansion until he died in 1919, at age 67. The mansion still stands on North Vermont Avenue, near the Roosevelt Golf Course. But the Arcadia Hotel's 22-year life ended in 1909, when it was torn down. Loews Santa Monica Beach Hotel now stands on the same site, near the Santa Monica Pier.

To commemorate the 100th birthday of Griffith's most enduring legacy, a 14-foot, $100,000 statue of the colonel sculpted by Venice artist Jonathon Bickart was placed at the park's main entrance in 1996.

He is not carrying a gun. And there is no accompanying statue of his long-suffering wife, the one-eyed Christina Griffith.

Griffith's attorney, the legendary Earl Rogers, was himself familiar with the effects of prolonged drinking. He tried to "prove that Mrs. Griffith had too much religion, and the colonel too much champagne."

A 1921 photo shows the 4,000-plus acres above the Los Feliz neighborhood that Griffith gave the city for use as a park.

Scorn for Wife Hexes Mayor's Life

He was the chief of police who couldn't stop getting arrested. Handsome, charismatic Charles Edward Sebastian seemed like one of the luckiest fellows who ever rose to prominence in L.A. public life—a hail-fellow-well-met kind of guy who in a short time worked his way up from beat cop to chief of police. And not long after, Sebastian was elected mayor, becoming the first and only person ever to hold both offices in Los Angeles.

But along with his prominence came a seemingly endless series of personal scandals. Between political enemies who were bent on destroying him and his own penchant for putting his foot in it, it wasn't long before Sebastian, a former flatfoot, was more or less back on the street.

In an era of inbred political clout, the Missouri-born Sebastian worked first as a ranch foreman, railroad grip man and sanitation inspector before joing the city's police force.

His bold initiative on the patrol beat drew attention from his superiors, and his good looks caused Angelenas to sigh when he passed them on the street. After only 10 years on the force, he was appointed chief of police. His legend grew when he defused a crisis that could easily have become an unthinkable tragedy.

A deranged railroad employee walked into the police station one day strapped with 53 sticks of dynamite. The human bomb, his face hidden behind a grotesque mask, declared that he was on a suicide mission to blow up the place and everyone in it. Sebastian stepped up and managed to talk him out of it. After that, his supporters begged him to run for mayor.

But as soon as he announced his candidacy, his luck began to turn.

Three months before the 1915 election, Sebastian and a high-ranking police officer were indicted in the death of William Jackson, a disabled homeless man who was beaten to death in jail. The matter was dropped within days, having apparently been concocted by his political enemies.

But it gave Sebastian second thoughts about running, lest the campaign disclose his long-standing relationship with a woman named Lillian Pratt.

When he persisted in the race, his political enemies tried anew. Two months before the election, Sebastian was arrested again and accused of contributing to the delinquency of a minor—Pratt's sister, 16-year-old Edith Serkin.

Serkin, who always accompanied her sister when she visited Sebastian in Room 17 of the Arizona Hotel at 330 W. 1st Street, testified that she had watched them "dally sexually."

Sebastian, a married man, insisted that his relationship with Lillian Pratt was merely an affair of the heart. The sister, Sebastian said, was always present as a chaperone. The public believed him.

His attorney, Earl Rogers, in a spectacular bit of showmanship, destroyed the case against Sebastian when he dragged into the courtroom an entire wall from the hotel room where the alleged misconduct took

Mayor Charles E. Sebastian and wife Elsie, the woman he called "the Old Haybag."

Sebastian, a married man, insisted that his relationship with Lillian Pratt was merely an affair of the heart. The sister, Sebastian said, was always present as a chaperone. The public believed him.

place, and proved that given the placement of a peephole in the wall, the sister could not have witnessed what she claimed.

Sebastian was acquitted. Thousands hailed the verdict with a torchlight parade down Broadway. Sebastian, in his uniform as chief of police, waved and bowed from a chauffeur-driven automobile.

On May 31, the eve of the election, someone fired two shots at Sebastian, barely missing. Either in spite of it or because of it, he was elected mayor. In a bizarre twist, his enemies tried to turn the incident to their advantage: Sebastian was arrested on the very day of his election and charged with framing an assassination plot to boost his campaign. But these charges, too, were soon dropped.

Despite all the scandal and turmoil, Sebastian continued to see Pratt. As the mayor, he became bolder. If his feelings for Pratt had been merely friendly before, they now deepened. On an official trip with his wife, Elsie, he wrote Pratt several love letters. One said: "I wish you could have been along, instead of the Old Haybag." Sebastian neglected to mail the epistles, and Mrs. Sebastian discovered them.

Her rage was so great that she took the letters to the *Record,* a newspaper that shared her disappointment with the mayor. The paper ran the letters on Page 1 under this large headline: "THE HAYBAG LETTERS!"

Now the good folk who had once cheered him turned their backs. The publication of the letters so embarrassed Sebastian that after a three-day drinking binge, he resigned from the city's highest office, claiming poor health. He'd been mayor for barely a year.

After that, Sebastian tried to run a grocery store. He sold drinks at a dance pavilion. He even attempted to open a detective agency but was denied a license by the prison board "in the best interest of the public."

The district attorney who'd once tried to put him behind bars finally gave him a job as an investigator.

Lillian Pratt, Sebastian's longtime mistress.

But Sebastian soon left the district attorney's office and began what was to prove his last career: running a gas station at Vermont Avenue and Santa Monica Boulevard. He earned enough to send his only son, Charles Francis Sebastian, through Stanford Medical School. (The boy went on to become a prominent Los Angeles surgeon.)

In 1921, Mrs. Sebastian tried for a third time to divorce her husband. (Her earlier attempts, charging desertion, failure to provide and mental suffering, had been denied by the court for insufficient evidence.) This time her accusations involved social standing. Her husband had let his membership in the Masonic Lodge lapse, causing her to lose her position in the Order of the Eastern Star, the Masonic auxiliary. A judge granted the divorce.

On an official trip with his wife, Elsie, he wrote Pratt several love letters. One said: "I wish you could have been along, instead of the Old Haybag." Sebastian neglected to mail the epistles, and Mrs. Sebastian discovered them.

Lillian Pratt had remained in Sebastian's life through scandal and divorce. Together with their dog, Barker, they rented a secluded cottage in Venice.

But scarcely had they found their happiness together when Sebastian suffered a stroke that left him hardly able to move or speak. Thereafter, he was wheeled up and down the street by his loyal longtime mistress.

On April 17, 1929, Sebastian died at the age of 56 in the arms of the woman who had shared his triumphs and shame, but never his name.

The Passion and Pain Of the Star of the Bar

He was one of the most brilliant defense attorneys this city has ever seen, and also one of the most colorful and tormented. For at least 25 years, from the turn of the 20th century forward, he dominated Los Angeles courtrooms, defending 77 accused murderers and winning acquittals for all but one.

But on the one occasion when he turned prosecutor—and sent the accused to his death at San Quentin—his remorse was so great that it worsened his lifelong drinking problem and helped lead to his downfall.

The son of a minister, Earl Rogers despised the death penalty. Perhaps this was the passion that drove him. "As long as there is such an inhuman and ungodly law as capital punishment," he wrote in an appeal to the Supreme Court, "I will defend with my last breath any man who might be its victim."

In his day, it was common for accused murderers to clamor "Get me Earl Rogers!" Even baseball fans would shout at ballplayers arguing with the umpire: "Go ahead and kill him, we'll get you Earl Rogers."

Rogers came to L.A. in 1894 with his first wife, Hazel Belle Green, whom he'd met at Syracuse University in New York, and their new baby, Adela. Fascinated by the law, he soon became the protégé of prominent attorney and future U.S. Senator Stephen White.

White liked Rogers' quick mind and confident style. They had in common a bottomless capacity for both knowledge and booze. But their friendship was destined to break up in court. Soon after Rogers began practicing, he defended an unemployed plumber accused of murdering a popular young lawyer over a $4 plumbing bill. White was working for the prosecution.

Rogers won, stunning the city and his onetime mentor. For the first

Earl Rogers

Rogers considered himself a defender of the lost, pleading on behalf of whores, pimps, robbers and death-dealers. He clung to the belief of his Methodist minister father that justice should serve the poor.

time, White had been beaten in court. And upon the "Little Giant's" fall, Rogers rose to glory.

Eventually his celebrity clients would include Charlie Sebastian, the L.A. police chief turned mayor; the philanthropist-scoundrel Col. Griffith J. Griffith, who came to trial after he shot his wife in the eye during a drunken rampage; and famed attorney Clarence Darrow. When Darrow was accused of bribing a jury during his defense of union activist J. B. McNamara in the 1910 bombing of the *Los Angeles Times,* Darrow hired Rogers to defend him. Rogers won an acquittal.

But mainly, Rogers considered himself a defender of the lost, pleading on behalf of whores, pimps, robbers and death-dealers. He clung to the belief of his Methodist minister father that justice should serve the poor.

His reputation and stature soon towered over others'; he was earning more than $100,000 a year in the second decade of the century. He was a courtroom showman who introduced innovative cross-examination techniques. Author Jack London called him "an authentic legal genius."

Enhancing Rogers' legend was his personal style: slim, elegant and dynamic. He was always immaculate, with a gardenia in his lapel and a different suit each day. He carried a lorgnette—golden eyeglasses at the end of a gold handle—through which he would peer at witnesses. The device became his trademark, pictured in newspapers around the world.

But throughout all this, Rogers' personal life was in turmoil: He

After one man was acquitted of murdering his wife, he turned to Rogers and gloated: "The truth will prevail, Earl." Rogers reportedly snarled, "Get away from me, you slimy pimp! You know you're guilty as hell."

divorced and remarried Hazel Belle three times before they finally called it quits.

And whatever was driving Rogers, it certainly wasn't belief in the innocence of his clients. After one man was acquitted of murdering his wife, he turned to Rogers and gloated: "The truth will prevail, Earl." Rogers reportedly snarled, "Get away from me, you slimy pimp! You know you're guilty as hell."

In 1906, Rogers was persuaded for the first time to switch roles and assist the district attorney in prosecuting Morrison Buck, the former chauffeur of Los Angeles oil magnate Charles A. Canfield. Buck had asked Canfield for a loan of $2,600, but when Canfield refused, he shot Canfield's wife, Chloe, twice in the head. The defense tried to prove Buck was insane, but Rogers proved he was sane, and Buck was hanged.

Yet the victory filled him with a remorse that never healed. Only seconds after Buck was pronounced dead at San Quentin, Rogers wailed, "We're all wrong. ...Who are we to take life?...I can't forgive myself."

He found some solace in the arms of Edna (Teddy) Landers, a tall, red-headed Irish-Canadian with a beautiful singing voice. In 1916 she gave

up her Roman Catholic faith to marry Rogers, who was almost twice her age. Their fairy-tale marriage ended three years later, when she died in a worldwide influenza epidemic at the age of 29.

From that point, the drinking problem that had plagued him grew worse, accelerated, friends said, by the guilt he carried for sending Buck to the gallows.

Rogers' daughter, Adela Rogers St. John, became a well-known journalist for the Hearst newspapers. She wrote articles perpetuating her father's reputation as a brilliant legal tactician and bon vivant. But she soon found herself facing him from the witness stand in the saddest courtroom scenario of his career.

By then, Rogers had sunk into drunken irresponsibility. His eldest son, fearing for his welfare, signed a complaint to have him committed to a sanitarium. Adela was called to appear in court against him. Rogers, defending himself this time, approached the witness box, tapping his famed lorgnette against his palm. "Nora," he said softly, using his pet name for her, "look at me, please. You don't think I'm crazy, do you, honey?"

"No, papa," she replied.

"Then do you want to go on with this farce and have me locked up?" he asked her.

Adela burst into tears. Earl Rogers had prevailed, and the complaint was dismissed.

But he had won only the freedom to destroy himself. After that, Rogers was in and out of hospitals until 1922, when he was found dead at age 51 in his room at the New Broadway Hotel, on Bunker Hill between 1st Street and Temple—a block away from the courthouse.

A Savior to the Stars

When Lana Turner was accused of knifing her gangster lover Johnny Stompanato, it was Jerry Giesler whom she called to defend her. When actor Errol Flynn was facing charges of statutory rape, he trusted Giesler to save his career.

Jerry Giesler, left, with Errol Flynn, who selected Giesler to defend him on statutory rape charges.

"Get me Giesler" became the byword of the day for anyone facing a tough rap.

"My clients don't want justice; they want off," Giesler once said. And with him at their side, they usually got what they wanted.

For more than 50 years—from 1910 until his death in 1962—Giesler set the pace for other criminal lawyers in Los Angeles, arguing more than 70 murder cases and saving his clients' lives every time. Some regained their freedom; others at least avoided the gallows.

He credited most of his success to the great Earl Rogers, who had been his mentor and the source of most of his legal education. "Every day I remember something else that Earl Rogers taught me, and I put it to use," Giesler said toward the end of his career. "What I learned from him has been priceless to me."

The baton was passed through a chance meeting. From Iowa, young Harold Lee "Jerry" Giesler had come to L.A. to enroll in law school at USC. While still a student, he ran a collection agency to support himself. One day his duties called for him to collect a bill at the office of the city's most famous barrister. His methods so impressed Rogers—

"My clients don't want justice; they want off," Giesler once said. And with him at their side, they usually got what they wanted.

Grateful client Lili St. Cyr gives Giesler a big hug after a jury acquitted the famed nightclub stripper of indecent performance in 1951.
Dangling in St. Cyr's left hand are her lacy bra and panties, Exhibits "A" and "B" at her trial.

who nevertheless refused to pay the bill—that he hired Giesler on the spot.

Giesler quit law school to become the great man's protégé (it was common in those days to study law under a mentor), and in 1910 was admitted to the bar.

He recalled that his association with Rogers gave him credentials so solid that he was allowed to skip the exam. "Since it was past the lunch hour, they only asked me two questions: What is your name, and what is your address," he said.

Giesler was hardly a casting director's notion of a crack defense attorney. He was short and plump, with a thin, reedy voice. But his zeal, tenacity and creative way of approaching a problem or applying the law ran circles around his competitors and dazzled juries over and over.

In those days, before the advent of radio and television, Angelenos packed the courtroom to catch the proceedings of well-publicized trials. In one such case, famed attorney Clarence Darrow was on trial for allegedly bribing a jury during his

defense of J.B. McNamara, a union activist charged with the 1910 bombing of the *Los Angeles Times*.

Rogers took Giesler along "to help carry the briefcases." When Giesler was asked to look up a point of law, he came back with 40 pages of research. And when Rogers disappeared during the trial on one of his unfortunate drinking binges, Giesler took over. His name quickly went up in gold leaf on Rogers' office window.

"I felt like a New York Yankee batboy being told he was going to pitch in the World Series," Giesler recalled.

The junior attorney got his real break when he won a spectacular reversal of fate for one of the richest and most prominent men in California, theater magnate Alexander Pantages.

Pantages had been accused of raping a 17-year-old showgirl in his office. Despite some questions as to the girl's credibility and motives, the judge threw the book at the powerful Greek immigrant, sentencing him to 50 years at San Quentin.

But Giesler, who had defended Pantages, refused to give up. He prepared an appeal so lengthy and creative that it set precedents in cases of statutory rape that remained unchallenged for nearly 50 years. He also coaxed out a formerly reluctant witness who was able to destroy the victim's credibility.

By the time Giesler was done, Pantages was acquitted. (Years later, on her deathbed, the showgirl confessed that she'd been paid to frame the theater magnate.)

With the Pantages reversal of fortune, Giesler's career took off. He subsequently won hung juries and acquittals for many of the rich and famous, including Flynn, mobster Benjamin "Bugsy" Siegel and stripteaser Lili St. Cyr.

But he also defended ordinary people. In one of his most sensational cases, he waived his $100,000 fee to come to the aid of Glendale resident Paul Wright, 38, who in a crime of passion had shot and killed his wife, Evelyn, and her lover John Kimmel, 36, an airline pilot.

The press called it the "White Flame Murder" because Wright said a white flame had exploded in his head when he awoke in his bedroom to hear a single note repeated over and over on the piano, and then found his wife making love to his best friend on the piano bench.

To this day, Giesler is commemorated each year by L.A.'s Criminal Courts Bar Association, which honors outstanding criminal lawyers with the Jerry Giesler Memorial Award.

Filled with uncontrollable rage, Wright got a pistol, walked back to the living room, and fired nine rounds at his wife and friend.

When he "came to his senses," he called the police and said, "Get me Giesler."

With his skilled attorney's help, Wright was convicted only of manslaughter. And at the subsequent sanity hearing, Giesler won the unprecedented right to make both the opening and closing arguments, and convinced the jury that Wright was insane at the time of the murder. Later, a new set of psychologists would find that Wright had regained his sanity and set him free.

One thing is certain: Wright wasn't crazy when he said "Get me Giesler."

To this day, Giesler is commemorated each year by L.A.'s Criminal Courts Bar Association, which honors outstanding criminal lawyers with the Jerry Giesler Memorial Award.

The master barrister died of a heart attack on New Year's Day 1962 after more than half a century of practicing law.

Giesler, right, stands next to client Robert Mitchum as the actor is sentenced to 60 days in jail for marijuana possession in 1949. Actress Lila Leeds, far left, was similarly sentenced. On her left is her attorney, Grant Cooper.

Crimes of Fashion,
Crimes of Passion

Of all the colorful, spotlight-stealing attorneys who have performed in Los Angeles courtrooms, there is really none to match Gladys Towles Root.

Gladys Towles Root in one of her aerodynamic hats.

"Hurricane Gladys" might have been a fitting tag for this tireless force of nature, but the press more commonly called her "The Lady in Purple," for the most prevalent color in a wardrobe that could modestly be called astonishing.

And while her choice of clientele would hardly have endeared her to feminists—she mainly represented men accused of sex crimes—she nonetheless made her mark for nearly half a century in a male-dominated world.

Root was born in Los Angeles September 9, 1905. An attention seeker early on, she wanted to be an actress but eventually changed her mind to please her father, who had given up law school to raise a family. He grew wealthy in business, and Root enjoyed a privileged upbringing, insulated from the seamy side of life.

That was to change the minute she opened her first law office, at 7th and Spring streets, in 1929.

Her first client, Louis Osuna, walked into her office demanding a quick divorce from his wife for her infidelity. But the next day, when he came home to find her in bed with another man, he decided the wheels of justice turned too slowly, and he shot her to death.

Osuna was in deep trouble. But he knew he was onto something when he met Root. He immediately told his jailmates about her. A cry of "Get me Gladys" went up. That got her career rolling.

Fifteen of the derelicts Osuna had tipped off sought out Root the first month—some of them able to repay her only with live poultry.

Osuna's instincts were on target. Root got him off with a 10-month sentence for manslaughter. And after that, she was in business.

Most of her clients, at least early on, were accused child molesters, rapists or peeping Toms—the sort few other lawyers would represent. Root didn't judge. At a time when rape was punishable by death in some states, she believed rapists had a glandular disorder and should receive hospital treatment. Her clients would claim they had been railroaded or that the children were lying. Sometimes it proved to be true.

"My mother told me when I was a young girl that I must be broad-minded toward unusual behavior," said Root. "She told me to think of those people as loose spokes on the wheel of life."

Root had nerve, style and energy to spare. At her height, she was making an average of 75 court appearances a month. She defended thousands of clients, becoming wealthy along the way. She found time to have two children: a son with her first husband, sheriff's Deputy Frank Root, whom she married right out of USC law school, and a daughter with her second, Jay C. Geiger, a fellow eccentric who was employed by a fashion magazine.

In Geiger she found a kindred spirit. They showed off their outlandish wardrobes at parties and restaurants. Geiger always had a green parrot named Pablo perched on his mink-covered lapels; at Perino's one day, Pablo took a bite out of the neck of a judge Root disliked.

Enough cannot be said about Root's wardrobe; the word "flamboy-

She was once seen walking down Wilshire Boulevard holding two lambs on leashes, each dyed pink to match her hair. Asked why, Root said, "I'm a screwball. I should have joined a circus."

ant" is inadequate.

She had begun making her own clothes as a girl, tacking them together in bursts of creativity from whatever offbeat materials were at hand. As a courtoom attorney she wore hats with the wingspan of a 747, collars that looked capable of levitating her, exotic furs and skirts containing 20 yards of taffeta. Her costume jewelry was bigger than big and gaudier than gaudy. Her hair was tinted purple, pink, mint, magenta or green—every color in the rainbow, to match her wardrobe. She was once seen walking down Wilshire Boulevard holding two lambs on leashes, each dyed pink to match her hair.

Asked why, Root said, "I'm a screwball. I should have joined a circus."

Friends theorized that her outrageous self-presentation helped offset the grimness of the sordid stories her clients brought into her life.

Not all of Root's cases involved perversion. In a 1931 victory, she got the state to reverse part of a 1906 state law barring marriage between certain races. A Filipino and a white woman who was pregnant with his child had begged Root to find a way they could be married. Root found that the law did not include the racial group from which Filipinos are descended. The high court agreed.

In the year 1959 alone, she tried nine murder cases, five of them women accused of killing their husbands. All were acquitted.

She was vehemently opposed to laws that punished consenting adults for homosexual acts, and to laws against prostitution.

After she bought a mansion in Hancock Park, she was among the residents who refused to sign a petition to stop entertainer Nat King Cole from buying a house there.

Unlike many attorneys who celebrated their victories with alcohol, Root never drank. Instead, she rewarded herself with chocolates.

On one memorable occasion, she didn't get her sweets. It happened with a client accused of molesting a 10-year-old girl. Root had the man walk to and from the witness stand with a white cane denoting blindness, and the judge dismissed the case, saying no blind man could possibly have done what the child had claimed.

As the defendant stood and faced the judge, he said, "Thank you. The moment I looked at you, I knew you had an honest face." Root, appalled, whispered to her assistant, "I swear, I didn't know."

In 1964, Root was stung by accusations of perjury during her defense of the men who kidnapped Frank Sinatra, Jr., from a Lake Tahoe resort.

Federal prosecutors indicted her for maintaining that the young singer had willingly participated in the kidnap as a publicity stunt. Famed attorney Morris Lavine defended her, and after a four-year battle, the charges were dropped.

In 1982, Root was still working hard and spectacularly attired—in gold—when she suffered a fatal heart attack in a Pomona courtroom while defending two brothers accused in a sodomy-rape case. She was 77.

Attorney for The Damned

He was a master of the written appeal who found his destiny as a lawyer when he appealed his own way out of jail during the lowest point of his life.

Morris Lavine with client Gladys Towles Root during her trial on perjury charges stemming from the kidnapping of Frank Sinatra, Jr.

Gangster Mickey Cohen was one of the many he sprung from jail. His other colorful clients included Teamsters chief Jimmy Hoffa.

Where other famed attorneys made their mark with fancy flights of courtroom rhetoric, Morris Lavine turned his talents to principle and precedent, arguing in papers reviewed only by a judge the reasons why a defendant should win a new trial.

Since his clients had already been convicted, Lavine once told columnist Walter Winchell that he wanted to be recognized as "the attorney for the damned."

Lavine wrote more than a thousand appeals in his career, including two that resulted in landmark Supreme Court decisions.

Gangster Mickey Cohen was one of the many he sprung from jail. His other colorful clients included Teamsters chief Jimmy Hoffa, alleged mafioso John Roselli, boyfriend killer Louise Peete and the wife murderer known as "Rattlesnake" James.

A native of Cleveland, the gifted Lavine came to L.A. as a youth in the early years of the 20th century, and by the age of 14 was already writing for local newspapers. By the time he graduated from law school at the tender age of 20, he had mastered four languages.

Lavine then served in World War I as a naval officer, and during that time acted as defense attorney in more than 300 courts-martial. But after the war, his enthusiasm for the daily deadline lured him back to journalism. As a reporter for the Hearst paper the *Los Angeles Examiner*, he shone, often going beyond the call of duty to trump the competition.

In one memorable incident, Lavine discovered the whereabouts of fugitive Clara "Tiger Woman" Phillips, who had broken out of jail and fled to Honduras. He persuaded her to give herself up; then, according to some accounts, he tipped off authorities, who brought her back in handcuffs.

Lavine's glory lasted until 1930, when he got in over his head by acting as a collection agent for a trio of organized crime figures, presumably to get the lowdown on their activities. One of them was the notoriously treacherous crime boss Charles Crawford. After Lavine accepted a payment of $75,000, Crawford accused him in court of extorting the money in exchange for agreeing to keep their names out of a damning story about an oil stock swindle.

Lavine went to jail. After 10 months, he wrote and won his own appeal. Five years later he received a full pardon from the governor and was reinstated as a lawyer.

He went on to a memorable career. After he got gangster Cohen released from prison in 1951 pending appeal of an income tax conviction, Cohen threw his short arms around Lavine's neck and said, "It's wonderful, Morrie—wonderful, wonderful!" and kissed Lavine on the cheek.

In another well-publicized case, Lavine helped defend the men convicted in the 1963 kidnapping of Frank Sinatra, Jr., from a Lake Tahoe hotel. He won an appeal for one of the three. When his colleague on the case, the always colorfully dressed attorney Gladys Towles Root, was charged with perjury for claiming that young Sinatra let himself be kidnapped as a publicity stunt, Lavine got her indictment overturned.

Later he made two pro bono appeals on behalf of indigents that resulted in landmark U.S. Supreme Court decisions, in 1965 and 1967,

Among Angelenos, Lavine is perhaps best remembered for the time he tried to fight City Hall, taking the battle all the way to the Supreme Court on behalf of Los Angeles taxpayers.

that prohibited prosecutors from drawing inferences of guilt from a defendant's refusal to testify under his Fifth Amendment rights.

Still, among Angelenos, Lavine is perhaps best remembered for the time he tried to fight City Hall, taking the battle all the way to the Supreme Court on behalf of Los Angeles taxpayers.

The dispute was over the intended use of the block of downtown land, fronting on Temple Street between Grand and Hill streets, that Cardinal Roger M. Mahony has now chosen for Our Lady of the Angels cathedral.

Lavine was once a part owner of this 5.5-acre parcel, having inherited it from his mother. But in 1947, when the land was occupied by tenants who lived in Victorian houses, the county Board of Supervisors chose it as the site for a proposed new courthouse.

They condemned the land and paid Lavine and the co-owner about $60,000 each. They ousted the ten-

ants and bulldozed the houses. Then they decided to build the courthouse at the corner of 1st and Hill streets instead.

That's when Lavine's battle began. First he sued on his own behalf, and lost. Then taxpayers sued, charging officials with conspiracy, fraud, misrepresentation and for wasting $2.2 million on the scrapped plan.

While bulldozers turned the property into a parking lot, Lavine carried the taxpayers' fight all the way to the Supreme Court. The battle went on for 10 years, rivaling the Chavez Ravine case in the way it stirred up the city. But the right of eminent domain prevailed, and Lavine and the taxpayers lost.

Lavine's peers honored him in 1956, naming him president of the local Criminal Courts Bar Association, succeeding another legendary attorney, Jerry Giesler.

The champion of appellate matters died in 1982 at age 86.

An 1889 view of the land, looking north from the corner of Broadway and Temple streets, that Lavine sold to the county in the late 1940s. The land was selected in 1997 for the site of Los Angeles' new Roman Catholic cathedral, Our Lady of the Angels.

High Theater For High Crimes

Two of Charles Manson's followers, Sandra Good, left, and Lyn "Squeaky" Fromme, kept vigil outside the Hall of Justice during Manson's sensational trial in 1970.

What stories the cracked and peeling walls of the abandoned former Hall of Justice might tell, if only stone and mortar could talk.

For more than 70 years, this 15-story Italian Renaissance building at the corner of Temple and Spring streets was at the heart of the county's justice system. It witnessed defendants like actor Errol Flynn, accused of statutory rape, and gangster Bugsy Siegel, on trial for murder, and gunman Sirhan Sirhan, assassin of Robert F. Kennedy; dramatic—and success-ful—defense attorneys such as Jerry Giesler; the pop of flashbulbs as news hounds captured their daily exits from the courtrooms, the crush of crowds anxious to catch a glimpse of the famous and infamous, the rush that crime always arouses.

By mid-1994, the building had been officially abandoned, a victim of damage inflicted in the North-ridge earthquake earlier that year. But with moviemakers and histori-ans occasionally visiting, city plan-ners raised the possibility a few years later of using the hall for fed-eral trials.

No matter what happens to the imposing gray granite structure, there's no denying that it was once home to some of the great courtroom dramas of the era.

CONSIDER:

1926—Supporters crowded in to cheer on radio evangelist Aimee Semple McPherson, accused of filing a false police report after her mysterious disappearance from Venice Beach. Dist. Atty. Asa Keyes dropped the misdemeanor charges in midtrial. (It was rumored that Keyes took $30,000 to withdraw the charges.)

1927—A near-riot occurred when a judge began to issue reserved seats to his political cronies for the trial of William Edward Hickman, who had kidnapped a 12-year-old girl and then returned her, apparently alive, for ransom. But the girl was dead—he had sewn her eyes open to make her appear alive and deceive rescuers.

1929—Within days of each other, and with the same judge and defense attorney, theater magnate Alexander Pantages was tried for statutory rape, and his wife was tried for vehicular manslaughter. So great was the curiosity that carpenters built barricades outside the courtroom to keep people in line.

Vaudeville performer Eunice Pringle, 17, in ponytail and little-girl clothes, testified that Pantages had raped her in his office. Ordered to come to court the next day in the clothes she wore the day of the alleged rape, she appeared as a seductive woman. But the jury convicted Pantages, who was notorious as a seducer of aspiring showgirls, and the judge sentenced the multimillionaire to 50 years in San Quentin. He went free after an appeal mounted by up-and-coming attorney Jerry Giesler. His accuser admitted on her deathbed that she had been paid to frame him.

Days before, Lois Pantages was convicted of killing another

Theater magnate Alexander Pantages, left, with his attorney, Jerry Giesler, during Pantages' 1929 trial on statutory rape charges.

motorist, a Japanese gardener. She was sentenced to 10 years' probation and a $78,500 fine. She collapsed at the verdict; all five women jurors burst into tears.

1931—Hundreds lined up for the murder trial of a popular prosecutor who wound up on the wrong side of the law. Deputy Dist. Atty. Dave Clark was accused of shotgunning crime boss Charles Crawford and former newspaperman Herbert Spencer. After arguing self-defense, Clark was acquitted of Spencer's death, and charges were dropped in the Crawford case. Clark had been running for municipal judge at the time of the slaying; even with murder charges against him, he received 60,000 votes (though he was not elected).

1940-1941—Movie actor George Raft testified for his friend Bugsy Siegel, on trial for the murder of Harry (Big Greeny) Greenburg, a witness to a mob killing. Though he was a notorious gangster, Siegel was set free after two star witnesses were shot, gangland style. Years later, a

friend of Siegel's willed $10,000 to the jail physician for supposedly giving Siegel special privileges while behind bars in one of the Hall of Justice's 520 cells. Siegel was back in the old Hall in 1944 on gambling charges. He pleaded guilty and paid a $250 fine.

1942—Jerry Giesler, by now a renowned defense attorney, won acquittal for matinee idol Errol Flynn on statutory rape charges involving two teenage girls aboard his yacht. Movie fans jammed the Hall.

1943—Authorities fearing a "zoot suit" riot guarded the courtroom where 22 Latino youths, called *pachucos* for their gang lifestyle, stood trial for the murder of fellow pachuco José Díaz. Díaz was found dead after a fight at a party near an abandoned Eastside quarry that the press dubbed "Sleepy Lagoon." Twelve were convicted of murder, and five more on lesser charges; five were acquitted. In 1944, all the con-

Women lined up to gaze at movie idol Errol Flynn during his 1943 trial on statutory rape charges involving two teenage girls. Flynn is accompanied by his attorney, Jerry Giesler.

victions were reversed on an appeal mounted by civil rights activists.

1943—Convicted murderer Louise Peete was on trial a second time for robbing and murdering a woman who had testified to her innocence in the first trial. A matronly but alluring woman, the persuasive Peete had been married four times, with each husband supposedly committing suicide when she rejected him. She was finally brought up on charges of murdering a boyfriend, and found guilty. Her second trial drew quite a crowd. Peete was executed in the gas chamber in 1947.

For more than 70 years, this 15-story Italian Renaissance building at the corner of Temple and Spring streets was at the heart of the county's justice system.

1957—L. Ewing Scott was on trial for the murder of his wealthy wife, who disappeared from their Bel-Air home. His lawyer argued that no body had been found and that the alleged victim "might walk through this courtroom door at any time."

"Aha," he said as the jurors looked expectantly toward the door. "That shows you are not convinced 'beyond a reasonable doubt' that she is dead." Then came the prosecu-

Hall of Justice, circa 1930.

tor's turn. "Every head in this courtroom turned toward that door just now," J. Miller Leavy noted. "Except one—that of the defendant. And he didn't bother to look because he knows she's not going to walk through that door. He killed her." Scott received a life sentence, was paroled in 1978 and died in 1987.

1968—To try Sirhan in the assassination of Robert Kennedy, the county built a high-security courtroom on the 13th floor, just a few paces from his cell.

1970–1971—When the Manson family was on trial for killing actress Sharon Tate and six others, Manson's "girls" kept vigil outside. The barefoot young women carved X's into their foreheads and promised to remain "until our father is released." Inside, Manson was barred from the courtroom after he leapt to within a few feet of Judge Charles Older.

Two years later, the new Criminal Courts Building opened across the street.

Stranger Than Fiction

3

The Blond Ambition Of Gorgeous George

He was billed as the "Human Orchid," the "Toast of the Coast" and the "Sensation of the Nation." With his fussy blond ringlets and frilly robes, he paved the way for future generations of gender-bending athletes and entertainers, outraging and delighting wrestling fans along the way.

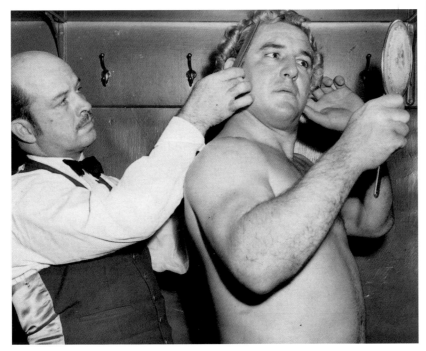

Gorgeous George arranges his marcelled ringlets with the help of his valet before making his entrance into the wrestling ring in 1949.

In the late 1940s, when the advent of television helped professional wrestling bounce back from the scandals of the 1930s, the man who called himself Gorgeous George became one of live television's first superstars. He kept legions of fans glued to their newly purchased TV consoles, and also filled the seats each week in such historic Los Angeles venues as Hollywood Legion Stadium and Olympic Auditorium.

Television demanded low-cost spectacles guaranteed to draw viewers, and George knew how to fill the bill. He had 250 pounds of pre-steroid muscle going for him, as well as a cunning assessment of the needs of the human psyche.

Although few fans ever knew it, George had been a psychiatrist in New York City but put that career aside in favor of the riches, fun, fame and glory he believed he could find through the staged spectacles of professional wrestling. "The more the fans hate me, the more they'll be free to love one another," he wrote in his autobiography, *Is There a Doctor in the Ring?* He believed that wrestling's overt violence could have therapeutic effects for fans.

The future golden-haired gladiator was born George Raymond Wagner in Nebraska, the son of a house painter. He began wrestling at age 13 and was twice named amateur champion of Texas. But as George reached adulthood, Mob ties and payola scandals were putting the kibosh on the world of professional wrestling, and he chose to pursue a more respectable career in psychiatry. Then television changed all that.

Professional wrestling made its television debut in 1948, appearing as part of a Tuesday-night lineup that included "The Milton Berle Show" and "Kukla, Fran & Ollie." The sport's biggest stars, Gorgeous George and the Mighty Atlas, were soon household names. The next year, George topped the card at the Olympic Auditorium, selling out the house 27 times. On each occasion he wore a different one of his 100 purple robes, each of which cost as much as $2,000.

"I got the biggest ovation of my life there," he later recalled of the Olympic. "They couldn't announce the match. The announcer burst out laughing, but I didn't mind. I was a sensation."

When he first decided to turn pro, George took the high road, trying to carve out an image by wearing spats and a homburg and carrying a cane. But dapper wasn't doing it, so George figured out a way to really get under people's skin.

He hired famed Hollywood hairstylists Frank and Joseph, who curled and bleached his hair. To complement the beautiful waves of his coiffure, he began wearing lacy, frilly gowns and sequined lavender robes. His nails were manicured and brightly polished, and he began to toss gold-colored bobby pins that he called "Georgie" pins to members of the audience.

His act shocked the sensibilities of a macho era. The crowd's response was often unruly—fights broke out in the grandstands—but

George, the so-called Human Orchid, promoting his television coverage of the 1951 Tournament of Roses parade.

attendance grew, and Gorgeous George was what audiences paid to see. As a red carpet rolled out and his theme song, "Pomp and Circumstance," played, his personal valet used a sterling silver spray gun to fill the ring with "Chanel No. 10," lest the scent of exertion from the previous match offend his boss' olfactory sense.

There was, of course, no such thing as a perfume called Chanel No. 10. But that didn't really bother fans, nor did they care that the matches were fixed.

In his autobiography, Dr. Wagner (aka George) expounded the theory that watching a contest between a "good guy" and a rule-breaking "bad guy" could be cathartic for fans. He was happy to cast himself as the bad guy. He dispensed savvy pearls of wrestling wisdom, such as: "Win if you can, lose if you must, but always cheat."

"I really don't think I'm gorgeous," he always said. "But what's my opinion against millions?"

Whether reviled or adored by his fans, he learned to withstand the whistles and wisecracks, taunting as much as he was taunted. But he couldn't stand someone pulling or touching his curls. Thirty-five percent of his fans were women, according to sponsors. Men often found him infuriating. During one bout, a male spectator extinguished his cigar on the back of George's calf. His expensive robes were sometimes stolen and torn to shreds by the crowd. "I really don't think I'm gorgeous," he always said. "But what's my opinion against millions?"

To friends and special admirers, who called him "G.G.," he gave 14-karat versions of his signature trinket "Georgie pins," making them take an oath: "I solemnly swear and promise to never confuse this gold Georgie pin with a common, ordinary bobby pin, so help me Gorgeous George."

In 1951, students at Woodbury College interviewed 5,000 owners of television sets about their viewing preferences. The study found that Angelenos most enjoyed watching 200- to 400-pound berserkers sit on the heads of their rivals and tie each other's limbs into square knots. Wrestling, with its bear hugs, power slams, eye-gouging and crotch-kick-

Television demanded low-cost spectacles guaranteed to draw viewers, and George knew how to fill the bill. He had 250 pounds of pre-steroid muscle going for him, as well as a cunning assessment of the needs of the human psyche.

ing, was by far the most popular TV event, with cigarette-puffing little old ladies responding 5 to 1 in its favor.

At his height, George wrestled five to six nights a week. During the day, he ruffled a few feathers at his 195-acre ranch in Beaumont, where he raised 35,000 "Gorgeous George" turkeys. George handled his own marketing and had the birds delivered to stores in limos with orchids emblazed on the doors.

To taunt his opponents, he sometimes had live turkeys delivered to their houses.

But if his fans were working out their emotions while George wrestled, their hero apparently wasn't. His relationships with women—and he had many, despite his flamboyant act—were turbulent and marred by violence and drinking.

After his wife Cherice, with whom he had two children, instigated divorce proceedings, his beloved ranch was tied up in litigation for years.

Meanwhile, wrestling's appeal began to fade. George, who had remarried and fathered three more children, retired in 1962 and opened a tavern on Sepulveda Boulevard called Gorgeous George's Ringside Bar. Patrons, remembering wrestling's glory days, would ask him whether the sport was phony and the matches faked. "I think you have phony and fake misconstrued with showmanship," he was known to reply sweetly.

Only a year into his new enterprise, he suffered a heart attack and died on Christmas Day 1963. He was 48 years old, and broke.

The Los Angeles City Council adjourned that week with a resolution in his memory. At his funeral, both of his former wives—seated on opposite sides of the church—cried uncontrollably. His last girlfriend, a stripper, sobbed and collapsed next to the orchid-colored casket covered with fresh orchids.

His memory is preserved in the large collection of Gorgeous George memorabilia maintained at Slammers Wrestling Gym in Studio City.

Feisty fan threatens to throw her purse at Gorgeous George during a 1948 wrestling match at the Olympic Auditorium.

A Turn-of-the-Century Dr. Feelgood

Dr. Alfred Guido Randolph Castles. Courtesy of The Magic Castle Archives.

Glamour, scandal, way-out religions and crackpot medical therapies—they all flourished in the Southern California sunshine during the first decades of the 20th century, as thousands of new residents flocked to Los Angeles to avail themselves of one of these attractions.

The more adventurous of those who came in pursuit of better health would often find their way to a European-style castle overlooking then undeveloped Hollywood. It was home and clinic for a physician whose name resembled his dwelling: Dr. Alfred Guido Randolph Castles.

Those who knew him described the flamboyant doctor as short in stature but long on ambition and self-aggrandizement. He described himself as a "glandular specialist" and was a world traveler and art collector. Courtly in manner, he was a true eccentric who went about town in heavy makeup, a frock coat and a top hat, enjoying the stir he created.

The Viennese-educated physician had changed his name from Schloesser (German for "castles") amid the anti-German sentiment of World War I. He lived up to both his names by building not one but two Hollywood castles, Glengarry and Sans Souci, where he staged musicales and entertained European royalty.

Castles was born in 1851 in Chicago. After graduating from Rush Medical College there and continuing his studies in Europe, he married a fellow American, Emma Marie Rose McDonell, in 1874.

At the turn of the century, after striking it rich in the Nevada silver mines, the couple and their four children moved to Hollywood, where the doctor built Glengarry, a copy of his wife's ancestral home in Inverness, Scotland.

Soon this castle proved too small for Castles' burgeoning social life and medical practice. So in 1912 he built Castle Sans Souci ("without care") on a three-acre plot at Franklin and Argyle avenues.

Sans Souci was distinguished by leaded glass windows, corner turrets, a crenelated roof line and a 100-foot tower poking up from its central keep. Its Gothic great hall had a 25-foot-high beamed ceiling, stained-glass windows, suits of armor and an organ loft.

The patient list claimed by the doctor read like a Who's Who of the contemporary rich and famous, including Monsignor Joseph Tonello, former secretary to Pope Leo XIII. Philanthropists, princes

Castle Sans Souci, Castles' home, stood on the corner of Argyle and Franklin avenues from 1912 to 1928, where the Castle Argyle Arms apartments are now located. Courtesy of The Magic Castle Archives.

and princesses, countesses, barons and counts were numbered among other guests and patients—or so the doctor said.

When Castles wasn't entertaining the rich and famous, he was striving to rejuvenate them. He advertised a technique that he claimed would reverse the aging process. His method—noninvasive by the standards of the time—involved ingesting pellets made from the glands of sheep and goats.

But as his remedies fell into disrepute, Castles began dabbling in real estate. He tore down Sans Souci and invested in a seven-story luxury apartment building.

The Castle Argyle Arms apartments, opened in 1928, attracted a new breed of royalty: moviemakers. Residents there over the next two decades were to include Clark Gable, Howard Hughes, Ronald Reagan and Cecil B. DeMille.

Castles died five years later, but his legacy still stands in Hollywood at the corner of Franklin and Argyle, its eccentric history known to few if any of the new residents.

When Castles wasn't entertaining the rich and famous, he was striving to rejuvenate them. He advertised a technique that he claimed would reverse the aging process.

Typecast as An Outlaw

He was a lawman who turned desperado—and liked it. Later, the real-life gunslinger worked on more than 100 Western movies as a technical advisor, actor and yarn-spinner. He might have become a leading man had he been as tall as his tales, but alas, one of the Old West's living legends stood a mere five feet tall with his boots on.

Al Jennings holds copy of the pardon he received in 1907 from President Theodore Roosevelt that ended his life sentence for a wild four-state crime spree in the late 1800s.

Al Jennings was born in Tazewell County, Virginia, in 1863, the son of a preacher-lawyer-musician. He ran away from home at age 11 and roamed from state to state. While working as a ranch hand, he learned to draw fast and shoot straight. He also met such legendary Westerners as Jesse James, Bat Masterson, Doc Holliday and Wyatt Earp.

In later years, he loved to tell tales about those encounters. "When I was 14, standing around Dodge City with Bat Masterson," Jennings once said, "an actor wearing a stovepipe hat and a long black coat got off the train. Bat pulled his gun and said, 'I'll plug that hat.' He fired, and the man fell dead. 'Guess I shot too low,' Bat said."

Fascinated by the law, the young Jennings read every legal text he could get his hands on. He moved to Kansas, where he was admitted to the Comanche County bar at age 20. In 1892, Jennings—ever restless—was elected district attorney in El Reno, Oklahoma

But two years into Jennings' tenure as a prosecutor, his brother Ed, also a lawyer, was shot in the back and killed by men who were disgruntled over his victory in a trial.

Jennings, swearing vengeance, tracked down the killers and shot three of them to death in a gunfight. He came out of it with an ankle wound, a $5,000 price on his head and a new destiny—as an outlaw.

He subsequently joined and became the leader of a band of outlaws he called the "Long Riders."

But stealing cattle and robbing trains wasn't as profitable as he had hoped, said Jennings. "Guess we robbed about 15 to 20 trains and most didn't have any money on them, so we had to take up a collection from the passengers—just like in church."

He once took a bullet in the face, and had his lips and chin stitched up by a surgeon to close the wound. "Took my liquor through a funnel for dang near a month," he lamented. But in later years, Jennings would cheerfully admit that he liked being an outlaw. "Some of the finest men I ever met were horse thieves," he said.

Jennings' technique as an armed robber was sometimes worthy of a comedy Western. Once, he was nearly run over when an engineer ignored him as he stood menacingly on the tracks, attempting to flag down the train.

The outlaw's luck ran out in the late 1890s, when he was captured by U.S. marshals after an attempted train robbery in which he blew up a U.S. mail car while trying to open a safe. His booty in that heist consisted of $12.60, a bunch of bananas and a jug of whiskey. Though he went peaceably, without a shot being fired, he was tried and sentenced to life in prison.

Experienced in the law, Jennings wrote letters and persuaded a U.S. senator to champion his cause. When President William McKinley heard of Jennings' case, he reduced his life sentence to five years. In 1904, the former prosecutor got a pardon from President Theodore Roosevelt.

A free man, Jennings hung up his guns and got hitched. His wife Maude would stand at his side—and tower over him—for more than half a century. The couple settled in Oklahoma, where Jennings resumed the practice of law. He later ran for governor but became disillusioned by politics, saying, "There's more honesty among train robbers than among some public officials."

He lost the election by a handful of votes, prompting another career change. This time he tried writing, describing his life as an outlaw in the 1914 book *Beating Back*. In 1921 came a book about a fellow prison inmate, *Through the Shadows With O. Henry*, an account of his friendship with the famous short-story writer.

Meanwhile, Jennings and his wife had been lured west to Hollywood.

His background won him a job as a technical adviser and actor in more than 100 early Westerns, including the biographical *Al Jennings in Oklahoma*. In 1945, when he sued a broadcasting company for allegedly defaming his character, his flair as a teller of tall tales kept jurors spellbound as they listened to his life story in court.

He told them that the popular "Lone Ranger" radio serial had libeled him by falsely accusing him of trying to persuade a 17-year-old boy to join his outlaw gang. Worse, the program's writers had belittled his prowess as a gunman. "They made me mad. They had this Lone Ranger shooting a gun out of my hand, and me an expert." The jurors were entertained, but Jennings lost the case.

By the early 1940s, Jennings and his wife had settled in the San Fernando Valley. Once again, his trigger-happy ways led to brushes with the law on those occasions when police were called to investigate gunfire at his modest ranch at 18824 Hatteras Street in Tarzana. When Jennings was 94, he once grabbed his six-shooter in the middle of the night to pursue a chicken thief, and in the excitement, accidentally gunned down one of his own roosters.

As late as 1957, the old-time gunfighter could be found working as a technical adviser to Hollywood. That year, actor Hugh O'Brian, who was playing television's Wyatt Earp, paid a home visit to Jennings for some tips on gunplay. Concerned neighbors called the police after the two faced off in a shooting duel—but the gunshots they heard turned out to be blanks.

In an incident two years later, Jennings picked up his old Colt .45 from the mantel and began emptying bullets from its chamber. As his old friend, Al Graves, stood by watching, Jennings started showing off with the gun and shot his friend in the elbow. He had forgotten the last bullet.

Despite a life filled with gunfire and bravado, Jennings lasted until the age of 97. When he died in 1961, he was buried next to Maude at Oakwood Memorial Park in Chatsworth—with his boots off.

Police rushed to the Jennings home in 1957 when neighbors reported hearing shots. It turned out that Jennings, then age 93, was showing actor Hugh O'Brian, TV's Wyatt Earp, how Colt revolvers were handled in his true-life outlaw days.

Bring Your Own Sunblock

He preached the benefits of nudism—
for the mind and the body—and he altered the
image of nudists from sex-crazed social lepers to
open-minded naturists.

Ed Lange in 1994

It was on bucolic, grassy, eucalyptus-scented grounds in woodsy Topanga Canyon that Ed Lange created the nudist paradise of Elysium Fields—the first nudist resort to adopt a "clothing-optional" policy rather than requiring all visitors to disrobe. It still exists, 30 years after he founded it.

Lange, the son of strict Chicago Baptists, believed in baring his soul and everything else to commune with nature, and spent his adult life trying to demystify the nudist way of life.

"Nude doesn't necessarily mean lewd," said Lange. "This place is about what you see—the birds, the bees, the sounds of water. It's a supportive, protective environment."

Lange said he wanted to help neutralize the "climate of fear" in which Americans viewed nudity and human sexuality. He got the Supreme Court to change its mind about whether nudist magazines could be sent through the mails, and Kodak to change its policy about printing nudist pictures.

He went on early talk shows—fully clad—to promote the nudist line.

Lange died in 1995, but his secluded paradise, Los Angeles' only nudist colony, has thrived for three decades, despite prayer vigils outside its gates, persistent efforts by the county government to shut it down, and dismayed neighbors who might not have realized what the place was until after they moved in.

Elysium Fields casts itself not as a playland for swingers or a mecca for voyeurs, but as an "educational facility and clothing-optional resort," a place for families. Sex and "provocative play" are prohibited—repeat, prohibited. Visitors are invited to shed their problems along with their attire and get in touch with their senses—to smell the grass, enjoy the fresh air and count the clouds. Though some outsiders referred to the camp as a "sin bin," Lange maintains nothing racier than body-painting ever took place there.

As a teenager in Chicago, Lange became fascinated with nudism after buying an early nudist magazine, *Sunshine & Health*, sold under the counter at a drugstore. Unlike most other young men, Lange was drawn to the articles more than the pictures.

Abandoning Chicago, he moved to Los Angeles in 1940, working as a set designer and as a freelance pho-

Hundreds of members flocked to the 20th anniversary party of the Elysium Institute in Topanga Canyon.

"Nude doesn't necessarily mean lewd," said Lange. "This place is about what you see—the birds, the bees, the sounds of water. It's a supportive, protective environment."

tographer for *Life*, *Vogue* and *Harper's Bazaar*. But his true career path opened up when he heard about what happened to Laura Glassey.

Glassey was a pioneer in the nudist movement, and she had opened the Elysia nudist park in the hills above Tujunga. But hostile newspaper accounts of alleged lewd behavior and hints of "unspeakable orgies" behind the "impenetrable wall" prompted authorities to act. Glassey was on the brink of losing her park.

To forestall it, members complied with a 1939 county law prohibiting nudism, and took to wearing G-strings. But when an unsuspecting sunbather dropped hers to go skinny-dipping, sheriff's deputies—who'd drawn the interesting assignment of peering through binoculars from the hills above—swooped in. Glassey was arrested and eventually had to close Elysia.

Through the ordeal, Lange was one of her biggest supporters. He set out to improve conditions for nudists and change what he considered an unhealthy attitude about sex and the human body. He and his wife June formed the Sundial Club, a social group for nudists that met in the

Langes' Hollywood apartment in the early 1950s.

He did not yet have the law on his side, but he had history.

Benjamin Franklin regularly took "air baths," sitting naked in front of an open window and breathing deeply. James Burnett, the Scottish scientist who was one of the first to suggest that man descended from apes, was a nudist, as was Charles Richter, inventor of the earthquake scale.

Lange waged numerous legal battles. He won a 1956 U.S. Supreme Court decision granting second-class mailing privileges for nudist publications. Five years later, he began publishing his quarterly nudist pamphlet, the *Journal of the Senses*, and wrote books promoting nudity, including *Beyond Nakedness* and *As Nature Intended*.

He persuaded Eastman Kodak to change its policy of refusing to return prints of nudes sent in for developing. Though he was fully clothed, he scandalized daytime TV viewers in the early 1960s by appearing on "Art Linkletter's House Party" to promote the lifestyle.

With his different-drummer tune, Lange had a pied piper ability to attract followers and promote a healthier attitude toward body acceptance, health and self-esteem. But even in Topanga—whose comfortably bohemian residents pride themselves on their reputation for tolerance—Lange encountered resistance to the project he began in 1968.

He said he had found his heaven, his ideal naturist resort, on the edge of Topanga State Park. On his eight acres—with one fig tree—he built an oasis of tranquillity where two common status symbols, clothes and cars, still have no currency. Indeed, cars, loudspeakers and radios are banned to this day.

On warm weekends, waitresses and teachers still mingle with doctors and lawyers. Some play tennis in nothing but sneakers, while others swim in the buff in the pool. Children squeal and romp across the lawn.

But the retreat has had troubles since it opened in 1968. Curious neighbors climbed to the top of the hills surrounding Lange's property, peeked over and called the sheriff. Deputies arrested Lange and two dozen others on successive weekends, charging them with indecent exposure.

Benjamin Franklin regularly took "air baths," sitting naked in front of an open window and breathing deeply. James Burnett, the Scottish scientist who was one of the first to suggest that man descended from apes, was a nudist, as was Charles Richter, inventor of the earthquake scale.

Determined to overthrow the ordinance, Lange began his first legal fight. He challenged the county code and won. The county appealed and Lange prevailed again. The state Court of Appeal finally upheld the right to assemble on private property, whether clothed or unclothed, as constitutionally protected.

Thwarted on one front, officials continued to battle over zoning and land issues until 1992, when they finally gave up and recognized the camp's right to exist.

Spanning almost three decades, the battle to gain legal and community acceptance cost Lange more than $1 million. The same local business leadership and the Topanga Chamber of Commerce that once shunned him and would not sell him a ticket to the group's annual dinner named Lange Man of the Year in 1994, a year before he died.

Today, Elysium Institute (which includes Elysium Growth Press, the publishing company that supports the resort and its educational facilities) is carried on by one of Lange's daughters.

With the passage of time, Elysium Fields—where the clothed and unclothed can mingle in harmony—has become what Lange intended, just another part of a colorful California landscape, rather than a risqué spot on a titillation tour of Los Angeles.

Even More Jinxed Than the MTA

In a city enmeshed in a freeway and mass transit nightmare, it's tempting to imagine the futuristic utopia we might be enjoying had an inventor named Joseph Wesley Fawkes been more successful.

Nearly a century ago, amid the bountiful apricot orchards of Burbank, Fawkes, a visionary and farmer, pondered the problem of linking his growing area with downtown. What Fawkes imagined was a future that ran through the air on one rail.

By 1910 he had built a contraption that he dubbed the Aerial Swallow. He claimed it would haul 50 to 55 passengers at speeds up to 60 mph. But investors didn't share his confidence, and the propeller-driven vehicle, which swung from an overhead track in the inventor's orchard, became known as Fawkes' Folly.

Locals called the Swallow's builder "Crazy Fawkes," though "eccentric" would have been a more precise—and kinder—description. He was a loner with few friends but his wife, Emma, who unlike her husband was known for her sunny disposition.

Born in 1861, Fawkes grew up during a period when mass trans-

Joseph Fawkes, seated in front of his airborne mass transit apparatus, poses with his Burbank neighbors in 1912 after completion of his visionary contraption. Courtesy of Earl Dufur.

portation was just developing. He loved speed. In smartly tailored clothes and sporting a waxed mustache, he raced around town in a carriage drawn by a pair of spirited horses with two Dalmatians running behind.

He owned a 20-acre ranch of walnut and apricot trees on Olive Avenue between Victory Boulevard and Flower Street. It was there that he hung a quarter-mile-long iron rail for the Swallow. The vehicle was about 40 feet long and powered by a Franklin air-cooled engine, which turned the propeller. A hot-air dirigible was supposed to be attached above the rail to give the machine the lift it needed to alleviate the weight of passengers and help it move faster, but the balloon never got off the drawing board.

Even before Fawkes' prototype was ready, the transportation crusader formed the Aerial Trolley Car Co. and started selling stock. He claimed that given the right of way, his monorail could speed from the Valley to downtown Los Angeles in 10 minutes.

But while Fawkes labored frantically to raise capital as well as rails, the Pacific Electric Red Cars spread their network across the metropolitan area, derailing his efforts.

That didn't faze Fawkes, however. On July 4, 1912, with iron determination, he invited a group of potential investors to a party on his ranch, with firecrackers, dinners and free rides in the prototype Swallow. Passengers entered the weird open car from a platform mounted

In 1913, the *Times* ran an artist's conception of a futuristic mass transit system that would provide "relief of over-crowded streets" by offering a monorail and people mover.

Locals called the Swallow's builder "Crazy Fawkes," though "eccentric" would have been a more precise—and kinder—description. He was a loner with few friends but his wife, Emma.

Most of his potential investors shrugged and kept their hands firmly in their pockets.

But others remained fascinated with Fawkes' concept. In 1913, the *Times* ran a futuristic drawing of a transit system that would provide "relief of overcrowded streets"; it included such features as a monorail and people mover.

For his part, Fawkes agitated fruitlessly for recognition.

As time went on, he also became a thorn in the side of Burbank officials. He locked horns with bureaucrats on numerous issues other than his beloved monorail. For years he had vehemently opposed cityhood for Burbank, and on a few occasions backed moves to annex the city—incorporated in 1911—to Los Angeles.

In 1918, when he decided to run for city treasurer, only 48 Burbank voters gave their support to the entrepreneur turned aspiring politician.

Fawkes died in 1928 at the age of 67, his dream unfulfilled. In 1947 his monorail prototype was carted off as junk, rusted and dilapidated. A thriving steel company now stands where the Aerial Swallow once tried to fly.

on a sawhorse. A sharp whistle announced that the Swallow was ready to roll—and it did, reaching a brisk three miles per hour. Less desirably, however, the contraption had to be pushed back manually to its starting point after each run.

"Back me, and with this setup I can glide straight over Mount Hollywood if they won't let me go along the river," he declared. "Once we build a line into Los Angeles, it'll revolutionize interurban travel. I can cross creeks and arroyos without bridges. It'll be a gold mine. In 10 years it'll put the P.E. in a museum."

Humping Along Route 66

Way before the Okies fled the Dust Bowl and followed this asphalt ribbon out West, and nearly a hundred years before the Beat generation would traverse it in search of kicks, the trail that became U.S. Route 66 was blazed by a most unusual pioneer.

He came leading a caravan of camels.

Lt. Edward Fitzgerald Beale, a surveyor in the U.S. Army, had been selected to discover whether these spitting, swaying, sand-loving beasts were better suited than horses for settling the West.

While testing the camel's usefulness in the New West, he charted a 450-mile stretch of desert from New Mexico to the Pacific Coast that would be famous and vital for more than a century. It became known as "Beale's Trail."

The Gold Rush had brought new settlers to California, and the government was now seeking a more effective supply route from East to West. Beale came leading the Army's first (and only) Camel Corps—a caravan of 25 camels, 56 soldiers and camel drivers, eight covered wagons and 350 sheep. Some say the camels were Beale's idea, that he had read about them in another explorer's North African journal. He convinced Jefferson Davis, then secretary of war, to finance the experiment. Four years

later it came to an end in Los Angeles, where the dromedaries and Bactrians, or two-humped camels, were corralled on Main Street in 1861 and then sold at public auction.

But for decades afterward, tales of the West included sightings of stray camels wandering the wastelands.

Long before the camels, Beale had made a name for himself as a fearless scout with a knack for making friends in high places. In 1828, as a boy, he was brawling in a street near the White House with another youth when a tall passerby grabbed them and asked why they were fighting. Beale said it was because his playmate had called newly elected President Andrew Jackson a "jackass."

The passerby, amused, told Beale to come see him in his new house. "Sir, who are you?" Beale asked. "I'm the jackass," said President Jackson.

In 1836, Jackson appointed the 14-year-old to the Navy. Ten years later, in the Mexican War during the Battle of San Pasqual, Beale and

Edward Fitzgerald Beale. Courtesy of National Trust for Historic Preservation.

more than a hundred others retreated to a hilltop in Escondido. Beale and his lifelong friend, the scout Kit Carson, volunteered to sneak through enemy lines commanded by Andres Pico to summon the Marines, who marched to the rescue.

Later, when the U.S. military got early word of the January 1848 California gold strike at Sutter's Mill, Beale was selected to smuggle an eight-pound lump back to Washington, D.C., as proof. He carved off a bit of gold for a wedding ring, married his fiancee and took off on what would be a career spent shuttling across the West, exploring desert trails and mountain passes for the military.

In 1853, with a presidential appointment as superintendent of Indian affairs for California and Nevada, Beale set up California's first federal Indian reservation, at the foot of the Tehachapis. More than 2,500 Yokuts from the San Joaquin Valley settled at Sebastian Reservation—diplomatically named by Beale for his patron, Arkansas Sen. William Sebastian.

When cattle rustlers became a problem in the "Grapevine Canyon" between Los Angeles and Kern County, Beale called for a military fort. Ft. Tejon, just this side of Bakersfield, became the outpost of military and social life in the 100 or so miles between there and Los Angeles, and Beale was at its center.

The Army later took Beale on as national surveyor general of roads. That same year, as Mexican land-grant families were selling off their vast holdings, Beale went on a buying spree. Eventually he would hold 270,000 acres that he named the Tejon Ranch. President Abraham Lincoln later refused to reappoint Beale as surveyor general, saying, "I will not have a surveyor who becomes monarch of all he surveyed."

He charted a 450-mile stretch of desert from New Mexico to the Pacific Coast that would be famous and vital for more than a century. It became known as "Beale's Trail."

Getting supplies to the fort was difficult; the heat killed pack horses and mules. Beale wanted to invest in camels. With Davis' support, he got Congress to appropriate $30,000 for the venture.

In 1857, the caravan—with Beale at its helm and the camels' brass bells clanging—started off from the New Mexico Territory for Los Angeles.

"This will eventually be the greatest emigrant road to California," Beale wrote in his journal as he jotted down watering holes on a route that had been explored but only vaguely mapped before.

The trip ended at Ft. Tejon 60 days later. By then the 25 camels numbered 28; three had been born. Beale noted only a few problems: The camels' lurching pace made some soldiers seasick. On the upside, the camels carried up to half a ton of cargo. Their feet could plod over sharp rocks. They fed on prickly pear cactus. And their water economy was legendary.

Thereafter, a team of camels often pulled Beale's surrey into town on his frequent trips to Los Angeles. Though some drivers characterized them as mean, Beale praised the gentleness of these four-legged "ships of the desert." He learned Syrian so he could talk to them. "I look forward to the day," Beale wrote, "when every mail route across the continent will be conducted…with this economical and noble brute."

But it never happened. Most of the drivers were poorly trained, and their ill treatment of the beasts brought ill results. Competing mule markets vied for favor in Washington. And with the coming of the Civil War, the Army had a new set of priorities. The camels' chief booster, Davis, became president of the Confederacy. By the time the war was over, the "iron horse," or railroad train, was speeding westward with more cargo than any beast could ever carry.

Copy of a sketch showing a camel caravan resting at the Playa Church at El Pueblo de Los Angeles on its way from the city to Ft. Tejon in 1857. The sketch is contained in the book "The City That Grew" by Boyle Workman.

A photo re-creation that depicts an actual jump over Beale's Cut made by a stuntman for the 1923 Tom Mix movie *Three Jumps Ahead*. Courtesy of The Robert S. Birchard Collection.

After the Army stabled the camels in downtown Los Angeles, they were put to work for a time transporting freight between the harbor and downtown. About 37 were then sold at public auction, most of them to a former driver who in turn sold them to circuses and parks. Others were released to roam the desert, where they bred for a time, startling many a cowboy who'd had a few drinks.

But the camels' most enduring legacy is still visible today. In an effort to get his caravan through the Santa Susanas, Beale used soldiers armed with picks and shovels, plus $5,000 from the Los Angeles County Board of Supervisors, to hack a narrow cut through the mountains. It was 90 feet deep, 240 feet long and 13 feet wide. It opened up trade and transit between L.A. and the north. The toll was two bits for horse and rider, $2 for teams of a dozen or more, and a dime a head for loose animals. For half a century, until the Newhall Tunnel was dug with newer technology, traffic flowed through Beale's Cut.

Though eroded in the El Niño rains of 1998, the pass remains virtually intact and can be reached from Sierra Highway off the Antelope Valley Freeway near Clampitt Road.

Beale went on to serve as U.S. minister to Austria in 1876, and he died at home in Washington in 1893. His Tejon Ranch was sold in 1912 to a business group that included Times Mirror, which has since sold its interest in the property.

Beale blazed a trail that countless others followed. Now an eight-lane freeway bisects his rancho, and interstates have replaced Beale's Trail.

Greek George Of Daisy Dell

Few music lovers know it, but the Hollywood Bowl—renowned for the gentle pleasures of alfresco dining and classical music—was home to one of the wilder and more colorful characters ever to perform on the stage of early Los Angeles history.

George Caralambo. Courtesy of Steve Pastis.

On the very spot where the stage now sits, a rough wooden cabin was thrown up more than a hundred years ago by a uniquely colorful individual known as "Greek George" Caralambo.

Then called Daisy Dell, the barren acreage had belonged to the U.S. government, which bestowed it on the immigrant in return for his seven years of service in the U.S. Army Camel Corps.

Born in Smyrna, now called Izmir, Turkey, Caralambo had arrived in Texas in 1857 with the second load of camels purchased by the War Department as part of its attempt to introduce the four-legged "ship of the desert" into the American West under famed surveyor Edward Fitzgerald Beale.

Along with nine other Greek, Syrian and Turkish camel herders, Caralambo was paid $15 a month to drive the camels used to haul the supplies for building the famed and short-lived Butterfield overland mail route. The camels' Army career ended with the outbreak of the Civil War—though not before providing Caralambo with a typically colorful adventure. While leading the herd of camels back to Los Angeles from Ft. Mojave, he was shot at with bow and arrow by a Mojave Indian. George's thick beard stopped the arrow, which hung there, barely grazing his chin.

After all the camels were auctioned off, Caralambo caught gold fever and headed for Holcomb Valley, then known as the hellhole of the San Bernardino Mountains. He quickly established himself as kingpin of a particularly rowdy saloon. For Caralambo, one day's work involved shooting a bystander who cheered when Caralambo's horse ran second in a race, gunning down a cheat caught filing off the horn tips of a bull about to fight a grizzly bear, and shooting a cook. The motive for the latter assault remains obscure.

In 1865, Caralambo headed for New Mexico, where he shot and killed Alfred C. Bent, the popular son of New Mexico's first governor, in an apparently unprovoked attack. Bent's father, Charles, had died in a similar manner while still in office.

Caralambo fled, but then, fearful of capture, faked his own suicide. He left a note in which he confessed to the killing, describing the motive as "self-defense." The newspapers bought into his phony demise. Both the *New Mexican* and the *Santa Fe Weekly Gazette* ran articles saying he had "shot himself in the head" and noting the location of his burial.

Free from pursuit, Caralambo returned to Los Angeles, where he became a naturalized citizen and changed his name to George Allen.

Around that time, he petitioned the government to recognize his service and wound up with a large chunk of useless land west of the Cahuenga Pass in the future Hollywood Bowl.

In 1867 he built a wooden shack there. In the meantime, while Caralambo and his wife, Cornelia Lopez, were operating the La Brea Waystation near what is now Kings Road and Fountain Avenue in West Hollywood, a Slavic immigrant recalled only as "Marsovich" moved onto the property and filed a mineral claim.

Caralambo fumed, but uncharacteristically decided to handle the problem nonviolently: He sued Marsovich. After several years in the courts, Caralambo won, but Marsovich still refused to move. Returning to the tried and true, Caralambo bit off Marsovich's ear—a novel though effective form of eviction.

Not wanting any more trouble with squatters, Caralambo and his wife, who was ready to give birth, moved into the cabin in Daisy Dell, an area also referred to as Bolton Canyon. Their first house guests were the infamous bandit Tiburcio Vasquez and his lover, Rosario, who happened to be the wife of one of the bandit's trusted soldiers, as well as Cornelia Lopez's sister.

While Lopez screamed with labor pains, Caralambo galloped to town—not for a doctor, but to betray his house guest for a $15,000 reward.

On May 15, 1874, a posse of seven stormed the tiny cabin to capture the unarmed bandit. Lopez, who had just delivered a girl, had purposely moved Vasquez's gun to another room while fixing his meal.

For Caralambo, one day's work involved shooting a bystander who cheered when Caralambo's horse ran second in a race, gunning down a cheat caught filing off the horn tips of a bull about to fight a grizzly bear, and shooting a cook.

The heavily armed deputies stopped his attempt to escape by shooting him first in the shoulder, then peppering his backside with buckshot as he attempted to climb through a window.

After being hauled off to jail, he was tried, convicted and hanged in Northern California the following year.

However, Caralambo never collected his reward.

Before the turn of the century, his wife died, and Caralambo remarried and sold his Bolton Canyon property for $500.

Short of cash, he decided to try again for a government pension. This time he heard that Charles Lummis, onetime *Times* city editor, writer, craftsman, founder of the Southwest Museum and defender of the city's poor, was the man to help him.

In 1903, when he visited Lummis' home in the Arroyo Seco, Caralambo realized that almost 50 years earlier, he had camped with his camels on his way to Ft. Tejon under the huge, four-pronged sycamore tree in the center of Lummis' patio.

Lummis sympathized with the former herdsman and took up his case, but without any luck.

In 1913, living in a wooden shack at La Misión Vieja in Montebello (forerunner of Mission San Gabriel), penniless and a widower, "Greek George" Caralambo, the former trailblazer, died.

It looked as though Caralambo was destined to be forgotten. He was laid to rest in Mt. Olive Cemetery in Whittier. No headstone was placed to mark the grave. Nearly 50 years after his death, the Native Daughters of the Golden West commemorated his unmarked grave with a tombstone. In 1968, Mt. Olive and nearby Broadway Cemetery were condemned and the land was converted into Founders Memorial Park, leaving Caralambo's remains, along with a few thousand others, somewhere between a park bench and a picnic table.

After that, his chipped tombstone rested in a storage yard behind the Pio Pico Mansion.

The colorful, if tempestuous, Caralambo may yet be rescued from obscurity, though. Steve Pastis, editor of the Greek American publication *Hellenic Calendar*, is at work on a book, "Greek George and Hi Jolly," and Caralambo's great-great-granddaughter, Juliana Waychus, a Madera schoolteacher, has a documentary film in the works.

The Real McCoy Not Such a Genuine Guy

Kid McCoy jokes around with children at the beach in 1924.

His outrageous cheating in the boxing ring—like spraying ammonia in one opponent's eyes and strewing thumbtacks under the bare feet of another—ironically made him a glamorous sports figure. His moniker is still in the American vocabulary: The Real McCoy.

At the turn of the century, Norman Selby boxed as "Kid McCoy," a world middle-weight and welterweight champion who retired in New York at age 24 with a half million dollars. But after he made his way to Los Angeles, where he played bit parts in movies as a bad guy, his violent temper finally got the best of him. Following one particular night of mayhem, he wound up swinging a pickax on a prison chain gang instead of landing punches in the ring.

Famed for his "corkscrew punch," he relied on underhanded tactics to gain titles and fame. Against a deaf boxer, he pointed to the man's corner, indicating that the bell had ended the round. It hadn't. When the man turned away, McCoy knocked him cold.

McCoy said the name "The Real McCoy" came about thus: "I'm in a saloon with a charming young lady, as usual. A drunk is making passes at her. I try to brush him off without too much fuss. 'Beat it,' I says, 'I'm Kid McCoy.' He laughs and says, 'Yeah? Well, I'm George Washington.' I have to clip him a short one, and down he goes. He wakes up 10 minutes later, rubs his jaw and says, 'Jeez, it was the real McCoy!'"

In a 166-fight career, he lost only six times. Surprisingly popular despite his tactics, he used his winnings to open a cabaret in New York, where he entertained with this story and others, and rubbed elbows with the famous.

But he could keep neither his money nor his temper. Saloon slugfests increased as his fame waned. His fortune gone after eight divorces, McCoy, a flabby 51, came to Los Angeles, where he worked as a security guard while pursuing movie roles. He started dating Theresa Mors, whose husband, Albert, was a wealthy art and antiques dealer. Theresa moved in with McCoy, recalled 92-year-old Frances Pearlstein Grunnet, the Morses' former secretary and the only surviving witness to what would occur. She gave this account:

Theresa's friends Sam and Ann Schapp, who owned a dress shop next to the antiques store, told her that McCoy was a bum and only after her money.

On August 12, 1924, McCoy came home drunk. When Theresa told him what her friends had said, he knocked her teeth out, stabbed her and shot her in the head. McCoy drank all night and, by the next morning, set out to kill Albert Mors as well.

Mors wasn't at his shop when McCoy got there, so he kept 11 people hostage while he waited. He ordered three men to take off their pants to discourage escape. (One left anyway, and McCoy shot him in the leg.)

One of the hostages was 19-year-old Frances.

McCoy gathered up the hostages' money, giving $300 to the soon-to-be-married Frances as a wedding gift. (She later returned it to its owners.)

Her boss, Albert, "never showed up," she said in a recent interview.

He relied on underhanded tactics to gain titles and fame. Against a deaf boxer, he pointed to the man's corner, indicating that the bell had ended the round. It hadn't. When the man turned away, McCoy knocked him cold.

"He was off getting a haircut, and then his new Cadillac wouldn't start, which saved his life."

Frustrated by the wait, McCoy went in search of the Schapps. He shot and wounded them before racing through what is now MacArthur Park, where police caught him.

McCoy's attorney, Jerry Giesler, persuaded the jury to convict the former boxer on manslaughter, not murder, charges.

McCoy served eight years of a 24-year sentence. Even in prison, he got some lucky breaks. While swinging a pickax on a prison chain gang near San Simeon, he witness a nearby plane crash and saved an injured pilot from the wreckage. That led to a better job, as a tour guide at San Quentin.

Notables like Gen. Douglas MacArthur, actor Lionel Barrymore, U.S. Vice President Charles Curtis and others petitioned for his release and eventually won him a pardon from California's governor.

In 1932, the 59-year-old parolee and his new, ninth wife moved to Detroit, where the Ford Motor Co. created a job for him as "athletic director." Three years later, he rescued several people whose boat had overturned on Lake Michigan.

But in 1940, at 66, he took his own life with a bottle of sleeping pills. His farewell note read, "I can't endure this world's madness any longer."

McCoy had once warned a young inmate, "Remember that the bright lights go out the quickest. Kid McCoy knows."

Battle of Sitting Duck: Uncle Sam v. Wily Wife

Jackson Barnett doing what he loved to do best: direct traffic on Wilshire Boulevard.

He was called the "richest Indian in America," but his tastes didn't run to polo or champagne. Rather, Jackson Barnett's interests were—quite literally—pedestrian.

In the 1920s, Barnett was one of this city's living landmarks, standing day after day on the northeast corner of Rossmore Avenue and Wilshire Boulevard—always impeccably dressed in a three-piece suit and always doing the same thing: directing traffic.

Nearly everyone saw him as a harmless, rather charming character—except the federal government, which saw him as an easy mark. Many believed his lovely wife, who was half his age, did too. Before long, he was at the center of a protracted tussle that became one of the strangest sagas in Depression-era Los Angeles. For two decades, the government pursued Barnett and his wife through hundreds of court appearances in three states, and even dragged them before a U.S. Senate committee.

Barnett, a Creek, was born around 1841 in the territory that eventually became Oklahoma. After a fight with U.S. soldiers attempting to force his people onto a reservation, Barnett fell from his horse, sustaining a head injury that left him with a childlike mind. As a consequence, he never learned to read or write.

When the government officially turned Oklahoma into "Indian Territory," Barnett received 160 rocky, unusable acres near what would become the town of Henryetta. It looked like a raw deal—until oil began gushing from the rocks on Barnett's property in 1912.

Hearing of the gusher, the good men in government felt they had to act on Barnett's behalf. That very year, they went to court and had Barnett declared mentally incompetent. A guardian appointed by the feds quickly leased Barnett's land to an oil company on favorable terms.

For almost a decade, the federal government gave Barnett an allowance of $40 a month from the riches it was earning from his land. Then one day he answered a knock on the door of his shack to meet Anna Laura Lowe, a pretty 40-year-old divorcee who literally took him from rags to riches.

In 1920, when Barnett was 79, he married Lowe, who persuaded the government to increase her hus-

Barnett with his wife, Anna Laura Lowe. Courtesy of Clinedinst Studio.

"My wife is pretty damn smart. Why, she can make change for any amount of money, even a $50 bill——yes, sir——quick as anything and right every time. They can't fool her," said Barnett.

band's income to $2,500 a month.

"My wife is pretty damn smart. Why, she can make change for any amount of money, even a $50 bill—yes, sir—quick as anything and right every time. They can't fool her," said Barnett.

But Lowe had her eye on more than small change, and she got it.

The government objected when it discovered that Barnett had given away more than $1 million in Liberty bonds that Lowe had helped him extract from his federal trust. He'd spent $550,000 on a charity for the endowment of Indian schools in Oklahoma, and had bestowed an equal amount on his wife.

In 1923, a federal judge in New York ordered that the bonds be returned and that all of Barnett's funds be handed over to the Department of the Interior to be held in trust. The action was blocked while Barnett's lawyers appealed. Meanwhile, the couple moved to Los Angeles, where Lowe got them set up in a 15-room colonial mansion on Wilshire Boulevard.

Three years later, federal marshals compelled the couple to appear before Senate hearings in New York, Washington and Oklahoma. The government sought to prove that Barnett's wife had "kidnapped him by seductive wiles, petting and persuasion and married him only for his money."

Many believed the government was right: that Lowe was an opportunist who had found her prey after learning the whereabouts of a sitting duck in Oklahoma.

Others believed she was the best thing that had ever happened to him. He seemed to adore her and loved riding in the car they had purchased, or on the horses they kept on a 100-acre ranch in Coldwater Canyon.

Nearly everyone saw him as a harmless, rather charming character—except the federal government, which saw him as an easy mark. Many believed his lovely wife, who was half his age, did too.

While suits, countersuits and appeals continued, Barnett spent his days directing traffic near his mid-Wilshire home. He passed out chewing gum to the neighborhood children, and on Halloween he gave them popcorn balls.

On May 29, 1934, Barnett died in his sleep at age 93, ending his romance with the woman who fondly called him "the chief."

Three months later, a U.S. district judge ruled that Barnett had been incompetent to make decisions, and his marriage was therefore declared invalid. All his property was ordered turned over to the Department of the Interior to be held until a court could determine who his heirs should be. In 1936 the U.S. Supreme Court upheld the decision.

More than 800 people subsequently sought a share of Barnett's $3-million estate. A federal court decided that 33 Creeks and a Caucasian relative were the heirs. Lowe got nothing.

More lawsuits were filed by the widow's creditors and attorneys, and the government seized her accounts and Coldwater Canyon property.

Nothing was left except the mansion on Wilshire, partially paid for with $40,000 from Lowe's daughter from a former marriage.

Lowe was jailed for contempt of court after failing to relinquish her rugs, tapestries and furniture. The government tried to take her to court for not watering her lawn, but backed down in the face of adverse publicity.

Thousands of women in Los Angeles were outraged by her plight and rallied to her cause, signing petitions and sending them to congressmen, senators, and to Franklin and Eleanor Roosevelt in the White House.

But Washington ignored their pleas, and the grace period on Lowe's eviction notice neared its end. Newsreel cameras were set up in front of her house as the press anticipated her dramatic removal.

On October 30, 1938, in front of a crowd of a thousand or more, federal officers pelted her home with tear gas canisters. The widow, brandishing an ax, emerged crying, screaming and kicking, along with her daughter. The police dragged both into waiting cars and took them to jail.

They were released not long afterward and moved into a small house in Los Angeles. In 1952, the chief's widow died penniless in her daughter's arms.

A Pioneer in Petticoats

Julian Eltinge, as he appeared in *Nine O'Clock Revue*.

He was a 200-pound man who squeezed himself into size 4 high-heeled shoes and a corset with a 23-inch waist. And for many years he laughed all the way to the bank, for at the turn of the century, his outrageous antics brought him a salary greater than that of the president of the United States.

Julian Eltinge, the original King of Drag, pioneered modern female impersonation, becoming the world's most flamboyant illusionist on stage and screen from before World War I into the 1930s. "It's a crime that the most beautiful woman in the world is a man," wrote a theater critic of the time.

As sidelines, Eltinge published a beauty magazine, sold sheet music, founded a line of cold cream and a Hollywood social club, and endorsed the Norda corset that reduced his 38-inch waist to 23 inches. He even built a shrine to himself—The Eltinge Theater—on 42nd Street, in the heart of New York's Broadway district.

He also legally changed his name to spare his family embarrassment.

Eltinge was born William Dalton in 1883 in Massachusetts. By age 10, he could no longer resist a visit to the frilly side of the wardrobe rack. He made his stage debut in a dress at the Boston Cadet School's annual theatrical presentation. His convincing female stage presence made him such a hit that the next year, when he was 11, the show was written around him.

Though the practice of men playing women onstage dates back at least to ancient Greece and was the standard in Shakespeare's era, it wasn't until Eltinge was a teenager, and a smattering of drag queens were tentatively sashaying about, that the American public took female impersonators to heart.

Eltinge made his Broadway debut at 21, in the musical comedy "Mr. Wix of Wickham." The show failed, but Eltinge was such a success as a showgirl that he put together other acts and toured the country and London for the next five years. One of his biggest hit musicals was *The Fascinating Widow*, in which he played both bride and bridegroom, and a bathing beauty.

Kings, queens and emperors—his unfailing cheerleaders—showered him with gifts, among them a bulldog named Smith, a gift from King Edward VII.

Eltinge's onstage persona and the fact that he never married led to speculation about his sexuality. He went out of his way to assert his masculinity. He once battled a "bunch of hoodlums" in a saloon who ribbed him about being a

Eltinge, ca. 1930. Courtesy of The Institute of the American Musical, Inc.

"swish." He punched out a stagehand who called him "Lucy." The same stagehand also let it be known that Eltinge was friends with the founder of a cutlery company in Sheffield, England. When the businessman died in 1907, Eltinge inherited his entire $1-million estate.

In 1912, when Eltinge's weekly salary of $1,625 made him the best-paid act in vaudeville and exceeded that of President Taft, he and two colleagues opened the only theater ever built by a drag queen: the Eltinge Theater, later called the Empire, on West 42nd Street in New York.

In 1912, when Eltinge's weekly salary of $1,625 made him the best-paid act in vaudeville and exceeded that of President Taft, he and two colleagues opened the only theater ever built by a drag queen: the Eltinge Theater, later called the Empire, on West 42nd Street in New York.

As different as Eltinge himself, the theater offered seats for thin, average and plump patrons. (The facade of the building still stands, though it was recently moved about 70 feet to make room for a new multiplex theater.)

Persuaded by film producer Jesse Lasky to come west and star in silent movies, Eltinge arrived in Hollywood in 1917, launching his film career in *The Clever Mrs. Carfax*. As in the other films he would make, he was portrayed at his insistence as a clean-cut straight man forced into drag through some plot device.

To balance his drag persona with a more "butch" one off-stage, his public relations firm photographed him laboring in overalls and in an unconvincing boxing match with "Gentleman Jim" Corbett. He also was often seen puffing on a cigar.

Eltinge preferred being called an actor or "America's Leading Sex Simulator," but others still referred to him as a "gay deceiver" and "the queerest woman in the world."

The brand-new Hollywood film industry loved him. He thrived as a featured player in several comedies, including *The Countess Charming* (1917), *Over the Rhine* (1917) and *The Widow's Might* (1918). Perhaps his chief footnote to fame was starring in *The Isle of Love* in 1922;

The grand living room of Eltinge's Moorish-style home in Silverlake reflected his interest in fine fabrics and furnishings. Courtesy of Charles Knill.

Eltinge preferred being called an actor or "America's Leading Sex Simulator," but others still referred to him as a "gay deceiver" and "the queerest woman in the world."

a young actor named Rudolph Valentino had a supporting role.

Choosing Silvelake as his home, Eltinge built a Moorish mansion he called Villa Capistrana. In the home's Chinese Room, a red chamber with an enormous dragon artistically rendered on one wall, he entertained members of the actors' colony, including Lasky, Mary Pickford and Geraldine Farrar.

Despite the party atmosphere, he brought his parents to live with him and hired one of Los Angeles' first landscape architects, Charles Gibbs Adams, who added a tropical garden of palms and fountains that still survives on the Baxter Street property.

When he took off his high heels, Eltinge sometimes donned cowboy boots, and he opened a dude ranch called Sierra Vista, east of San Diego. The 100-room ranch, which he touted as a retreat for men only, was the first financial mistake of his career. The second—the stock market crash—would not be of his own making.

The crash put a dent in Eltinge's substantial fortune; nature would take a toll on his career.

After the release of *Madame Behave* in 1925 and *Maid to Order* in 1930, he decided to semiretire and hang up his frock. The films did fairly well, but the chin straps he used couldn't disguise the fact that he was well over 40 and looked matronly on film.

More than that, though, there was a new puritanical sensibility in the nation. Drag was thought to be a byproduct of homosexuality and, as such, a threat to society. Eltinge found his once highly respected career criticized as immoral.

He rarely performed thereafter. Booked in 1940 at the Rendez-vous—a somewhat seedy L.A. nightclub—Eltinge was forced to forgo drag and emcee in a tux. The same year, a local ordinance required all female impersonators to take psychiatric exams before working professionally.

His final appearance came a year before his death in 1941, when he played a cameo role with other vaudevillians in Bing Crosby's *If I Had My Way*.

Today, his gender-bending legacy survives in movie, musical and comedy acts, and his villa, the house that drag built, still stands.

No Juliet for The 'Romeo of Song'

At the height of Hollywood's Golden Age, Russ Columbo was one of the town's most sought-after bachelors. He was a crooner and Valentino lookalike with flashing eyes and a charming smile. His composition "Prisoner of Love" became his vocal trademark. He was taller than his principal competitor, Bing Crosby, and most Hollywood insiders considered him more handsome, better dressed and more formidable at the microphone.

Russ Columbo dining with actress Sally Blane, younger sister of Loretta Young, at the Brown Derby restaurant in 1933. Rumor had it that the two were engaged, but a year later Columbo died in a bizarre accident on the day he was to have announced his engagement to Carole Lombard.

But a career like Crosby's was not to be. Columbo's life ended abruptly in 1934 in what appeared to be a freak accident. But even now, his untimely end remains shrouded in tantalizing mystery.

Born Ruggiero Eugenio de Rodolfo Columbo in San Francisco in 1908, he was of Italian descent, the 12th son of a 12th son. After his family moved to Los Angeles, he attended Belmont High, where he became a violinist with the school orchestra. He was soon earning money as a musician, playing in theaters for silent films. He dropped out of school and in short order was hired to play "emotion" music for silent film vamp Pola Negri's love scenes.

Negri was instrumental in helping Columbo get bit parts in films and later played a major part in publicizing his career.

In the late 1920s, shortly after Rudy Vallee made "crooning" and dancing cheek-to-cheek a national craze, Columbo burst onto the national scene as the new pop style's prime exponent. When he wasn't singing, he was swinging on his violin with other leading performers, such as George Eckhart's orchestra, which performed at the Mayfair Hotel in downtown Los Angeles; Slim Martin's band at the Pantages Theater in Hollywood; and Professor

Columbo was billed as "Radio's Valentino" and the "Romeo of Song." The combination of his sensuous voice and good looks created a magnetism that few women could resist.

Moore's orchestra at the Hollywood Roosevelt Hotel.

He even performed with Crosby. In 1928, when Columbo joined the Gus Arnheim Orchestra at the Cocoanut Grove as a violinist, he would croon tunes with the band's talented young vocalist. After Crosby left the act, Columbo took over.

Columbo received skyrocketing profits from early talkies in which he costarred: *Wolf Song* (1929), *Street Girl* (1929), *Dynamite* (1929) and *Moulin Rouge* (1930).

While he continued making movies, Columbo organized his own band and opened a dinner theater, Club Pyramid, in a converted warehouse on Hollywood Boulevard, where he showcased orchestras and other entertainment.

By the early 1930s, Columbo was in the middle of "the battle of the baritones," with Crosby singing on CBS radio and Columbo on NBC's Blue Network. (Crosby was indirectly responsible for launching Columbo's radio career. Columbo and his agent were broke and needed to get back to New York for Columbo's broadcast debut. The agent scraped up the money by selling Crosby an old car.)

Columbo was billed as "Radio's Valentino" and the "Romeo of Song." The combination of his sensuous voice and good looks created

a magnetism that few women could resist. His long list of romantic "interests," as the era's popular fan magazines described them, included Constance Bennett, Sally Blane, Dorothy Dell and Carole Lombard.

As his career took off with his radio show, nightclub, theater appearances, films, orchestra and composing, Columbo was making as much as $7,500 a week. He spent many hours singing and writing about the powers and pitfalls of love, including "You Call It Madness (But I Call It Love)."

But at the height of his career, tragedy came suddenly.

September 2, 1934, was to have been a big day for the 26-year-old Columbo. He intended to announce his engagement to Carole Lombard that afternoon. But shortly after lunch, he went to visit his best friend, portrait photographer Lansing Brown, who lived on Lillian Way in the Wilshire district. As they were looking at Brown's Civil War—era dueling pistols, Brown's went off, ricocheting off the top of a mahogany desk, piercing Columbo's left eye and entering his brain.

He died on the spot. His pallbearers included such movie greats as Crosby, Gilbert Roland, Walter

Lang, Stuart Peters, Lowell Sherman and Sheldon Keate Callaway.

But questions surrounded his relationship with Brown. Had they merely been friends, or was there more to it? Had Columbo's life ended in a tragic accident or a jealous argument? No charges were ever brought against Brown. An insurance company ruled the death accidental.

Meanwhile, Columbo's aging mother had suffered a heart attack and had been hospitalized in Santa Monica just two days before his death. Fearing the news of her son's death would kill her, family and friends kept it from her.

The charade continued for more than a decade after Columbo's death, while his mother remained in poor health and partially blind. Family members faked letters and telegrams each month from London, where they said her son was working. A monthly check arrived for $398, supposedly sent from his earnings. The payments were actually from a double-indemnity $25,000 life insurance policy.

At the end, that was all that remained of Russ Columbo's short-lived but frenetic plunge into music, glamour and romance.

Sin and Sincerity

chapter

4

The Multiracial Ministry Of William Seymour

Fate deprived William Joseph Seymour of sight in one eye, but the fiery African American preacher's vision of a colorblind Christianity—reinvigorated by what its adherents called "the gifts of the spirit"—briefly changed the face of American religion.

William Joseph Seymour with his wife, Jennie. Courtesy of Fred Berry, Joshua Ministries.

In 1906, from the porch of an unpretentious wood-frame house on Bonnie Brae Street near downtown Los Angeles, Seymour, the son of slaves and a former waiter, began proclaiming his enthusiastic version of the Gospel, attracting ever-growing multiracial crowds.

It was the beginning of what we now call Pentecostalism.

The unbridled fervor of his multiethnic flock soon drew the enmity of the neighbors, and Seymour was forced to move to a onetime stable in what is now Little Tokyo. This small mission became the vortex of an ecstatic Pentecostal worship—known as the Azusa Street Revival—that rapidly spread throughout the world.

But the racially integrated aspect of Seymour's joyous revival was short-lived. As Pentecostalism spawned new Protestant denominations, white believers who were willing to adjust to speaking in tongues and faith healing increasingly drew the line at sharing their pews with blacks and Latinos.

But Seymour kept the faith, proclaiming that "one token of the Lord's coming is that He is melting all races and nations together, and they are filled with the power and glory of God."

Louisiana-born in 1870, Seymour worked from childhood in the cane fields with his parents and siblings. A bout with smallpox brought him close to death and cost him the sight in one eye. Soon after, while he struggled with his conventional Methodist upbringing, he felt what he believed was a spiritual calling and left home to attend a Texas Bible school.

Armed with a rudimentary scriptural education, he came to Los Angeles, where he began holding prayer meetings in the home of Richard and Ruth Asbery, a black couple living at 216 N. Bonnie Brae Stree.

What began with fewer than a dozen worshipers soon overflowed into the street. Jennie Evans Moore, a neighbor who would become Seymour's wife, walked over to see what all the fuss was about and began speaking in tongues and banging out tunes on the piano—though she had no musical experience.

For five days, seekers came to listen and participate. They beheld "a plain, common-looking man with a short beard and glass eye, not given to outburst," the Rev. Lawrence Catley of Pasadena told the *Times* years later, recalling the meetings he attended as a 10-year-old.

Soon the porch caved in under the visitors' weight. The neighbors complained, and the group moved to a church converted from a stable on Azusa Street, in what was then a predominantly black neighborhood. There, revival meetings began at 10 a.m. and often lasted past midnight.

For three years, Seymour and his partner, a white Methodist preacher named Hiram Smith, were considered the "best show in town for free."

As 1,500 people jammed into the 40-by-60-foot sanctuary, vigorous hand-clapping blended with the sounds of "bones" (cows' ribs), a washboard and thimbles, creating what was called "music of the spirit." Seymour's wife, Jennie, added the sound of the piano, and a violin player joined in. But the fiddle didn't last; too many people believed it had the devil in it and associated it with dance hall music.

"The power of the Lord was so great...it seemed to tingle your spine, and your hair stood on end," Catley recalled.

Hundreds of spirit-filled seekers received baptism by water at Terminal Island in San Pedro, while others were baptized in the Holy Spirit—without water—in the upper prayer chamber, or "tarrying room," at the church. The walls were lined with

This small mission became the vortex of an ecstatic Pentecostal worship—known as the Azusa Street Revival—that rapidly spread throughout the world.

canes, crutches and pipes left by the lame who claimed cures and the smokers who reformed.

Offerings were placed in tin mailboxes nailed to the walls of the barnlike main room. Seymour's fund-raising approach always was low-key; he never pleaded for more money or passed a plate or basket.

From 1906 to 1908, the Azusa Street Revival church printed a religious newspaper called the *Apostolic Faith* that achieved a circulation of 50,000. But the racial split that would weaken the church prevailed there, too: Two Caucasian women who worked on the staff left the paper and took the subscription list to start their own publication in Oregon.

Meanwhile, newspaper reports on the phenomenon created by Seymour ranged from condescendingly skeptical to racially hostile.

One contemporary account described the Azusa Street services thus: "Disgraceful intermingling of the races, they cry and make howling noises all day and into the night. They run, jump, shake all over, shout to the top of their voice, spin around in circles, fall out on the sawdust-blanketed floor jerking, kicking and rolling all over it. Some of them pass out and do not move for hours as though they were dead.

"These people appear to be mad, mentally deranged or under a spell. They claim to be filled with the

The converted stable, still standing today, from which Seymour ran the Azusa Street Revival Church. Courtesy of Fred Berry, Joshua Ministries.

Jennie Evans Moore, a neighbor who would become Seymour's wife, walked over to see what all the fuss was about and began speaking in tongues and banging out tunes on the piano—though she had no musical experience.

Spirit. They have a one-eyed, illiterate Negro as their preacher who stays on his knees much of the time with his head hidden between wooden milk crates. He doesn't talk very much, but at times he can be heard shouting 'Repent!' and he's supposed to be running the thing."

But while some were quick to criticize, others were even quicker to join in.

The humble and famous from around the country flocked to the church, eager to catch the spiritual fever. Arabella Huntington, wife of industrialist Henry Huntington, attended on at least two occasions.

Out-of-town ministers—concerned even then that Sunday is the most segregated day of the week in America—secretly sought to learn Seymour's success in bringing blacks and whites together. But in 1909 his own congregation bowed to the racial prejudices of the time and split along black-white lines. Members left and began constructing separate churches and denominations that still exist apart today.

Against formidable odds, Seymour's Azusa Street Revival survived for almost three decades. After his death in 1922, his wife continued preaching until about 1930, when the members were working-class families who had the spirit, but not the money, to keep the church alive.

Seymour's radical experiment in multiracial worship didn't last, because whites were unable to accept a sustained role by black leadership, says Cecil M. Robeck Jr., a professor of church history at Fuller Theological Seminary who is writing a book on Seymour.

The little house on Bonnie Brae Street is being renovated as a museum and bookstore by Pentecostal Heritage Inc., a nonprofit organization that represents several Pentecostal groups. The organization also plans to honor the birthplace of the movement with a plaque and memorial wall at the former site of the Azusa Street Church, where the Japanese American Cultural and Community Center now stands.

Sister, Sister On the Air Were You Treated Foul or Fair?

Of all the evangelists who have blended showmanship with spiritual fervor, perhaps none is remembered in Los Angeles as fondly as the remarkable—and pioneering—Aimee Semple McPherson.

In the 1920s, Sister Aimee became the biggest show in town by blending outrageous, vaudeville-style theatrics with her upbeat cheerleading for Jesus. She established her own church, the Foursquare Gospel, on the Pentecostal tenets of baptism, physical healing, the Second Coming and redemption. Within five years of her arrival in Los Angeles, 240 Foursquare Gospel churches had sprung up in Southern California alone, with another 200 scattered throughout the country.

But at the zenith of her popularity, she was involved in a strange and possibly self-arranged "disappearance" that saw her reappear days after an elaborate memorial service

had been held in her honor. She claimed to have been kidnapped, but authorities called it a hoax and hauled her into court. Her reputation never fully recovered.

The Canadian-born Aimee Kennedy originally wanted to become an actress, but began to think of turning the stage into a pulpit after she attended a revival meeting at age 18. She later wrote that she gave herself to Christ in response to the preaching of Robert Semple, an Irish Pentecostalist whom she married.

Two years later, Semple died of dysentery in Hong Kong, where they had gone as missionaries. Aimee returned to America with a baby daughter, desolate and depressed. A year and a half later, she married Harold (Mack) McPherson, a solid, unglamorous accountant with whom she had a son.

The honeymoon was soon over. But Aimee recovered her zest for life after she decided she wanted to preach and discovered her gift for rousing a crowd. Mack wanted no part of a preacher's life and took off.

Aimee Semple McPherson in a 1935 portrait.

The honey-haired Aimee barely noticed.

With her children and her iron-willed mother, Minnie (Ma) Kennedy, she hit the road with $100, leaving Philadelphia in an Oldsmobile and arriving in Los Angeles in 1918.

To kick-start her church, she donned a leather cap with goggles and scattered religious leaflets from an airplane to promote revival meetings that she held at the Los Angeles Philharmonic Hall and in tents. It was a hint of the showmanship that would soon draw huge crowds and fill her collection plates to overflowing.

On New Year's Day 1923, Sister Aimee dedicated her newly built Angelus Temple, which still stands on Glendale Boulevard overlooking Echo Park Lake. The immense concrete building, with twin broadcasting towers and a revolving, neon-lit cross on its domed roof, became an instant landmark as the spiritual and theatrical base for the by then world-famous "Lady Evangelist."

She had designed it like a Broadway theater. Arranged in tiered rows, 5,300 seats dropped to the orchestra pit, where a young Anthony Quinn once played saxophone in the band, and then to the stage, where Sister Aimee sat on a red velvet–cushioned chair.

Her voice was backed by music from the temple's 30-foot golden organ; behind it all was a mural of Jesus with his hands outstretched toward Sister Aimee's flock.

From that point on, she was as famous and popular as any movie star, never failing to deliver a good show and sermon. She once compared Jesus Christ to the Lone Ranger, and once drove—dressed as a cop—onto the church stage on a motorcycle. "Stop!" she cried to the faithful. "You're speeding to ruin!"

She was as effective at raising money as she was at saving souls.

She would tell her Sabbath crowds: "I have a disease, an incurable disease. It is aggravated by the clinking of metal . . . but the rustle of that green soothes it!" She was also known to instruct her congregation of 30,000 at collection time: "Sister has a headache tonight. Just quiet money, please."

As the collection plates filled with money, so did the "miracle room" fill with crutches and wheelchairs discarded by the healed. Her claims to miraculous healing through the Lord brought in thousands, some of them suffering from incurable diseases, but many more hoping to witness firsthand the miracle cures they had heard of. One 10-year-old polio victim carried his shoes with him when he was brought up to her, so confident was he that he would walk again. And he did.

Her reach extended way beyond the lakefront church. A year after the temple opened, Sister Aimee began broadcasting "The Sunshine Hour" every morning over radio station KFSG, which stood for Kalling Foursquare Gospel, the name of her church.

At the zenith of her popularity, she was involved in a strange and possibly self-arranged "disappearance" that saw her reappear days after an elaborate memorial service had been held in her honor.

Postcards depicting Sister Aimee superimposed on the Pacific Ocean were passed out as souvenirs in the 1920s.

At one point, the station was shut down by the Commerce Department for "jumping frequencies." McPherson sent Herbert Hoover, who headed the department, this telegram: "Please order your minions of Satan to leave my station alone. You cannot expect the Almighty to abide by your wavelength nonsense. When I offer my prayers to Him I must fit into His wave reception. Open this station at once."

But the government minions stood firm on their wavelength nonsense, and Sister Aimee was forced to find a more competent engineer before the station could reopen.

It was a former engineer at the station—a married man named Kenneth Ormiston—who was to get Sister Aimee into trouble once again.

Dedicated in 1923, Angelus Temple still stands on Glendale Boulevard across from Echo Park Lake.

On May 18, 1926, Sister Aimee, then 36, disappeared while swimming at Venice Beach. Hundreds knelt on the beach for days, praying and scanning the horizon for her. The story made worldwide news. An airplane was chartered to drop rose petals on the waves.

Sister Aimee finally resurfaced 36 days later in Douglas, Arizona, telling a harrowing tale of kidnap by "Jake," "Rose" and "Steve." Her return to Los Angeles was a major triumph. She stepped from the train onto a carpet of roses, and as she paraded through the city, at least 100,000 lined the streets to greet her rose-draped car.

Her followers believed her story, but authorities did not. A major backlash followed her public triumph—perhaps, historian Carey McWilliams has speculated, because the Protestant establishment was irritated by her immense popularity. She was charged with "criminal [conspiracy] to commit acts injurious to public morals and to prevent and obstruct justice" and brought to trial.

For months, the burning question in a Los Angeles courtroom was whether Aimee Semple McPherson had been kidnapped, as she claimed, or had run off to Carmel with Ormiston, as authorities, who never found Jake, Steve or Rose, believed. Although the district attorney introduced evidence of some clandestine rendezvous in a Carmel motel during the lurid court proceedings, the charges were eventually dropped.

Sister Aimee called the scandal a plot hatched by the devil, and she embarked on a "Vindication Tour."

Although the most faithful among Aimee's following remained steadfast, her blemished reputation undercut efforts to increase the flock. She even lost face with the press.

Suffering from a severe mood disorder and estranged from her daughter, Sister Aimee was treated for a nervous breakdown in 1930 and put on medication. The pills became a habit, and in 1944 she died of a Seconal overdose while touring Oakland.

Her body was brought back to Los Angeles, where more than 40,000 mourners paid their respects. She was buried with a live telephone in her coffin, but there have been no reports that she ever placed a call from the beyond.

In her life, Aimee had blazed a trail for other women ministers. Nearly half the 411 churches she helped establish were headed by women. She was succeeded as president of the Foursquare Gospel Church by her son, Rolf McPherson.

By the 1990s, the International Church of the Foursquare Gospel claimed 1.73 million members at 25,300 churches and meeting sites worldwide. The church celebrates October 9, Sister Aimee's birthday, as Founder's Day.

L.A.'s Close Encounter With the Ballards

As an incubator of exotic spirituality, Los Angeles has been unparalleled from the start. No other place in America has given rise to as many mystic and spiritual alternatives, cults and creeds.

The editors of *Life* magazine called Los Angeles in the 1930s "a cuckoo land" and said "nowhere else do eccentrics flourish in such close abundance—or is undisciplined gullibility so widespread."

Of all the cults that have sprung up here, perhaps none has been so entertaining and indigenous-seeming as the I AM movement.

Founded by two self-described angels, it featured a blend of space travel accounts and prosperity tips that were a magnet to legions of the desperate during the Great Depression. To be sure, the cult's teachings brought prosperity to its founders, a former salesman and a storefront medium—neither particularly angelic—who launched the movement in the early 1930s and, ultimately, numbered their adherents at more than 1 million.

It all began—as so many religions have—with a vision atop a mountain.

En route to Los Angeles from Chicago, a former stock salesman named Guy W. Ballard took a side

Edna Ballard and son Donald as they were about to surrender to the U.S. marshal on charges of mail fraud.

journey to Mt. Shasta, the highest peak in the Cascades, near the Oregon border. Ballard had been obsessed since his childhood in the flat Kansas terrain with visions of a mother lode of buried gold and jewels and claimed to have "felt the energy" of this great mountain pulling him.

During his climb he said that he encountered a "majestic figure, God-like in appearance, clad in jeweled robes, eyes sparkling with light and love." His new master, whom he later identified, inexplicably, as St. Germain, tapped him on the shoulder and offered him a cup filled with "pure electronic essence," he said.

After Ballard imbibed it, the apparition proffered a tiny wafer of

"concentrated energy" that Ballard said he also consumed. Soon he and St. Germain were surrounded by a "white flame which formed a circle about 50 feet in diameter," Ballard said, and together they whizzed through time and space, visiting fabled cities and discovering a cache of gold and jewels.

Empowered by the divine messenger, Ballard raced to Los Angeles with his wife Edna, a former storefront medium. They formed a religion based on God's identification of himself as "I AM"—a sort of *Reader's Digest* condensed version of the Hebrew deity's proclamation, "I am who I am."

In 1934, under the pen name Godfre Ray King, Ballard shared his experiences—for a fee—in the treatise *Unveiled Mysteries*, which sold like hotcakes for the then-hefty sum of $2.50 a copy. His strange creed, lifted from a dozen sources, promised the faithful the power to acquire wealth and convinced them that he was bestowed with the gift to heal. His theology basically had two symbols, wealth and energy, and demanded that members abstain from tobacco, liquor and sex, which tended to divert the "divine energy."

As the "love offerings" rolled in from lectures and the sales of such religious artifacts as records, jewelry, photographs, cold cream and some sort of electrical device equipped with colored lights called "Flame in Action," the Ballards were able to buy radio time and rent the Shrine Auditorium for their preachings.

For a short time, the inner circle found a home in a rambling downtown tabernacle from the top of which a blazing neon light flashed "Mighty I AM." Buxom beauties, clad in evening gowns with orchid and gardenia corsages, ushered in the faithful.

The cult spread across the nation, enrolling converts through letters stating that the end of the world was coming and that the faithful should withdraw their funds from banks and life insurance policies and turn the money over to their immortal leaders. The high cost of spiritual enlightenment left many deeply in debt to family, friends and banks.

In 1939, the sect suffered a small setback when the immortal Ballard discarded the body that bound him to the physical universe and set off on his next phase of spiritual exploration.

A year after what skeptics insisted on calling his death, the I AM movement almost—but not quite—dis-

His theology basically had two symbols, wealth and energy, and demanded that members abstain from tobacco, liquor and sex, which tended to divert the "divine energy."

solved when guru Edna, her son Donald and eight others from the "inner circle" were indicted on 18 counts of mail fraud for collecting about $3 million from followers. Undaunted, hundreds of chanting supporters filled the streets outside the courthouse during their trials.

The defense said the nation's safety depended on Guy Ballard's divine power and influence. Before his death, the attorneys argued, an invisible force called K-17 had come to Ballard's aid and miraculously sunk a flotilla of undetected Japanese submarines ready to attack the United States.

Prosecutors declined to produce rebuttal witnesses.

Disappointed former disciples came forward with accounts of how the organization promised to restore the eyesight of a blind senator, but failed. Another member, a destitute 75-year-old woman, was assured she would be taken care of for the rest of her life and guaranteed protection in "the next world" after handing over thousands of dollars in jewels and cash.

"We're no more obliged to return the money or pay her bills than any ministers would be," Edna Ballard said angrily. "I know how to turn their evil back into them. If she'd brought as much love and blessing into the world as I have, she wouldn't be in this fix."

Atypically for the time, the trial was conducted with scrupulous care for the defendants' First Amendment rights. U.S. District Judge Leon R. Yankwich even swapped his black robe for a light-colored business suit out of deference to those on trial. "Many people here honestly believe that light and bright colors have a favorable effect on their soul's welfare," he said, "and I am not one to flout another's religious belief. I feel that if the situation warranted it, I could function as well in a bathing suit."

Two trials later, Edna Ballard and son Donald were convicted of mail fraud. After an appeal, the U.S. Supreme Court upheld the conviction, but later reversed that decision on a rehearing. Justice William O. Douglas wrote that people "may not be put to the proof of their religious doctrines or beliefs," even when their creed "may be incomprehensible to others."

Rejoicing and leaving their scandalous past behind, mother and son, along with 300 loyal followers, packed and fled to Santa Fe, New Mexico, in the late 1940s.

But the "white flame" continues to lure many followers. Now headquartered in Chicago as the Saint Germain Foundation, the group still has several Southern California temples and claims members in many countries, from Sweden to West Africa to Brazil. For three days each August, the I AM stages an outdoor reenactment of the life of Christ on a hillside near Mt. Shasta, their own holy mountain.

The annual summer conference, held on a 20-building, 200-acre property the foundation maintains near Shasta, draws "I AM" students from around the world.

Air Raids From the Pulpit

Seventy years before there was a 700 Club or a Christian Coalition, there was the Rev. "Fighting Bob" Shuler, whose fire-and-brimstone preaching won him not only one of the world's largest radio audiences but also a powerful voice in the politics of his adopted city—Los Angeles.

He led successful campaigns to drive officials from office and to make the Bible compulsory reading in state schools. At the zenith of his popularity, he narrowly missed being elected to the U.S. Senate.

And though he bears no relation to the Rev. Robert Schuller, who established the Crystal Cathedral "megachurch" in Orange County, Fighting Bob's congregation grew to 6,000 at its height. It was the largest Southern California congregation of its day and the precursor of today's evangelical powerhouses.

Fighting Bob was an equal-opportunity attacker.

At various times during the 1920s, his targets included the YMCA, the Los Angeles Public Library and the Knights of Columbus. From his bully pulpit at the downtown Trinity Methodist Church, he showered political brimstone, linking scriptural revelation and tabloid gossip in accusations against the politicians and lawyers he labeled the "criminals who spoil paradise."

Another frequent target was rival Aimee Semple McPherson, a Pentecostal evangelist with a huge L.A. following whose fame sometimes eclipsed Shuler's.

Like Sister Aimee, Shuler had his own radio station, KGEF. His nightly broadcasts were all the more popular for his readiness to shoot from the lip at the hint of a rumor. Shuler was always promising and delivering lurid revelations—true or not—to his eager audience.

Although he had a propensity for making trouble and publicity for himself, Shuler also was the most visible leader of the good-government Progressive movement, which campaigned to shut down Los Angeles' quasi-legal, police-protected gambling dives, saloons and houses of prostitution.

Shuler was born in 1880, the son of a Methodist minister in Virginia. Ordained at 23, he began preaching in the backwoods of his home state, Kentucky and Tennessee. He moved to Texas and then to Los Angeles in 1920, along with his wife and six children. Here he assumed the pastorate of the struggling Trinity Methodist Church, organized a half century earlier with only a handful of members.

His new congregation was eager for a taste of the unyielding evangelical revival then sweeping the country. Shuler didn't disappoint them. His fiery, revival-style preaching

Robert Shuler in 1929 court appearance on charges of contempt of court.

poured from the pulpit at 12th and Flower streets and from the pages of his privately published *Bob Shuler* magazine.

Like so many of his kind, Shuler also had a flair for promotion. One year, Shuler advertised a Mother's Day gift for the woman who brought the largest family to church. The winner, a Mrs. Hahn, arrived with her seven sons, including 2-year-old Kenneth, who later would become one of Los Angeles' master politicians. In fact, the widowed Mrs. Hahn so impressed Shuler that he instantly called for a special collection in her honor. It took in $20.

In 1923, Shuler got a tip that Los Angeles Police Chief Louis D. Oakes was spending his evenings in dissolute fashion. After catching the chief emerging from a sleazy hotel with a young woman on each arm, Shuler crucified him in a series of blazing sermons. Oakes was re-

He blasted away at the "real criminals," like the YWCA, which staged Saturday night dances that sometimes carried over to the Sabbath.

Shuler's church, Trinity Methodist, at 12th and Flower streets where he preached his hellfire and brimstone. It was torn down in 1982.

moved from office by the mayor, denied a disability pension, then fired from the LAPD for chronic alcoholism and adultery.

Shuler launched KGEF in 1927 with the help of a $25,000 contribution, and Los Angeles was never the same. He campaigned tirelessly for stronger morals laws and implored listeners to see the error of their ways.

He blasted away at the "real criminals," like the YWCA, which staged Saturday night dances that sometimes carried over to the Sabbath, and the Los Angeles Public Library, for putting books on its shelves better suited to "heathen China or anarchistic Russia."

Then as now, Shuler's brand of activism was bound to make its way into the courtroom, and there he met with a mixed response.

In 1927, Shuler and his right-hand man, the Rev. Gustav Briegleb of St. Paul's Presbyterian Church, went to the Follies Theater to see the much-talked-about "Hot Mamma Revue." The police commissioner was informed, and the theater was soon raided.

Although the pastors' testimony stirred up a storm during the week-long trial, it still took only six hours for an all-male jury to exonerate the 27 women accused of indecent exposure.

The Knights of Columbus were stung by Shuler's rabid anti-Catholicism, and he outraged the unflappable Mayor George Cryer by linking him to crime overlord Charlie Crawford—"the Wolf of Spring Street." Both the Knights and the mayor sued Shuler for libel, unsuccessfully.

Not long after the Follies fiasco, Shuler took to the radio and newspapers to denounce his former comrade Briegleb for accepting a donation of $25,000 and a $3,500 diamond ring from the now-reformed crime kingpin Crawford, who dropped the ring into the collection plate at St. Paul's. Shuler insisted that he would "baptize a skunk" before accepting an offering from Crawford. Briegleb held out for Christian charity while conceding that the church's building fund had a deficit.

In 1929, theater magnate Alexander Pantages was tried for statutory rape. Shuler charged on the radio that Pantages had bribed the jurors. When a guilty verdict was read, the bar association went after the preacher. Shuler was accused of contempt of court and sentenced to 30 days. He loudly claimed that he had been railroaded and that he welcomed his martyrdom.

Two years later, the Federal Radio Commission, precursor to the FCC, took away Shuler's broadcasting license for numerous abuses, including charging the president of USC with "monkey business" (allowing the theory of evolution to be taught) and the city health officer with ordering medical examinations of women by men (he hadn't).

Undeterred, Shuler unsuccessfully ran for the U.S. Senate in 1932 on the Prohibition ticket, receiving 564,000 votes in the general election.

His popularity dwindled further when he lost the 12th Congressional District race in 1942. "Many of the men in Washington charged with thinking and dealing with the destiny of the world are half drunk," he raved in the campaign.

Calling it quits in 1953—after wearing the clerical collar for a half century and ordaining almost 60 ministers from his Trinity congregation, including three sons—Shuler retired, yielding the pulpit to son Bob Jr.

In 1982, almost two decades after Shuler's death, the 80-year-old Trinity Methodist Church was torn down.

Fighting Fire With Love

Way before the rest of Southern California had discovered peace, love, long hair and beads, a way-out visionary who called himself Krishna Venta established a utopian commune in the crags above Chatsworth Reservoir.

He called it the WKFL Foundation of the World—for Wisdom, Knowledge, Faith and Love—and in 1948 he built a monastery among the sandstone formations of Box Canyon. His followers became known as angels of mercy in the 1950s for the aid they offered to disaster victims and others in need.

But their leader was a little too loving to suit some of his followers. Jealous because they believed he was sleeping with their wives, two male members of the cult blew it sky high with dynamite in 1958.

Born into this world as Francis Pencovic, Venta lived in Berkeley and toiled as an industrial worker before making his way to Los Angeles. To his new followers, he claimed he was born in a Himalayan valley and brought into existence directly by God, without human parents. He had no bellybutton—which he pointed out as proof of his divine origin. The cult in Box Canyon quickly grew to 53 adults and children.

"I may as well say it, I am Christ," Venta announced in 1949 upon returning from a trip to Europe. Even without a bellybutton, there was no convincing Pope Pius XII, who Venta said refused to meet with him.

The same year, after the performance of a Christmas Passion play, his followers—still in their costumes of cotton robes and bare feet—decided they would no longer wear shoes, or cut their hair, or dress in anything but long robes until the world was at peace.

The core values of Venta's faith were simple: universal love and equality, study and knowledge, and tolerance. He also taught that smoking is good for health, and that mankind came to Earth in 12 rocket ships powered by cosmic energy.

The premise of Venta's philosophy was contained in a chant: "Love one. Love ye one another. Love all. Serve ye one another."

His followers took the message to heart. They aided earthquake and flood victims, helped out in homes when there was illness. When a plane crashed in the canyon, they helped carry out the dead. They maintained a food bank for the homeless, and over the years the commune became a shelter for battered women and a rehabilitation center for alcoholics and drug addicts.

Most enthusastically—and controversially—they were volunteer firefighters who went as far as Bakersfield to battle flames. A *Times* article dated March 28, 1953, called the group "a disaster aid order" whose "gowns have been flecked by burning cinders of many fires."

But the Ventura County fire department didn't seem to want their help, and a miniature turf war erupted. In 1956, a fire captain refused to let any group members help fight fires farther than 200 yards from their monastery, even though other volunteers were called in to help.

He thought their long robes and bare feet were dangerous in fires. Even after cult members bought their own firefighting clothes, boots and equipment, firefighters were ordered to turn off the sirens when firetrucks left the station so sect members would not be alerted to a fire and follow the engines.

Meanwhile, Venta was crossing the authorities in other ways. He was charged with writing bad checks and, in 1949, was briefly jailed for nonpayment of child support.

But for the most part, the group was able to persist with its good

Krishna Venta shown in 1940 in jail, where he spent two hours on charges that he failed to provide support for his ex-wife and their two children.

He claimed he was born in a Himalayan valley and brought into existence directly by God, without human parents. He had no bellybutton—which he pointed out as proof of his divine origin.

Members of the WKFL Fountain of the World kneel in prayer at their Box Canyon colony in 1954.

The premise of Venta's philosophy was contained in a chant: "Love one. Love ye one another. Love all. Serve ye one another."

deeds until December 10, 1958. That was when Brother Peter (Elzibah) Kamenoff and Brother Ralph (Jeroham) Muller, who believed that their leader was having sex with their wives, set off a bomb with 20 sticks of dynamite, killing Venta, themselves and six others. Venta had recently thrown Kamenoff and Muller out of the order for disloyalty. They left a two-hour tape recording explaining their reasons, along with notes asking for forgiveness.

The explosion could be heard more than 20 miles away. The fire it touched off burned more than 150 acres. Surviving followers voiced the belief that, like Christ, Venta would rise from the dead. A few remained at the monastery; the rest moved to Alaska to join Venta's widow, Mother Ruth.

In the 1960s, the few cult members remaining in the canyon offered food and shelter for three days to another bearded man with a Messiah complex—the then unknown Charles Manson. He had dropped in for a little spiritual renewal before moving over the hill to the Spahn Movie Ranch in Chatsworth, and then to mayhem.

In the 1970s, several former members of the WKFL joined the Rev. Jim Jones' People's Temple and later died with 912 others in mass murder-suicides in Guyana in 1978. Other members went back to ordinary lives.

Venta, who called himself "The Voice," had said he could help his followers gain knowledge on their journey of 4,304,272,100 years to the spiritual realm. His mortal self is buried at Valhalla Memorial Park in North Hollywood.

Standing Their Ground

chapter

5

The Ballad of Pedro Gonzalez

Pedro Gonzalez was a Spanish-language balladeer and broadcaster who became a hero to the Mexican Americans of Los Angeles during his tireless fight for social justice. He came of age in the time of Pancho Villa and lived to be 99, but part of his life was stolen when he was railroaded into prison by political enemies.

Pedro Gonzales during his days as a radio singer in Los Angeles in the 1930s.

Banned from the United States upon his release, he resumed his broadcasts from Tijuana and lived out a life worthy of the *corridos*, or folk ballads, that he sang so beautifully.

In 1910 Gonzalez was working as a teenage telegrapher in a dusty village in Chihuahua, Mexico, when he was pressed into service at gunpoint by soldiers of Revolution leader Francisco "Pancho" Villa. Gonzalez had been working for the other side, secretly telegraphing reports of the insurgents' movements to government officials in Mexico City. Villa offered him a choice: Join the revolution or die.

Gonzalez saw the light, acquiring not only a new vocation but a social conscience he never lost. While escaping with Villa's men into U.S. territory, Gonzalez was shot by U.S. Army troops. He returned to Mexico to recover from his wounds and was apprehended by government forces. As he stood in front of the firing squad, several village children were instructed by their teacher to stand between Gonzalez and his executioners; they spared him rather than shoot the children. Years later, at a village fiesta, Gonzalez was introduced to one of his saviors, by then grown. Her name was Maria. They danced and, not long after, were wed.

In 1923, Gonzalez and his family emigrated to Los Angeles at a time when border crossings were freely allowed. Gifted with a rich tenor voice, he auditioned as a singer for a popular variety hour on radio station KMPC, but the station manager sent him away because he sang in Spanish. Undeterred, Gonzalez got his foot in the door by doing commercials for the station in Spanish, showing the manager the way to a previously untapped source of revenue.

Gonzalez and his newly formed band, Los Madrugadores (The Early Risers), were soon broadcasting a daily 4 a.m. wake-up call to L.A.'s growing Latino community. The ballads he composed, including the classic "Sonora Querida," were recorded and released by the Columbia label.

He became an instant folk hero, but his popularity with Latino listeners did not endear him to the city's white establishment, which soon labeled Gonzalez a rabble-rouser.

After he announced over the radio that workers were needed to clear some land, hundreds of Latinos arrived in downtown Los Angeles with picks and axes, ready for work. Police, fearing they were armed for some kind of uprising, responded by throwing them into paddy wagons. Gonzalez denounced the roundup on radio, and attempts were soon made to cancel his broadcasting license.

In the early 1930s, a few years before Los Angeles would roll up the welcome mat for Dust Bowl immigrants, it shut its doors to Mexican migrants. Immigration and Naturalization Service sweeps plucked about 600,000 Latinos, many of them U.S. citizens, off the streets of Los Angeles and summarily deported them to Mexico.

Gonzalez blasted the architects of the sweep as the "real criminals. . . . They say that this deportation campaign is to secure jobs for North American citizens. It's a trick. It isn't true. It's really nothing more than a racist attack against all Mexicans. We are neither illegals nor undesirables," he said during one broadcast.

He became an instant folk hero, but his popularity with Latino listeners did not endear him to the city's white establishment, which soon labeled Gonzalez a rabble-rouser.

Gonzales, shown here at age 89, was honored in 1984 during a celebration at the Centro Cultural de la Raza in San Diego.

His on-the-air opposition to the U.S. Department of Labor's "Operation Deportation"—which his folk-singer contemporary Woody Guthrie soon would condemn in his own ballad, "Deportees"—got Gonzalez in trouble with Dist. Atty. Buron Fitts.

Saddled by rumors that he had ties to organized gambling, Fitts needed help in getting out the Mexican American vote for his reelection. But after Fitts bought political ads on Gonzalez's radio program while at the same time stoking the anti-Mexican sentiments of white voters, Gonzalez turned against him on the air.

A year later, in 1934, Fitts had Gonzalez indicted on a trumped-up rape charge.

Gonzalez was convicted of assaulting 16-year-old Dora Versus and sentenced to one to 50 years in San Quentin. There he endured solitary confinement in a tiny cell and was once dunked in the prison sewer tank by malicious guards. Unbowed, he continued to agitate, organizing hunger strikes for improved conditions.

Versus soon recanted her accusation, admitting that she had been induced by authorities to lie. But a judge refused to admit the new evidence, citing a technicality.

Maria and Pedro Gonzalez at home in 1987. The couple was married shortly after Gonzalez was introduced to Maria as one of the young children who had spared him from a Mexican firing squad by interrupting the execution.

In 1984 Mayor Tom Bradley proclaimed December 22 "Pedro J. Gonzalez Day" in Los Angeles. His life story inspired a documentary as well as a 1987 feature film, *Break of Dawn.*

After a steady stream of Latino protests—including appeals by two Mexican presidents—and support orchestrated and sustained mostly by his wife, Gonzalez was paroled after serving six years and was ordered deported to Mexico.

On the day of his release in 1940, his train stopped at Union Station, where a crowd of thousands cheered him. He entertained them with ballads and songs for hours, until the train left for the border.

Settling near Tijuana, he formed a band and resumed his broadcasts, speaking out against social injustice.

In 1971 the Gonzalezes were finally permitted to return to the United States and become citizens, ending years of separation from their five U.S.-born children, two daughters and three sons.

In 1984 Mayor Tom Bradley proclaimed December 22 "Pedro J. Gonzalez Day" in Los Angeles. His life story inspired a documentary as well as a 1987 feature film, *Break of Dawn,* starring Mexican folk singer Carlos Chavez and Maria Rojo.

Pedro Gonzalez, unwilling revolutionary and unbending social activist, remained steadfast in dedication to his people on both sides of the border until his death near San Diego, at 99, in 1995.

Mrs. Rindge and Her Malibu Turf War

Few of those who scoot up the Pacific Coast Highway into Malibu or scamper along its golden beaches have heard of the woman who once waged war to keep them out of this paradise.

Her name was May Knight Rindge, and for three decades—from the turn of the century until the highway opened in 1928—she used lawyers, guns and money to protect the entire Malibu coast from public access.

To some older California landholders, she was a hero who would forever stand as a symbol of courage in the battle against the invading newcomers. But in a place like Los Angeles—for decades a mecca for sun worshipers—the public was destined to prevail.

The war was waged over one of the sweetest tracts of California ranchland ever to fall into private hands. A fertile valley overlooking the ocean, complete with a lake, a trout brook, wild trees and sandy beaches, it became a joyous retreat for millionaire Frederick Rindge and his family.

Rindge, a businessman and writer who'd inherited a fortune at age 26, bought the land for $10 an acre in 1892. Called the Rancho Topanga Malibu Sequit, it stretched 22 miles

May Knight Rindge, the "Queen of Malibu." Courtesy of The Seaver Center for Western History.

up the coast from Las Flores Canyon northward, reaching as far as three miles into the mountains.

In those days, the ranch offered splendid isolation; Rindge himself built the first road in from Santa Monica. But the isolation was not to last. As Los Angeles grew, travelers wanting a convenient crossing from Santa Monica to Oxnard came in a steady stream over Rindge's private roads by horse and by wagon.

The Southern Pacific Railroad wanted to run tracks across the sea-level property. The growing number

of motorists wanted a highway built along the coast.

Against them all, the Rindges wanted to enjoy the property they called "Sunset-Land" in peace and to spare its pristine beauty from careless campers and squatters, who set off dangerous brush fires. One of those fires devastated the land—and destroyed the ranch house—in 1903. Thereafter the Rindges raised their three children in town, in a magnificent home they built in the West Adams district near downtown. But they continued to use the ranch as a family sanctuary.

In 1905 Frederick Rindge fell ill and died. His grieving wife did not falter in the fight to preserve the land he had so loved. "Her eyes were brown and steady," recalled a friend, Lauretta Houston, about May Knight Rindge. "And there was no backing down when she made up her mind."

The press dubbed her "The Queen of Malibu." She became a formidable opponent to those who would corrupt her holdings, willing to spend a fortune and go to any extreme.

She built her own 15-mile railroad, complete with two major trestles at least 50 feet high, and used it to ship wheat and alfalfa down to her private pier and a waiting barge. Because a federal law prohibited the construction of parallel competing rail lines, the Southern Pacific was thwarted.

But that didn't stop the travelers or homesteaders who were encroaching on the land and were widely believed to be guilty of making a great many cows and pigs disappear from the working ranch.

In 1917 the Rindge family closed its private ranch roads to the public entirely. The only passage through was at low tide, along the beach. Homesteaders got an injunction, and county authorities opened the gates under a court order. Mrs. Rindge merely closed them again.

The battle escalated. The Rindges put up high fences and hired armed riders to patrol them and turn back all invaders.

In 1923 the courts established the state's right to eminent domain across "The Malibu," as the land was known. But state engineers and surveyors were blocked by the drawn pistols of Mrs. Rindge's small army of fence-riders. They retreated to avoid bloodshed.

Mrs. Rindge continued to fight them in court, but lost. In October 1925, a superior court handed down the decision that granted the state the right to proceed with the present Pacific Coast Highway (then called the Roosevelt Highway). The Rindges' Marblehead Land Co. was awarded $107,289 for damages to ranch property, a paltry sum compared to the $9,180,000 that Mrs. Rindge and her attorney had sought.

Sadly, Mrs. Rindge watched bulldozers encroach upon the Malibu. Soon a wide ribbon of concrete road divided her ranch, bringing the motoring world into her private domain. The highway was opened to traffic in 1928.

Among her losses, May Rindge could count in excess of $1 million a year in attorneys' fees—as well as her relationship with one of her sons, who sued her for bankrupting the family estate with the hundreds of criminal complaints and civil suits she had filed for trespass, libel and defamation of character.

As the battle wound down and her fortune dwindled, Mrs. Rindge began subdividing and selling off beachfront lots for $2,500 each in what became the Malibu Colony. The attraction was privacy as much as beauty. Uniformed guards at the entrances of the six-mile strip protected residents against sightseers and autograph hounds.

The Malibu Colony soon filled with movie people, among them Bing Crosby, Gloria Swanson, Gary Cooper, Ronald Colman, Barbara Stanwyck, Dolores del Rio, Jack Warner and Clara Bow. Adela Rogers St. John, journalist daughter of the great lawyer Earl Rogers, was also among the first to buy.

The Depression plunged Mrs. Rindge into bankruptcy. In 1941 she died at age 75 in her hilltop home on Harvard Boulevard in West Adams. Today the beautiful handiwork of its architect, Frederick Roehrig, endures, along with an inscription etched in gold above the grand ballroom fireplace by Frederick Rindge: "He who aims below the sky, aims too low."

In 1923 the courts established the state's right to eminent domain across "The Malibu," as the land was known. But state engineers and surveyors were blocked by the drawn pistols of Mrs. Rindge's small army of fence-riders. They retreated to avoid bloodshed.

The Rindge family built a magnificent mansion named "Sugar Hill" on a two-acre hilltop in the West Adams district in the early 1900s. Courtesy of Harold Greenberg.

Without Prejudice:
A Wartime Teenager's
Unswerving Friendship

He was an idealist who gave up his freedom to stick with his Japanese American friends while they endured one of America's worst social injustices.

When his teenage pals from L.A.'s Bunker Hill were rounded up and forced into internment camps during World War II, 16-year-old Ralph Lazo, who came from a Latino family, voluntarily went with them as a form of social protest.

With the others, he finished his high school years at Manzanar camp in the High Sierra, where he was so popular that he was elected president of his class.

Internment "was immoral. It was wrong, and I couldn't accept it," Lazo said later. The camps were a dehumanizing experience for many Japanese Americans, but the spirited Lazo tried to keep his friends laughing until the war was over and they were free.

On February 19, 1942—10 weeks after Japanese bombers devastated the American naval base at Pearl Harbor—President Franklin D. Roosevelt signed an executive order that approved the internment of

Ralph Lazo, circa 1985

120,000 Japanese Americans on the West Coast.

The controversial program was designed to protect national security, since all Japanese were perceived as potential spies. But groups like the American Legion, the California Farm Bureau, unions and all of California's leading newspapers demanded the internment not only of resident Japanese immigrants, but also of Americans of Japanese descent.

"Herd 'em up, pack 'em off and give 'em the inside room in the badlands. Let us have no patience with the enemy or with anyone whose veins carry his blood," wrote syndicated columnist Henry McLemore of the *San Francisco Examiner*.

Popular columnist Westbrook Pegler agreed. "To hell with habeas corpus," he wrote.

Among the handful of non-Japanese Americans willing to resist those hysterical sentiments was Lazo, a Mexican American who was growing up in the Temple Street neighborhood on Bunker Hill, in those days a melting pot of Japanese, Basques, Jews, Latinos, Filipinos, Koreans and African Americans.

His father—John Houston Lazo, a house painter and muralist—was a widower who spent long hours away from home working to support him and his sister, Virginia. Ralph Lazo frequently ate at the homes of his nisei (second-generation) Japanese American friends. He also played basketball on a Filipino Community Church team and enrolled at night in a Japanese language class at Central Junior High School.

"He was a real hustler who always made everyone laugh," said his high

Until his death in 1992, Lazo maintained close ties to the Japanese American community. He was one of 10 contributors who gave $1,000 or more to the fund initially used to prepare the class-action lawsuit against the U.S. government that finally won financial compensation for those who were interned.

school friend Yoshindo Shibuya, who is now a dentist in San Diego.

When his friends were pulled out of Belmont High and ordered to Manzanar, Lazo shared their pain and confusion. He helped in the sad task of hurriedly selling their personal belongings.

Soon afterward, Lazo resolved to go with them. When he told his father of his decision, he was purposely vague, allowing his father to believe he was going to a Boy Scout-type camp. Days later, when the headlines of a local newspaper roared "Mexican American passes for Japanese," his father knew the truth. But he made no effort to bring his son home. And despite the news story, internment camp authorities permitted him to stay. Aside from some who followed their spouses, he was the only non-Japanese in any of the internment camps.

Manzanar was located on barren, dusty land 200 miles northeast of Los Angeles in the Owens Valley. It was ringed by barbed wire and machine gun towers. For four harsh summers and four bitter winters, it

was home to 10,000 Japanese Americans, plus Lazo.

Everyone of Japanese descent was interned—young and old, sick and well, even 101 orphans and foster children, some as young as 6 months. Lazo was the only one who could walk out, but he didn't. He stayed and made more friends, who would remain steadfastly loyal to the country that had imprisoned them.

Lazo landed a job delivering mail for $12 a month. Later he was a $16-a-month recreation director. With his slight build, he became cheerleader for the camp football team, which played all its games at home because the squad was forbidden to leave Manzanar. He was elected president of his high school class, even though academically he ranked last among 150 students.

Toyo Miyatake, who was to become a famous photographer, was also interned there. With his contraband camera, he would point out to Lazo the beauty around them.

Despite the sacrifice he was already making, his country had no qualms about calling on Lazo to come to its aid. He was drafted in August 1944. A news release from the U.S. Department of the Interior, War Relocation Authority, announced: "America's only non-Japanese evacuee, Ralph Lazo . . . of Los Angeles will leave Manzanar Relocation Center soon to join the U.S. Army." Lazo served in the South Pacific, helping to liberate the Philippines, where he earned a Bronze Star for heroism in combat.

After the war he graduated from UCLA and later earned a master's degree in sociology from Cal State Northridge. He taught at several schools throughout Los Angeles and

Internment "was immoral. It was wrong, and I couldn't accept it," Lazo said later.

worked with gang members before becoming a counselor at Valley College, from which he retired in 1987.

Until his death in 1992, Lazo maintained close ties to the Japanese American community. He was one of 10 contributors who gave $1,000 or more to the fund initially used to prepare the class-action lawsuit against the U.S. government that finally won financial compensation for those who were interned.

His only regret: "that there was a Manzanar."

In 1994 the Manzanar High School Class of 1944 dedicated its reunion to the skinny Chicano kid from Bunker Hill, recording this sentiment:

"When 140 million Americans turned their backs on us and excluded us into remote, desolate prison camps, the separation was absolute—almost. Ralph Lazo's presence among us said, No, not everyone."

Members of the Lettermen Club of Manzanar High School. Lazo is on the far right end of the middle row. Courtesy of Archie Miyatake.

A Shot to the Heart

From the docks of San Pedro to the copper mines of Utah, Joe Hill was a legendary union agitator who helped form the Industrial Workers of the World and was immortalized in song and story.

Hill was the troubadour of the IWW, the Wobblies. His short and turbulent career was marked by a commitment to the downtrodden and a trademark sense of humor that endured to the moment of his execution by a Utah firing squad for a questionable murder conviction.

Although Hill's story will always be connected with his Utah trial and execution, it was in Los Angeles that he wrote the songs that inspired generations of workers and rebellious students.

He was best known for his bitter parodies of popular songs, published in the IWW's "Little Red Song Book," which proclaimed its purpose on its paper cover: "To Fan the Flames of Discontent."

Hill's masterpiece was "The Preacher and the Slave," set to the tune of "In the Sweet By-and-By." It made fun of "long-haired preachers" who console hungry workers with the promise that "you'll get pie in the sky when you die." Another was "Casey Jones— The Union Scab."

Founded in 1905, the IWW reached out to unskilled workers. Although many craft unions barred

Joe Hill, a prison photo. Courtesy of the Archives of Labor and Union Affairs, Wayne State University.

women and minorities, the Wobblies proposed one union for all. They sought to organize immigrants and the workers on the bottom of the economic heap, regardless of race or sex.

During the bitter union organizing that periodically convulsed Southern California in the early part of this century, the Wobblies filled L.A.'s jails and sang Hill's songs.

Born in Sweden in 1879, Joel Hagglund came to America in 1902, wandering across the country, working on the railroads and waterfronts.

He Americanized his name to Joseph Hillstrom and then simply to Joe Hill.

He drifted through life a loner, not knowing what he wanted or where he

I dreamed I saw Joe Hill last night,
Alive as you or me.
Says I, "But Joe, you're 10 years dead."
"I never died," says he . . .
And standing there, as big as life,
And smiling with his eyes,
Joe says, "What they forgot to kill
Went on to organize."
—Alfred Hayes and Earl Robinson

was going, until he reached Los Angeles, a fiercely anti-union town, in 1910.

Watching the Brotherhood of Railway Engineers strike against Southern Pacific, Hill became intent on rebuilding America as a socialist society and came to share the dream of creating one big union. He joined the IWW and began writing songs.

The Wobblies were not pacifists, and Hill was among those who believed that physical force was the best response to the violence sometimes used by management to suppress the unions.

A quiet man with a hot temper, Hill carried a pistol in a shoulder holster and hung out along notoriously tough Beacon Street near the fog-shrouded San Pedro docks. He found refuge at the waterfront's

Scandinavian Seamen's Mission, run by his preacher friend, Gus Lund. Hill, a teetotaler, drank coffee, wrote songs and played the piano for the homeless.

In 1913, Hill ran afoul of the Los Angeles Police Department, which habitually harassed radicals and what the *Los Angeles Times* then characterized as "union-labor parasites." After a streetcar robbery, the police went looking for Hill.

The charges were dropped when no one identified him as the holdup man, but Hill fled Los Angeles for Chicago, stopping in Utah to earn money. While staying with a Swedish family, he was arrested and accused of fatally shooting two people during a robbery.

Hill said he was innocent. No witness at the trial identified him as the gunman. No motive was introduced and no gun was found. When a friend of Hill swore to the police that the IWW man had been with him the night of the murder, the authorities ordered the friend to leave Utah.

But Hill refused to offer more than a cursory explanation of a gunshot wound he suffered the night of the robbery.

He said he was shot in the chest during a fight over a married woman, but gave no details and never revealed her name. Hill's gallantry, if his story was true, lent much to his mystique but seriously hampered his defense. In the end, prosecutors convinced the jury that a chain of circumstantial evidence, and Hill's failure to testify fully, was proof of guilt.

Hill was sentenced to death, but an international outcry ensued. More than 75,000 petitions for his pardon poured into Utah. Helen Keller publicly supported Hill, as

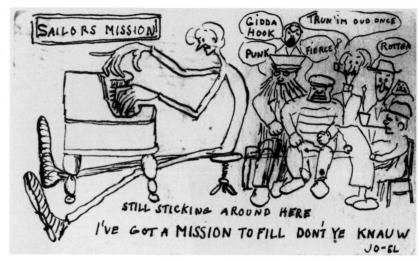

This postcard, drawn by Joe Hill, was sent in 1911 to a friend at Sailor Hall in San Francisco. Courtesy of the Archives of Labor and Union Affairs, Wayne State University.

did the Swedish ambassador and Samuel Gompers, founder of the American Federation of Labor.

When the uproar reached the White House, President Woodrow Wilson twice wired Utah Governor William Spry urging "a thorough reconsideration of the case." Spry responded by accusing the president of meddling.

On the eve of his execution, Hill sent a telegram to IWW chief "Big Bill" Haywood, asking that his body be hauled over the state line. "I don't want to be caught dead in Utah," Hill said.

Given a choice between hanging and a firing squad, Hill selected the latter. And in a final act of defiance, on November 19, 1915, while tied to a chair with a paper target over his heart, he yelled the order to fire.

His last wish was honored on May Day 1916, when tiny packets of his ashes were scattered to the winds, having been mailed to IWW

locals in several countries and every state—except Utah.

Hill's martyrdom made him a larger-than-life symbol during the next 25 years as the union movement accelerated. He had bequeathed his followers a legacy of courage and defiance, as well as a stern injunction: "Don't waste any time mourning. Organize!"

More than a half century later, Joe Hill was remembered at the 1969 Woodstock music festival, when Joan Baez sang these words: "From San Diego up to Maine, in every mine and mill, where working men defend their rights, it's there you'll find Joe Hill."

A decade later, on Hill's 100th birthday, labor leaders pressed the state of Utah to deliver a pardon. But the state attorney general's office refused, since the state's law contained no provision for pardoning the dead, however wronged.

A Man of Color's Unfading Passion

At the turn of the century, he came to California seeking opportunity and found discrimination instead. But rather than give up, young John Somerville resolved to make higher education his pathway to success—and, along the way, became a pioneer for social and economic development in African American Los Angeles.

The first black graduate of the USC School of Dentistry in 1907, he was joined in his practice by his wife, the former Vada Watson, who became USC's second black dental graduate. Together they threw their energies into creating a better Los Angeles, becoming leaders in the city's early civil rights movement.

John Alexander Somerville grew up in an educated family in Jamaica, where racial prejudice was unknown to him. A voracious reader, he fully expected to win a scholarship to college. When he didn't, he found work as a cabin boy on a ship and set out for America.

No sooner had he arrived in San Francisco than he and a friend were refused service in a restaurant because the establishment didn't serve blacks. Somerville was stunned. "It is hard to express the emotion that arose in my soul," he later wrote. "I was bluntly made to understand that because of the pigmentation of my skin, I was denied even the elementary necessities of life."

The following days brought more rejections: for housing and employment. But the 20-year-old would not be deterred. He resolved to work at any job, no matter how menial, until he could invest in a professional degree. "I wanted to earn a place where I would not have to ask any other fellow for a job," he said.

Drawn by a climate that reminded him of his homeland, he resettled in Southern California and worked in a bowling alley until he had saved the money to enroll in USC's dental school. But his presence caused an uproar. His new classmates convened a meeting and decided they would resign en masse unless Somerville was dismissed from the university.

They presented their ultimatum to the dean, Garrett Newkirk. But USC had issued a declaration in 1885 that said no student would be denied admission because of race, color, religion or sex. Newkirk called Somerville into the meeting and invited him to address the others.

Undaunted, Somerville spoke. "I am here today for the same purpose that you are: to seek an education leading to a profession through which I can minister to human needs," he told them. One day, he predicted, his fellows were likely to be ashamed that they had tried to block his progress "for no other reason than that the color of my face is different from yours."

Newkirk then informed the mob that USC intended to provide Somerville with an education, and any student who objected was free to resign. No one stepped forward.

Somerville went on to earn the highest grade point average in the class of 1907, even though he had to work his way through school. After he passed the state dental board exam with the highest score received up to that time, he set up his office at Fourth and Broadway, then the center of Los Angeles' black business district. He became a U.S. citizen and bought his first home at 1800 San Pedro St. By then he had also become the first black member of the chamber of commerce.

At USC he had kept company with Vada Watson, a liberal arts major raised by a mother who had instilled in her a strong social conscience and an appetite for achievement. In 1912 she and Somerville were married.

Meanwhile, L.A.'s growing black population, which had tripled in the first decade of the century, was being forced by restrictive housing covenants to reside almost solely in the Central Avenue district. Overcrowding was a serious problem.

In 1913 Somerville and others wrote a letter to W.E.B. DuBois, the black intellectual who had helped found the NAACP in 1911. DuBois came to Los Angeles to speak, and was put up in the Somervilles' guest room. That same year, the couple founded the Los Angeles chapter of the NAACP in their living room. John Somerville served as its president for 10 years.

As World War I approached, the Somervilles decided that Vada should become a dentist so she could carry on the practice if John were drafted. She was not just the sole black but the only woman in USC's dental class of 1918, and she became the school's second African American dental graduate.

But Somerville was not drafted, and so Dr. John and Dr. Vada shared the practice for more than a decade, until Dr. Vada retired to pursue a vigorous civic life.

Highly active in progressive politics, the couple hosted many distinguished visitors to the city, including Eleanor Roosevelt and Rosa Parks.

But Somerville wanted to do more to alleviate the housing crisis for African Americans. He decided to construct a first-class apartment building for blacks—but a bank president refused the loan, opining that Somerville couldn't attract "the class of tenants who are willing to pay the required rental."

It took Somerville only two weeks to secure advance commitments from 30 tenants eager for quality housing. He named the 26-unit building the La Vada apartments, for his wife, and opened it in 1925.

Even in the booming 1920s, most hotels in L.A. still refused to accommodate blacks. Somerville's response was to invest in the project that would become his lasting lega-

"It is hard to express the emotion that arose in my soul," he later wrote. "I was bluntly made to understand that because of the pigmentation of my skin, I was denied even the elementary necessities of life."

cy: the upscale Hotel Somerville, which rose at the corner of 41st Street and Central Avenue.

The hotel was a sensation. When it opened in June 1928, more than 5,000 people attended the gala. Among them was DuBois, who called it "a jewel done with loving hands" and "a beautiful inn with a soul."

Other investors took the hint, and capital began to flow into the Central Avenue district. The legendary Club Alabam jazz venue was built next door. Prominent African Americans like musicians Duke Ellington and Count Basie, dancer Bill "Bojangles" Robinson, comedian Eddie "Rochester" Anderson and writer Langston Hughes came to stay at the Hotel Somerville, and the NAACP chose it as the site of its national convention.

Somerville had stretched his resources to the limit to build the hotel, and when the stock market crashed in 1929, he was forced to sell it off. Still, it continued to thrive and play a vital role in the community. Its new owners called it the Dunbar, after black poet Paul Lawrence Dunbar. Under that name it became the center of Los Angeles'

John Somerville. Courtesy of the University of Southern California.

blues and jazz scene for more than two decades.

Somerville managed to recover his financial position and threw himself into political and civic activities. In 1936 he became California's first black delegate to a Democratic national convention. Ten years later he published an autobiography, *Man of Color*, and became the first black appointed to the Los Angeles Police Commission. In 1954 England's Queen Elizabeth II declared him an officer of the Order of the British Empire for his contributions to Anglo-American relations.

In 1972, shortly after the couple's 60th wedding anniversary, Vada Somerville died. Her husband, by then 91, died a few months later.

An inscription on a watercolor picture of a sailing vessel that hung in Somerville's home exemplified his attitude toward life: "Do not wait for your ship to come in. Row out and meet it."

Clearing the Air About Tokyo Rose

American GIs called her "Tokyo Rose," and in the public mind, she was painted as a traitor who broadcast sexy taunts over the airwaves to undermine the morale of soldiers far from home.

Iva Toguri, then 29, awaits trial in Japan in 1945 on charges of treason against the United States. She was one of more than 20 women whose voices were collectively known as Tokyo Rose during World War II.

The truth, when it finally came out, was just the opposite: She was a victim of wartime circumstances, a brave and loyal subversive who tried to come to the aid of her country and instead was imprisoned for treason.

Born on the fourth of July, 1916, in Los Angeles, Iva Ikuko Toguri grew up the daughter of Japanese immigrants in a mostly white neighborhood on Wilmington Avenue in Compton. She joined the Girl Scouts, had a crush on actor Jimmy Stewart, dreamed of becoming a doctor and graduated from UCLA in 1941 with a degree in zoology.

When her mother's sister in Japan was taken ill, Toguri was chosen to represent the family at her bedside. Toguri's mother was also seriously ill and would die the following year on her way to a U.S. internment camp.

Toguri took her first-ever trip to Japan at age 25, and in her haste to depart, left the U.S. without a passport. Instead, she had a certificate of identification issued by the State Department, with the assurance that it was sufficient to let her reenter the U.S.

But that was before the Japanese attacked Pearl Harbor. Suddenly the climate was rife with hysteria and paranoia, and Toguri was persona non grata in both countries.

In Japan she was classified as an enemy alien and constantly harassed by the Japanese government. The negative attention she brought upon their household became intolerable to her aunt and uncle, and they asked her to leave.

Penniless and hungry, Toguri asked Japanese authorities to imprison her with other American nationals, but they refused. With her English skills, she found work as a typist at Radio Tokyo, transcribing scripts to be broadcast as propaganda to American troops in the Pacific theater.

Here she met other English-speaking POWs who had been drafted into service, and made an exciting discovery: These Allied loyalists were waging a covert campaign to sabotage the Japanese propaganda effort. An Australian, Major Charles Cousens, wrote the scripts. Through on-air flubs, innuendo, double entendre and sarcastic, rushed or muffled readings, they spread their subversive high spirits to the GIs. When their Japanese supervisors got suspicious, they reverted to a robotic delivery to sound as though they were being forced to read at gunpoint.

The program was called "Zero Hour." Adopting the on-air name of "Orphan Ann," Toguri began taking her turn at the microphone, joining more than 20 other English-speaking women who took names like "Dutchy," "Little Margie" and "Madame Tojo."

Collectively, the female voices became referred to as "Tokyo Rose" in GI slang. Outsiders mistook Tokyo Rose for an actual person. The confusion would soon come to haunt Toguri. In fact, it would come to define her life and cost her years in prison.

Iva with her husband, Felipe d'Aquino, in 1948.

Collectively, the female voices became referred to as "Tokyo Rose" in GI slang. Outsiders mistook Tokyo Rose for an actual person. The confusion would soon come to haunt Toguri. In fact, it would come to define her life and cost her years in prison.

A typical "Orphan Ann" broadcast sounded something like this: "Hiya, keeds. I mean all you poor abandoned soldiers, sailors and Marines vacationing on those lovely tropical islands. Gets a little hot now and then, doesn't it? Well, just remember, fellas, while you're sweating it out on the islands, your sweet little patootie back home is having a hotcha time with some friendly defense worker. They're probably dancing right now to this number...it used to be your song... remember?"

Then music like Ray Noble's band playing "Good Night, Sweetheart" would crackle over the airwaves.

For war-weary soldiers and sailors in the Pacific theater, the broadcasts were a break in the boredom, not to be taken seriously. But the American government wasn't in on the joke; when the war ended, it arrested Toguri for investigation of treason.

She'd been singled out after she trusted an overreaching American journalist, Harry Bundridge, who was in Japan pursuing an interview with the mythical Tokyo Rose. He offered her a substantial sum of money to sign a contract identifying herself as "the one and only Tokyo Rose," and she agreed, unaware that Tokyo Rose was perceived as a traitor.

Later, when reporters asked her questions about her broadcasts of American troop movements and counterattacks, she was puzzled. On October 17, 1945, she was arrested by U.S. counterintelligence officers who didn't bother to tell her why. She spent a year in a six-by-nine-foot cell in Tokyo. Her husband, Felipe d'Aquino, whom she'd met while working at a news agency and been drawn to because he shared her pro-American feelings, was allowed to visit her only once a month.

When an exhaustive investigation by the Army, the FBI and the Justice Department failed to turn up evidence of treason, Toguri was released.

She rejoined her husband, and when she became pregnant, she applied for clearance to return home so her baby could be born in America. But her attempts were frustrated for lack of a passport.

Meanwhile, red-baiting columnist Walter Winchell was clamoring to have her put on trial in America. The American Legion and the Native Sons and Daughters of the Golden West issued strong protests against her return. Even the Los Angeles City Council joined in, passing a resolution against her return to her home city on the basis that she might adversely influence "loyal" Japanese Americans.

Ironically, Toguri had been the only civilian at Radio Tokyo who had refused to renounce her American citizenship.

Toguri was still stuck in Japan when her baby died at birth, perhaps due to her exhaustion and emotional duress. Shortly after that, Toguri was rearrested, charged with "treasonable conduct against the U.S." and brought to San Francisco on a troop ship.

For war-weary soldiers and sailors in the Pacific theater, the broadcasts were a break in the boredom, not to be taken seriously. But the American government wasn't in on the joke.

In 1949, when the jury deadlocked after a 56-day trial, the judge refused the jurors' request for dismissal, pointing out that the trial had been "long and expensive."

The jury returned two days later, finding Toguri not guilty on seven counts and guilty on one. Her offense boiled down to a single sentence: "Orphans of the Pacific, you are really orphans now. How will you get home now that your ships are sunk?"

Her attorneys had argued that this statement was not intended seriously and could not possibly have been taken that way, since the Allies had just won a major sea victory.

Stripped of her American citizenship, Toguri was sentenced to 10 years in prison and fined $10,000. She said goodbye forever to her husband, who had been forced to sign a statement saying he would never try to enter the U.S. again.

She served six years and two months at a women's reformatory in West Virginia, becoming a model prisoner. But the day she was freed, she was handed deportation papers sending her back to Japan. She spent two and a half years fighting the order, and won. The Justice Department also came after her, demanding payment of the $10,000 fine. It was paid in full from her father's estate when he died in 1972.

In the early 1970s a new generation of journalists began to reexamine her case. A campaign grew, contending that Toguri had been the victim of racism and wartime hysteria.

Twenty-seven years after her conviction, two witnesses who testified against her admitted they had been coached by the prosecutor and had testified under extreme duress. In 1977, President Gerald R. Ford granted her a full and unconditional pardon—the first time in U.S. history that a pardon had been given after a treason conviction. But she has never received an official apology.

Today, 81-year-old Toguri lives quietly in Chicago.

Iva Toguri d'Aquino waits on a customer in her small gift shop in Chicago in 1975.

Some Dreamed, Some Schemed

chapter

6

Winging It With a Million Ideas

In the years between the world wars, when California was the developing ground for almost every advancement in the field of aviation, much of the innovation was led by a restless and unconventional spirit named Jack Northrop.

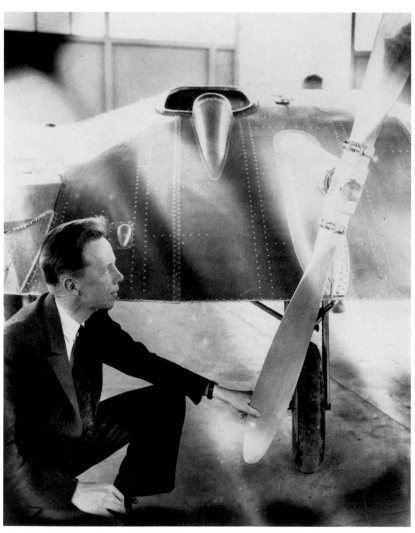

Jack Northrop studies pusher propeller of first flying wing design in 1929. Courtesy of Roy Wolford.

It was a time when the aircraft business looked a lot like the modern computer industry: a little luck and a lot of demand for a world-changing new technology transformed hard-driving backyard tinkerers and visionary mavericks into millionaire captains of industry.

But while competitors emphasized production and reaped fat government contracts, Northrop kept his focus on research and design, quitting company after company to start new ones whenever success threatened to slow him down.

Ultimately, his uncompromising spirit cost him his dearest dream when the Air Force scrapped production of his Flying Wing bomber after he refused an illegal order to merge his firm with a competitor's. It was a secret he kept for 30 years.

Born John Knudsen Northrop in 1895 in Newark, New Jersey, young Jack moved frequently with his parents until they settled in Santa Barbara, where he graduated from high school in 1913. He decided that school had nothing else to offer him.

"The idea in my family was that I should go to college, but I wouldn't do it," he said. "I thought I knew what it was I wanted to know, so I got a job that could teach me."

He became an auto mechanic for a brief time, and then a draftsman-engineer for three brothers who were building a twin-engine seaplane in a Santa Barbara garage. Their name

"Jack Northrop was a man with a million ideas, all of them good," Douglas would say of him later.

Northrop's new night fighter, as shown in late 1948. Courtesy of Roy Wolford.

was Loughhead, which they later spelled phonetically as Lockheed.

This happy partnership was interrupted by Jack's service in World War I. He tried to return to the Lockheeds after the war, but they had gone broke.

He hooked up with another future giant of aviation, Donald Douglas, who was hiring draftsmen to help build round-the-world biplanes. Northrop thrived there, and within four years had become a project engineer.

His response was to quit in order to focus on his own ideas—a move he would repeat over and over.

"The urge to back a few of my own ideas remained strong," said Northrop. In 1927 he partnered with Allan Loughhead and two other men in a new company, which they called Lockheed. Northrop was chief designer of their first project, a high-wing monoplane called the Vega, which was flown around the world by Wiley Post and across the Atlantic and Pacific by Amelia Earhart. It made their reputation.

No sooner had the aircraft taken wing than Northrop left Lockheed, in 1928, to found a company all his own.

"Jack Northrop was a man with a million ideas, all of them good," Douglas would say of him later.

Northrop's new company was called Avion Corp., and it focused on research in all-metal, stressed-skin construction. "I was following a dream," he admitted, "the flying wing."

Some called it his obsession: He believed he could reduce drag by incorporating all elements of an airplane, including fuselage and tail assembly, in the wing itself.

His first attempt with Avion made test flights in 1929 and 1930, but the aircraft was hampered by a tail assembly that hung behind the wing. "It was just the best I could do for the moment," said Northrop. That year, Avion was purchased by a unit of United Aircraft (which later became Boeing and United Airlines). Northrop was named chief designer and operating head, but he resigned to go his own way once again.

"I wanted to do things my own way," he said. "Having to check with a parent firm—even a good, forward-looking one—got on my nerves."

With W.K. Jay, who'd helped him form Avion, and supported by financial backing from Douglas, he formed the Northrop Co. in El Segundo. There he began work on the Gamma and Delta commercial aircraft, as well as the Army's A-17 attack planes, the BT-1 Navy dive bomber and other military aircraft. The firm prospered—so much so that Douglas used the clout of his financial interest to submerge it into his Douglas Aircraft.

Once again Northrop, who had been named general manager and vice president, resigned. He claimed he planned to take a six-week vacation and had "no plans of reentering the industry." No one believed him.

By early 1939 he had gathered the capital to set up a brand new company, with himself as president and chief designer-engineer. Located in Hawthorne, it would be called Northrop Aircraft. Its first project was a new Flying Wing.

"This time," said Northrop, "we did what I'd intended all along—a true Flying Wing—with pilot, power plants and cargo area all housed inside the wing structure."

The resulting airplane first flew in 1943 and led to many military innovations designed and built by Northrop. Among them were the highly successful P-61 (Black

Widow) night fighter and the F-16 Reporter, a photo-reconnaisance monoplane that could travel at 440 mph—fast for its time. Northrop also developed a sophisticated prosthetic arm for amputees and did pioneering work in celestial navigation systems that were the forerunners of the ones that guide modern missiles.

He received countless honors and awards, but in 1949 he suffered a severe and painful setback. By then his Flying Wing was poised to become the United States' prime strategic air weapon. He had developed a jet-powered version that had won a Defense Department competition, and he had a contract to build 35 of the tailless bombers for the Air Force, with a possible subsequent order for 200 or 300 more.

Then, abruptly, the Air Force canceled the contract and ordered the seven Flying Wings under construction destroyed. The order forbade Northrop even to save a single one for continued experimental flights or study. The explanation given was a vague "technical problems."

At the time, rumors that the Pentagon was using coercion in dealing with aircraft companies had led to an investigation by Congress. Northrop testified under oath that no coercion had been used against him or his firm in the Flying Wing contract.

Thirty years later, in a television interview, Northrop admitted he had lied. "Under pressure of the life or death of Northrop Corp.," he said, "I committed perjury."

He said the Flying Wing contract had been canceled after he refused an order from Stuart Symington, then secretary of the Air Force, to merge his firm with a competitor, Convair, which had taken a more conventional approach to designing strategic air weapons (Convair later got the bomber contract denied to Northrop).

He said he lied under oath, and kept silent later, because he feared further reprisal against the Northrop Corp. from Symington, who had become a U.S. senator and a powerful member of the Senate Armed Services Committee.

Symington denied Northrop's charges. "But that cancellation," Northrop said, "took the heart out of me. It stopped being fun." In 1953 he retired, saying he was doing so for reasons of health.

But he continued to work as a consultant and to write and lecture.

In February 1981 Northrop fell ill with pneumonia and died at a Glendale hospital. He was 85.

"Aviation was a fun job," he recalled in an interview shortly before his death. "I would get up in the morning eager to see what we could do with the planes. At night I would say, 'Tomorrow we'll see what we can do to make them fly better.' It was a big thrill every day.

"If I had it to do all over again, I would! And I don't think I'd change much of anything."

Northrop with the piston-powered XP-35 Flying Wing before its first flight, July 3, 1946. Courtesy of Roy Wolford.

"Aviation was a fun job," he recalled in an interview shortly before his death. "If I had it to do all over again, I would! And I don't think I'd change much of anything."

Earle Anthony's Well-Wheeled Future

In L.A., widely recognized as the birthplace of what has come to be called the "car culture," few recall the major role in that sort-of-blessed event played by Earle C. Anthony, a mechanic turned merchant prince to the motoring set.

Long before the internal combustion engine replaced equine transit on Los Angeles' streets, Anthony—a self-taught teenage mechanic—put the city on the horseless carriage map when he designed and built L.A.'s first electric vehicle: the "Anthony Special Runabout."

In 1897, about a decade after brothers Charles and Frank Duryea sold the nation's first gasoline-powered buggy, Anthony, whose friends called him "E.C.," shocked Angelenos with a half-horsepower converted buckboard that gasped and sputtered through the city's streets at the electrifying speed of 6 mph. (Anthony also was involved in L.A.'s first automobile crash when his "speedster" hit a pothole while accelerating down Beaudry Hill.)

The buckboard bender notwithstanding, young Earle had begun his full-throttle ascent on the road to success. Besides an automotive

Earle Anthony in the half-horsepower converted buckboard he built.

empire and gas station chain, his holdings would include a bus line, radio and television stations, neon signs, roads, bridges and a private castle called Villa San Giuseppe.

Illinois-born in 1880, Anthony arrived in L.A. with his family at age 12. While attending Los Angeles High School, he built his revolutionary runabout out of a buckboard, bicycle tires, wheelchair parts and a homemade battery.

Shortly afterward he headed north to study engineering at UC Berkeley. While there, he worked as a stringer for major newspapers and founded the school's humor magazine, the *Pelican*.

Returning to Los Angeles after graduating in 1903, he began to refine his vision of a future on wheels. Facing the challenge of making the city more friendly to the auto age, he took his $2,000 in sav-

Even while in San Francisco on business, Anthony kept up with is business operations to the south. He's shown here during the early 1940s at breakfast in San Francisco's posh Mark Hopkins Hotel.

Anthony, whose friends called him "E.C.," shocked Angelenos with a half-horsepower converted buckboard that gasped and sputtered through the city's streets at the electrifying speed of 6 mph. (Anthony also was involved in L.A.'s first automobile crash when his "speedster" hit a pothole while accelerating down Beaudry Hill.)

ings and purchased one of L.A.'s first car dealerships, at 4th and Hill streets. He soon was a distributor for 18 manufacturers, and by 1905 he had a toehold in the lucrative Packard franchise.

His influence helped his chums obtain the distributorships for other big car makers. Charlie Howard got Buick, and Don Lee took Cadillac. Another close friend, Bill Hewson, already had the Ford dealership.

Finding new ways of increasing car sales, this so-called "Big Four" bought the first full-page newspaper ads urging construction of a bridge across San Francisco Bay. These early road warriors led the way in the "good roads" movement that evolved into an interstate system.

Angelenos' passion for cars began to grow in 1909, when Anthony organized the first auto show in Southern California. In a tent at Pico Boulevard and Grand Avenue, thousands who had never seen a car looked in wide-eyed wonderment at the fanciful displays.

That same year, the city's first gas station (a farm wagon with a gas tank on top) sprang up at Wilshire Boulevard and La Brea Avenue. Fuel was 10 cents a gallon. Motorists unlucky enough to live too far from the proto-filling station had to continue searching out grocery and hardware stores where gas could be purchased.

Tired of the inconvenience, Anthony and a group of fellow entrepreneurs opened L.A.'s first full-service gas station at Washington Boulevard and Grand Avenue, selling 200 gallons of gas in two hours in 1913. Within a year, hundreds of National Supply stations dotted the coast in a red, white and blue color scheme. The group cashed in on its quick success, selling the chain to Standard Oil.

In 1922, pioneering the local use of radio, Anthony mounted a five-watt transmitter to a breadboard on his kitchen table and began advertising his Packards to surprised listeners. His radio station was KFI, which soon became the West's first 50,000-watt, clear-channel station.

Two years later, using his initials, he launched another station: KECA. It was sold in 1944 in the wake of a

In 1922, pioneering the local use of radio, Anthony mounted a five-watt transmitter to a breadboard on his kitchen table and began advertising his Packards to surprised listeners. His radio station was KFI, which soon became the West's first 50,000-watt, clear-channel station.

---

new antitrust law, and the new owners changed its call letters to KABC.

Always quick to recognize new advertising venues, Anthony returned from a 1923 trip to France with three neon signs—a commercial art form perfected by Frenchman Georges Claude a little more than a decade earlier. The signs were an immediate sensation, setting off a rage for neon across America. Two of the original signs went to Anthony's newly opened dealerships in Oakland and San Francisco, and the third was erected in downtown Los Angeles near 7th and Flower streets.

The 30-foot sign glowed the word PACKARD with the logo of Earle C. Anthony Inc. below in smaller script. Like a movie premiere, thousands flocked to see it. Later, a smaller sign would blaze over the 1000 S. Hope St. entrance of his new dealership, which opened in 1927.

Propelled by his motto—"Don't waste time dreaming about it! If it's worth thinking about, do it! If not, forget it!"—Anthony built a four-story Taj Mahal of auto showrooms, designed by architect Bernard Maybeck, at Hope Street and Olympic Boulevard.

On the rooftop, radio antennas pumped out the KFI signal while 25 gleaming new cars sat on floors of Spanish and Italian tile mixed with marble and polished stone. Neatly groomed, white-coated service representatives greeted and pampered

prospective buyers as well as those waiting for service, which always included a wash.

Gulping drinks during Prohibition, Anthony courted movie celebrities and agents, betting a little of their stardust would rub off on his cars—and, of course, boost sales. Errol Flynn received a Packard with his initials engraved on the door, and actress Jean Harlow tooled around town and parked her Packard in highly visible spaces.

To please his wife, Irene Kelly, Anthony built a hilltop castle on eight acres in the Los Feliz area. But even that soon began to resemble a business investment as the retreat he called Villa San Giuseppe turned into an elegant playground for entertaining celebrities, including Leo Carrillo, Hedda Hopper and Virginia Farrell.

His career was not without controversy. In the 1930s, when President Franklin Roosevelt took to the airwaves to deliver his fireside chats, Anthony refused him free time on KFI. In the 1950s, when Anthony

vigorously campaigned to bring the Dodgers west, certain city council members dragged their feet. Anthony's radio station announced their names and home phone numbers in the interest of "public service."

After World War II, demand for Anthony's Packards began to decline. Returning GIs who migrated westward seemed to prefer the Buicks and Stude-bakers they had known before the war. When Packard put its logo on Studebakers for a two-year period, it was a crushing blow to Anthony's luxury car business. By 1958 the showroom was filled with Lincolns and Mercurys.

The man who helped create the city's car culture died in 1961 at age 81. His successes had been marred by a bitter marriage, and he and his wife frequently fought over their pampered son, Kelly. The father eventually banned the son from the radio and TV stations. Kelly died broke, just three months after his father.

Anthony's splendid auto showroom closed in 1962 and was purchased by Union Bank. His radio station, sold in 1973, lives on under new ownership.

Villa San Giuseppe still stands, nestled amid oaks and sycamores in a prestigious neighborhood on Waverly Drive. It has become a retreat for the Sisters of the Immaculate Heart of Mary and a house of prayer for priests.

The Dawn of Sunset Strip

He was a master of glitz and glamour whose flashy, celebrity-studded restaurants turned a sleepy stretch of hillside street into the fabled Sunset Strip.

Billy Wilkerson was already the founder and publisher of the *Hollywood Reporter* when he began dotting a onetime cow path with elegant nocturnal playpens for the stars—the Vendome, Cafe Trocadero, Ciro's and Restaurant La Rue. He also found time to help kick-start Las Vegas' transformation from a sleepy desert village with a handful of gambling shacks into an internationally renowned resort city.

But the center of the tireless Wilkerson's attentions remained the 1.7-mile Sunset Strip, between Los Angeles and Beverly Hills, in its heyday the haunt of some of the most raucous and charming characters in Hollywood's turbulent history.

Surrounded by poinsettia fields and avocado groves, his restaurants and nightclubs on the Strip were the places savvy press agents took starlets to have their pictures taken with established stars, where only the most famous commanded a regular table and where studio heads decided the fate of unwitting actors seated two tables distant.

All of it, of course, made good copy and great photos for Wilkerson's industry newspaper.

Wilkerson was born into an Irish Catholic family in Nashville, Tennessee, in 1890, the son of a professional gambler who housed his family in either plantations or shacks—depending on how the cards, the ponies and his luck were running.

Wilkerson set out to become a doctor, but in 1916, before he could get his medical degree, his father died, leaving a mountain of debts. Billy quit school to help his family and managed a New York theater before moving on to more lucrative speakeasies.

In 1930 he migrated west to Hollywood, where he founded the *Daily Hollywood Reporter*, the first entertainment industry trade publication on the West Coast. Within six years, Wilkerson moved his upstart paper to 6715 Sunset Boulevard. The printing was done in back; the editorial and business offices were upstairs. On the ground floor, Wilkerson ran an exclusive barbershop and an elegant haberdashery.

He wrote daily front-page editorials called "Trade Views" that drove official Hollywood mad. The feature made and broke many film careers. Incensed studio heads regularly

barred Wilkerson from their lots; at one time, in 1931, he was locked out of all the studios. But they needed him as much as he needed them, and the relationship would eventually resume.

An actor named Ronald Reagan became so angry over the paper's scorn for his abilities that he twice stalked into Wilkerson's office, only to slip and fall each time on the polished parquet floor. F. Scott Fitzgerald became so enraged over criticism of his lover, gossip columnist Sheilah Graham, that he waited outside the paper, hoping to challenge Wilkerson to a duel. But the author of *The Great Gatsby* and *The Last Tycoon* finally departed without incident—presumably for his regular stool at the bar at nearby Musso's.

It was, perhaps, a fortunate departure, for although history records nothing of Wilkerson's marksmanship, he was a formidable adversary in print. His personal motto was "Never forget a friend, never forgive an enemy."

In 1947, Wilkerson helped fuel a campaign of anti-communist hysteria with his relentless exposure in the Hollywood Reporter of movie stars, writers and directors whom he believed were sympathetic to leftist causes. The inflammatory effort, now referred to as the Hollywood Witch Hunt, led to the creation of the Hollywood blacklist, a list of people who were denied work because of their political beliefs (real or imagined), and ruined careers and friendships throughout the entertainment industry.

Once, as Wilkerson raked an accountant over the coals for skim-

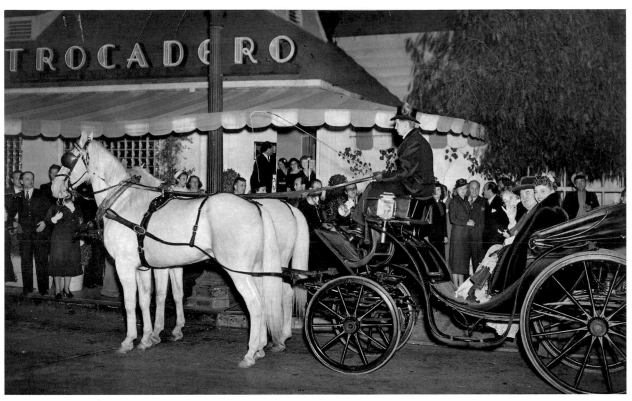

Guests at a Gay '90s party arrive at the Trocadero Club on the Sunset Strip in a carriage befitting the era they celebrate. The party was held in late 1937.

An actor named Ronald Reagan became so angry over the paper's scorn for his abilities that he twice stalked into Wilkerson's office, only to slip and fall each time on the polished parquet floor.

ming off the top, the unfortunate culprit suffered a heart attack and died. With no remorse, Wilkerson ordered the paramedics to take the body out the back door of his office, because a thief didn't deserve to exit through the front—not even into eternity.

Although the newspaper remained his passion, a visit to Paris convinced Wilkerson that Hollywood needed a restaurant with continental class. In 1934 he reopened a former roadhouse as the Cafe Trocadero, a smart French-themed late-night club at 8610 Sunset Boulevard. Soon agents began moving their offices to the Strip, where they were not only closer to their favorite tables but also exempt from city business taxes, because that part of

the street traversed unincorporated county territory.

Stars such as Lana Turner, Sonja Henie, Robert Taylor, Tyrone Power, Fred Astaire, Jean Harlow, Clark Gable, Bing Crosby and William Powell sat in the dining room, with its painted panoramas of the Parisian skyline, drinking champagne before taking to the dance floor as Nat King Cole sang or Harl Smith and his Continental Orchestra belted out a rumba. When Turner asked Wilkerson to be best man at her third wedding, he offered the use of his Bel-Air home for the ceremony.

His personal life was turbulent: He was married six times. Wife No. 3, Edith Gwynn, worked at the *Hollywood Reporter* even after their marriage ended. Wife No. 6, Tichi Wilkerson Kassel, helped guide the paper after her husband's death. She is now listed as publisher emerita.

Every Saturday night at the Troc, as it came to be known, the back room filled with the smoke from the cigars of Irving Thalberg, Darryl Zanuck, Carl Laemmle Jr., Joseph Schenck and Sam Goldwyn, who all had a penchant for high-stakes poker. Would-be stars such as Judy Garland, Phil Silvers and Jackie Gleason got their start by competing in "Amateur Hour" at the Troc on Sunday nights.

The chance to rub elbows with notorious but impeccably behaved mobsters such as Hollywood labor racketeer Willie Bioff, Tony Cornero, Mickey Cohen, Bugsy Siegel and Wilkerson's good friend Johnny Roselli only made the Troc seem more glamorous.

In less than three years, the Troc took in $3.8 million and was re-modeled three times at a cost of

$271,000. In 1937, Wilkerson sold it with the provisions that he and his family and guests could dine for free and that food and beverages would be delivered to his house, as well as to his mother's home, upon request.

In 1940 Wilkerson opened his next hot spot on the Strip, Ciro's, at 8433 Sunset (now occupied by the Comedy Store). LaRue followed. About the same time, he also opened the Arrowhead Springs Hotel, a gambling joint in the San Bernardino Mountains. But when he recruited three known mobsters from the local Clover Club to run his gaming operation, law enforcement officers raided the resort and closed it down for good.

Five years later, Wilkerson, whose compulsion to gamble sometimes cost him $20,000 a day, conceived a novel kind of recycling: He would open his own casino in Las Vegas, where such gaming was legal.

Three months before Benjamin "Bugsy" Siegel strutted into town, breaking hearts and noses, Wilkerson broke ground for the Flamingo on a 33-acre desert parcel purchased earlier that year for $84,000. But he had gambled away most of his construction money by the time Bugsy muscled him out of his ownership.

Wilkerson returned to his Bel-Air home and died in 1962.

The *Hollywood Reporter* has long since moved its offices to trade-paper row on Wilshire Boulevard. Its old Sunset Boulevard offices are now occupied by the *LA Weekly*. Wilkerson's ghost, however, is said to haunt what was once his second-floor office. Some say he sings during earthquakes, while others attribute to him a knocking sound that comes from beneath the original floor.

> F. Scott Fitzgerald became so enraged over criticism of his lover, gossip columnist Sheilah Graham, that he waited outside the paper, hoping to challenge Wilkerson to a duel.

Wilkerson, right, chats with actor Cary Grant, one of the many Hollywood stars who made the Trocadero a major celebrity hangout of its day. Courtesy of the Wilkerson Archives.

A Showplace In the Sky

Los Angeles has been home to many men of genius in the aviation field—from celebrated fliers to captains of industry. It's little known that some owed their early inspiration to a man who would never pilot a plane or even approach a drawing board, a visionary impresario named Dick Ferris.

Dick Ferris, left, with flyer Glenn Curtiss at the 1910 air show held at Dominguez Field.

A tireless promoter and man about town, Ferris had his hand in just about everything that was new and exciting in Los Angeles at the turn of the century and after.

An actor who headed his own theatrical company at the Philharmonic Auditorium, he also founded a racetrack, a sportsmen's resort in Baja California and the Yellow Taxi Cab Company. He was well known for throwing parties to celebrate his 38th birthday—year after year after year.

But Ferris is best known for mounting an event that would forever be remembered by some of the most influential figures in aviation.

In 1910, when planes were made of paper and pilots were made of brass, Los Angeles' aviation age sputtered to life in a beanfield.

On January 10, on a plateau overlooking San Pedro Bay, more than 20,000 flight enthusiasts gathered to witness the first International Air Meet in the country. Just seven years earlier, Orville and Wilbur Wright had sailed 40 yards over Kitty Hawk, N.C.

Ferris had visited France the previous year and witnessed the world's first air show. Back home, he pitched the idea to enthusiastic city fathers and town merchants. Soon an aviation committee was selected, and the ball was in motion.

Ferris mounted a campaign keying on the region's mild winter weather by naming each of the meet's 10 days after a city or state: Pasadena, San Diego, Arizona and so on.

City workers dug trenches for a gasoline line from a storage tank to the site. Potholes were filled on the unpaved roads, and three miles of wire fence went up to surround the 57-acre field. Huge tents were erected for the airplanes and mechanics. Three train-car loads of sawdust covered the grandstand and concession areas, and several water trucks would quench the crowd's thirst to the tune of 10 cents a glass—quite a price when you could get a beer for a nickel.

While the future was taking shape over their heads, 276,000 spectators arrived at the meet in buggies, mule-drawn wagons, trains and the then-six-year-old Red Cars.

Smack in the middle of farmland, donated by the Dominguez family, onlookers set their sights on the wild blue and watched as biplanes and monoplanes roared into dizzying flips and spirals to the accompaniment of a brass band.

Smack in the middle of farmland, donated by the Dominguez family, onlookers set their sights on the wild blue and watched as biplanes and monoplanes roared into dizzying flips and spirals to the accompaniment of a brass band.

Glenn Curtiss flew this plane at Ferris' 1910 air show. He broke a world record at the time by getting it airborne in 6.25 seconds and within 98 feet. The previous record was 8 seconds and 115 feet.

But all of a sudden the music stopped as the young and daring French aviator Louis Paulhan began climbing higher and higher into the sky. Ferris, with his coattails streaming in the breeze, ran onto the field shouting and shaking his finger for the band to continue. But it was useless. The bandleader and musicians stood transfixed, along with the audience, their mouths open in amazement as Paulhan reached a dizzying 4,165 feet, setting a world altitude record.

Ferris later said he had paid Paulhan $50,000 to participate in the event. With the notoriety the feat achieved, he got his money's worth.

Also at the meet was a tough 13-year-old street kid named Jimmy Doolittle, who one day would rise to become a World War II general and celebrated flier. Doolittle would later say the air meet changed his life forever.

Other pioneer aviators present were Roy Knabenshue, Edgar Smith, Waldo Dean Waterman, Charles Willard, Clifford B. Harmon and Lincoln Beachey, who five years later would fatally plunge his aircraft into San Francisco Bay, realistically, but inadvertently, demonstrating a suicide dive for 50,000 onlookers.

Georgia (Tiny) Broadwick, a 4-foot, 8-inch daredevil, thrilled spectators as she parachuted from a hot-air balloon hovering overhead, thus becoming the first woman skydiver.

There were only a few minor mishaps: Two pilots crashed before getting into the air, a plane caught fire on the ground and a pilot was struck on the back of the head by a propeller while trying to start his engine. He was not seriously injured.

The show generated a hefty profit and was considered a huge success. Gold medals were hung on the winners, who divided a $40,000 purse. The Rotary Club named Ferris "the father of Los Angeles aviation."

To a few, the sporting event was more than just romance and adventure. Like Doolittle, they had seen the future and would become the pioneers of the aircraft industry.

Five years after the meet, Glenn Martin, a professional "birdman" who would found the aerogiant Martin Marietta, started a company in Inglewood and hired Donald W. Douglas to work for him.

The following year, Douglas, an MIT graduate, opened his own business in a barbershop on Pico Boulevard. It was a business that would become synonymous with post-World War II commercial aviation construction before merging to become half of McDonnell Douglas and, now, a part of Boeing Corporation.

Today the site of the air meet is commemorated with two plaques. One was erected by the Native Daughters of the Golden West on the south side of Victoria Street, near the entrance to Cal State Dominguez Hills. The other, a California state landmark, is close by on Wilmington Avenue. A room filled with memorabilia and a detailed diorama of the meet can be seen at the Dominguez Ranch Adobe on Tuesday and Wednesday afternoons.

Most residents of the area are unaware that the nearby streets and a school are named for aviation pioneers such as Willard, Paulhan, Broadwick and Curtiss, and an entrepreneur who believed that "the sky's the limit."

Slaloming Along The Cahuenga Pass

Southern California has always been a place created by imagination: a desert that flourished with piped-in water; a sunny hamlet that became world famous for its photoplays; the home of Walt Disney, who created an empire from make-believe.

Joseph "Sepp" Benedikter shows off his moves on the slopes of the Cahuenga Pass to two appreciative "snow bunnies." Courtesy of Bill Southworth.

But for sheer novelty, few efforts have rivaled that of Joseph "Sepp" Benedikter, a daredevil Austrian downhill racer who, for one brief summer in 1939, established a thriving ski enterprise in a town where snowflakes are as rare as waiters with no acting aspirations.

Ski fever was just beginning to afflict the American West in June 1939, when Benedikter, encouraged by a group of film celebrities, opened his Pine Needle Ski Slope on a North Hollywood hillside.

Benedikter dumped 6,000 burlap sacks of pine needles on the hill, installed two rope tows and built a ski rental shop, where he introduced and promoted the new sport of dry-land skiing.

Under the gaze of grazing cows, Hollywood jet-setters and downtown professionals came out to play. Students included Ginger Rogers, Lori Saunders, Jane Wyman and Joan Bennett. Beneath a blazing summer sun, they dressed in fashionable bathing suits and shorts, strapped on long wooden skis and clung to a rope for dear life. They never had to use ski wax; the pine needles were slippery enough.

Benedikter began skiing at age 3 in his hometown of Badgastein, in the Austrian Alps. The next year, in 1915, he entered a race for children under 6 and won his first of more than 200 trophies.

He was one of five dashing ski enthusiasts imported to the U.S. from Austria, home to modern downhill skiing techniques, by W. Averill

Benedikter, far right, and some of his students. Courtesy of Bill Southworth.

Benedikter, encouraged by a group of film celebrities, opened his Pine Needle Ski Slope on a North Hollywood hillside.

Harriman, the railroad tycoon who had decided to boost business on his Idaho line by creating a ski resort at the Union Pacific's Sun Valley terminus. Along with others, Bene-dik-ter helped design the runs and organize the construction of the lodge. When Sun Valley opened in 1936, Benedikter was the first person to ride the world's first chairlift.

The innovation was modeled after banana boat conveyors that brought giant stalks ashore on hooks. At Sun Valley, they simply attached chairs instead of hooks to the cables. Before chairlifts, skiers used rope tows—or, in some cases, climbed six to eight hours with sealskins strapped to the bottoms of their skis to keep from sliding back downhill.

Hollywood stars flocked to the country's first true ski resort. Benedikter, with his chiseled good looks and toothpaste-ad smile, was soon sharing the limelight with them; he was typecast as a ski instructor in *I Met Him in Paris*, starring Claudette Colbert, Robert Young and Melvyn Douglas. In 1939 his Hollywood pals lured him to Los Angeles, where they'd formed the star-studded Wooden Wings Ski Club, which counted as members Gary Cooper, Errol Flynn, Henry Fonda, David Niven, Richard Greene, Tyrone Power, David O. Selznick and Lili Damita.

Benedikter's task was to teach them to ski. He made it pay by opening the enterprise to the public, after spreading pine needles all over the 800-foot hill between Lankershim and Cahuenga boulevards, where the Universal Sheraton hotel now stands.

But his craving for thrills and appetite for travel made him restless, and he left Los Angeles and the pine needles behind after one season to return to Sun Valley. There he won the first Diamond Sun medal for downhill racing in 1941.

The Idaho resort had taken off. Glenn Miller captured the nation's imagination with a new song, "It Happened in Sun Valley," as skiers arrived daily through the winter on a train called the City of Los Angeles. Again Benedikter was pulled away from his lucrative private ski instruction to double for Milton Berle in *Sun Valley Serenade*, starring Sonja Henie and John Payne.

The other Austrians who arrived with Benedikter at Sun Valley also prospered after their own fashion. Hans Hauser married gangland heartthrob Virginia Hill, the former lover of natty Bugsy Siegel. Friedl Pfeifer moved to Colorado to create a resort of his own, in a place called Aspen.

During the summers, Benedikter kept in shape by working at an Idaho logging camp, until a loaded truck rolled over on him and ruptured several discs.

Germany's annexation of Austria made him a citizen of the Third Reich, and even his show business connections couldn't keep Benedikter out of a World War II internment camp.

> **In July 1948, when snow was sparse, he jumped 110 feet across a highway lined with cars at Mt. Lassen in the Sierra Nevada. Later, lawmakers outlawed such antics after a less skilled leaper was killed.**

After the war, he returned to the Los Angeles area for good, settling in Tarzana and taking charge of ski schools at some of Southern California's newly opened mountain resorts. He supplied them with certified instructors from his latest business brainchild, the Far West Ski Instructors Assn., while still devoting part of his time to daredevil stunts.

In July 1948, when snow was sparse, he jumped 110 feet across a highway lined with cars at Mt. Lassen in the Sierra Nevada. Later, lawmakers outlawed such antics after a less skilled leaper was killed.

After developing Holiday Hill ski area (now called Mountain High East) near Wrightwood in 1949, where he built Southern California's longest double chairlift—more than a mile long—Benedikter again pushed the limits of sport with stunts.

To thrill hundreds of thousands of spectators, he built what was called the world's highest artificial ski jump at the Los Angeles County Fair in Pomona in 1951. He brought in the U.S. Olympic team for exhibition jumping off a 225-foot tower that sloped 500 feet. In the 100-degree weather, as much as 8 million pounds of crushed ice was blown onto the slope. It was packed down, in a preshow audience warm-up, by girls in shorts who tramped up the slope sideways on skis.

But when the drumroll came, no one on the team wanted to be the first to take the breathtaking leap. Benedikter stepped in and made the opening jump; reluctantly, the team followed. Each evening he led the team, weaving figure eights down the hill, illuminating their descent with torches. Later he reconstructed the jump at Dodger Stadium.

In 1956, after rain flooded the Los Angeles basin, Benedikter put on a pair of water skis and was towed by a car through a neighborhood at 23rd and Main streets. He even starred in a short-lived weekly TV show, "Ski Meisters," teaching viewers the art of skiing.

An "accidental engineer" who used his problem-solving skills throughout his skiing career, he also designed and built incline chairlifts and funiculars for apartment houses and homes on hillsides from Hawaii to Laguna. He later operated a general contracting business in Tarzana.

In 1964 Benedikter purchased a run-down ski area, Rebel Ridge near Big Bear, and converted it into a successful operation, drawing stars like Eddie Albert and Ann-Margret. He remained king of the mountain for five years, then sold it.

The skier's journey ended with his death in 1981, four years after he was inducted into the National Ski Hall of Fame.

Sin City, Three Miles Out

If you walk to the end of the Santa Monica Pier today, chances are you'll see sea gulls, sailboats and surfers on the waves. Half a century ago, if you had taken a similar stroll, you would also have seen the glittering gambling ships *Texas* and *Rex*, anchored just over three miles offshore. If you were feeling lucky, you might even have been among the 50,000 or so folks who ventured out onto the bay each week to test that luck.

In 1938, thousands of gamblers stood on the Santa Monica Pier each day waiting to be ferried out to the ships. Other floating casinos were anchored off Venice and Long Beach. But Santa Monica Bays *Rex* was the fanciest, and most lucrative, of all the gambling dens, taking in an estimated $20,000 a day from 300 slot machines, six roulette wheels, eight craps tables and a 500-seat bingo parlor.

Rex's owner, Anthony Cornero Stralla—better known as Tony Cornero—maintained that volume by catering to middle-class gamblers as well as Hollywood celebrities.

Cornero was an Italian immigrant who saw himself as a grateful, loyal citizen. His gambling ships merely provided outlets for his fellow citizens in their constitutionally protected right to the pursuit of happiness. If those outlets were illegal, well, there were ways to get around that.

Cornero's underworld career had begun during Prohibtion, when he reputedly made $1 million smuggling liquor from Canada into the United States. But his foray into the import business ended in 1928, when federal agents caught up with him as he tried to sneak 1,000 cases of foreign whiskey aboard an opulent gambling ship moored off Long Beach.

At his trial, Cornero said he was just trying to save millions of Americans from poisoning themselves on domestic bathtub booze. He was convicted anyway.

Never one to accept fate, Cornero escaped from the train taking him to prison. He spent two years in Europe—and engaged in more high-seas bootlegging—before deciding to surrender.

Two years later, when Cornero emerged from prison, he and his two brothers, Frank and Louie, sank their liquor money into a Las Vegas resort called the Meadows. But Cornero still had the sea in his blood. When Prohibition ended in 1933, he left the desert to invest his

Authorities circle the *Rex* in Santa Monica Bay during a nine-day confrontation in 1939 that led to the closing of Cornero's floating gambling operation.

Cornero was an Italian immigrant who saw himself as a grateful, loyal citizen. His gambling ships merely provided outlets for his fellow citizens in their constitutionally protected right to the pursuit of happiness.

Tony Cornero, far right, stands at the rail of the *Rex* with his assistants in August 1939 as they defy attempts by law enforcement officials to board the ship.

profits in Santa Monica's gambling ships.

For a time, Cornero and his new partners operated several gaming ships off the California coast—earning Tony the nickname "Admiral Cornero" in the press. But when he lost his share of the biggest boat, the *Tango*, on a roll of the dice, the self-made gambling czar decided to go into business for himself and set out to create a whole new standard for offshore gambling.

In May 1938, Cornero paid $23,000 for a 51-year-old fishing barge that he renamed the *Rex* and spent $200,000 to remodel. Tony didn't want any trouble with the law, so he did his homework and did everything by the book. He anchored the boat 3.1 miles offshore. By his reckoning, it was just outside California waters. To assure the public of his honest intentions, he placed a full-page ad in newspapers offering $100,000 to anyone who could prove any of the *Rex*'s games were fixed. He also asked the FBI to check the fingerprints of his employees, and said he would fire anyone with a criminal record.

Still, in a town that had grown notorious for backroom gambling and police payoffs, Cornero was anything but discreet. After all, keeping quiet about his boats wouldn't bring the public out to the docks in big numbers, and Cornero knew he was in a high-volume business. He hired stunt pilots to advertise the ship in the then exotic medium of skywriting, with two-mile-high letters spelling out REX over downtown. He took out full-page newspaper ads promising that "the *Rex* surpasses all the thrills of the Riviera, Monte Carlo, Biarritz and Cannes combined."

When reformer Fletcher Bowron (also known as "Old Chubby Cheeks") became mayor of Los Angeles in 1938, he promised to clean up the town's graft and corruption. But Bowron needed to get the goods on his enemies to do it. The mayor, a former judge and newspa-

During what became known as "The Battle of Santa Monica Bay," Cornero held out for nine days before law enforcement officers boarded the ship and began smashing gambling equipment and confiscating money.

At its height in 1938, the *Rex* attracted thousands of gamblers each day, including some who would have appeared more comfortable in a church bingo parlor.

per reporter, knew Cornero hated the city's dominant gambling syndicate because it had always barred him from operating in Los Angeles. So the mayor asked Cornero to meet with him at his home, high on a hill near the Hollywood Bowl. Cornero handed the mayor a list with the names of 26 of the police department's highest-ranking officers, who Cornero said were being paid off by the syndicate. The mayor had all the officers' phones tapped to gather the evidence he needed to fire them.

It worked. The police department was swept clean, and the town's dry-land gambling syndicate closed up shop overnight. But Bowron's gratitude was short-lived. Two months later he picked up a newspaper and saw the headline: "New Vice Setup in Los Angeles." A trusted employee of the mayor's had reported that Cornero and Bowron met "in a secret midnight meeting at the mayor's house." The story's implication was damning—that Bowron and Cornero were in cahoots, and Cornero was now assured of protection. To save his neck, Bowron quickly turned on his informant. He released a copy of an allegedly pre-dated letter to Attorney General Earl Warren seeking his help in putting Cornero's gambling ships out of commission.

Warren ordered an illegal wiretap on Cornero's phone and came up with a nuisance abatement charge that stated the casino "induced people to lead idle and dissolute lives."

On July 28, 1939, authorities in water taxis surrounded the *Rex*. The crew, under Cornero's command, erected a steel door over the gangway and fought off the invaders with fire hoses. During what became known as "The Battle of Santa Monica Bay," Cornero held out for nine days before law enforcement officers boarded the ship and began smashing gambling equipment and confiscating money.

During the battle, Cornero was heard to shout: "I will not give up the ship!" But he finally surrendered, dryly explaining that he needed a haircut. None of the material gained in Warren's wiretap was used in Cornero's trial, however, and he was cleared of violating state gambling laws.

Warren couldn't sink the flamboyant Italian immigrant for long. Cornero launched a new ship called the *Lux* in 1946, but was only able to keep it open a few days before Congress outlawed gambling in U.S. coastal waters.

The *Rex* was used as a supply ship during World War II, until it was sunk off the coast of South Africa by a German submarine.

On February 9, 1948, Cornero survived an attack by an unknown gunman who shot him at his Beverly Hills home, where he was living with his third wife. Ultimately he returned to Las Vegas to await the opening of his biggest project ever—the $6-million Stardust hotel. On July 31, 1955, Cornero died of a heart attack at a Desert Inn craps table. He was down $10,000 at the time.

L.A.'s Lord of the Rings

Sporting Los Angeles in the 1930s was home to racing dogs, floating craps games and that unique blend of machismo and show business called professional wrestling.

Lou Daro, who always wore a white carnation on his jacket lapel, returns on the train from New York, where he was elected president of the International Wrestling Promoters' Association in 1938.

Each week, all over the city, brawny men with colorful nicknames entered the ring to face opponents who would stomp, choke, slam or tackle them before hysterical crowds. Fans either didn't know or didn't care that the match had been rehearsed. Encouraged by splashy stories and pictures in the local press—written by journalists who were often on the promoters' payrolls—they bet wildly and illicitly on their favorites.

In the midst of this tarnished glamour stood Lou Daro, better known as "Carnation Lou." The robust, cigar-wielding wrestling promoter with the white carnation nattily pinned to his lapel had once been a circus strongman; he loved to boast that he had the greatest chest expanse of any man alive. But in the heyday of wrestling, he was keeping fit by lifting the sacks of cash that came his way.

Until the 1930s, professional wrestling in Los Angeles had been as legitimate as Wall Street—and almost as dull. Then Lou Daro arrived.

Daro had a show business flair and a booming, German-accented voice that rumbled across the Grand Olympic Auditorium, which had opened in 1925 at the corner of Olympic and Grand. Born in Austria in 1887, he ran away from home at age 10 to join a flying trapeze act with the Barnum & Bailey circus. He never went to school, but in his world travels he learned to speak eight languages.

By the time he was a young man, he had built up his physique and found a new angle: He was billed by the traveling circus as the "strongest man in the world." During performances at major venues like the New York Hippodrome and Madison Square Garden, he would lie in the center of the ring while an automobile loaded with passengers slowly rolled across his chest.

Daro came to love the greasepaint, the spectacle and the roar of the crowd. He challenged himself to create ever new ways to sell tickets. In the early 1920s, in what would be his last professional test of strength, he fought a tug-of-war with eight harnessed Clydesdales. One horse reared up in fright, and the injuries put Daro in a body cast.

He took what money he had and headed for Los Angeles with his brother, Jack.

No longer able to perform himself, Daro decided to test his mighty flair for show business in a new arena: performance wrestling. With Jack, he put together a stable of colorful figures who were willing to turn their contests into theater. The brothers' notoriety began in 1924, when they advertised instant cash to "anyone who can stay two minutes or three rounds with the Strangler"—Ed "Strangler" Lewis.

To guarantee a crowd, Daro gave away 50,000 free passes for a match in the downtown Philharmonic Auditorium, which had seats for only 5,000. As the masses pounded on the doors, Daro—to his delight— was arrested for inciting a riot, giving him publicity that kicked off his fortune.

The bouts used the basic choreography of today's "performance" matches, including such crowd-pleasing tactics as the flying tackle, the "belly bounce," the airplane spin and so on. Among the wrestlers Daro signed were heavyweights "Man Mountain" Dean and Jim Londos, known as the "Golden Greek," who smeared his body with olive oil.

After a decade of 433 wild, staged, overcrowded exhibitions and occasional riots at the Grand Olympic Auditorium, Daro's savvy showmanship had brought in more than $6 million in box office receipts.

But despite his riches, Daro was capable of ignoring his debts to others. Sometimes it came back to haunt him. An auto mechanic

The Olympic Auditorium, home to L.A.'s boxing and wrestling matches, shortly after its opening in 1925.

In the early 1920s he fought a tug-of-war with eight harnessed Clydesdales. One horse reared up in fright, and the injuries put Daro in a body cast. He took what money he had and headed for Los Angeles with his brother, Jack.

To guarantee a crowd, Daro gave away 50,000 free passes for a match in the downtown Philharmonic Auditorium, which had seats for only 5,000. As the masses pounded on the doors, Daro—to his delight—was arrested for inciting a riot, giving him publicity that kicked off his fortune.

Jack Daro, left, brother of wrestling impresario "Carnation Lou" Daro, poses with tow wrestlers he has just signed to meet at the Olympic Auditorium in a 1937 match-up. The two are Vincent Lopez, center, and Dean Detton.

named Leo Focher refused to give up on a $249 car repair bill that had gone unpaid for almost 10 years, since Daro's first impoverished days in Los Angeles. Focher showed up at the Olympic on July 10, 1935, to make another attempt to collect. Daro said he was too busy, and when Focher persisted in shouting at Daro, a Daro crony yelled, "It's a stickup!"

Focher ran to his car. When police arrived, Daro ordered, "Get that car!" A few blocks away, they stopped Focher; as he leaped out of his car, one officer shot him in the leg. Another shot him through the heart.

It was ruled justifiable homicide. But Focher's widow gave the blood-stained bill, which had been pierced by a bullet, to a reporter.

The reporter sent it to Daro and said he would clear Focher's name without mentioning the bill if Daro put $25,000 in a trust fund for Focher's family. Begrudgingly, Daro complied.

For a few more years he managed to stay ahead of trouble. In 1938 he was elected president of the International Wrestling Promoters Assn.

But the Daro brothers' misdeeds finally caught up with them. Their career as fight promoters ended in 1939 after a special state investigating committee found that the "wrestling czars of California" had an illegal monopoly and had paid more than $200,000 over four years to sportswriters, radio announcers, politicians and public relations firms for their alleged "good will, advice and entertainment."

Daro kept going for a time, but lawsuits and poor health eventually took their toll, and he died in 1958 at the age of 71. He was buried with his signature carnation in his lapel.

A One-Two Punch: Slapsie Maxie's Dual Career

"Slapsie" Maxie Rosenbloom takes a break from his workout at the gym in 1939 to check the day's opportunities at Hollywood Park.

He was a not-so-nice Jewish boy, a reform school graduate who nonetheless scored knockouts not only in the ring, but also on the stage and screen.

Famed as a fighter for his wild footwork and flurries of open-handed blows, "Slapsie" Maxie Rosenbloom parlayed his reign as light heavyweight champion of the world in the early 1930s into a successful comedy act and, later, a nightclub that became one of the era's Los Angeles landmarks.

Rosenbloom, who fought 289 professional bouts with 210 wins—only 18 by knockout—began his 15-year boxing career in 1923, when no less a figure than the legendary sportswriter Damon Runyon dubbed him "Slapsie" Maxie.

Born in New York in 1904, Rosenbloom started boxing his way out of Jewish Harlem at age 12, a year after he'd hit a teacher and knocked out two of her teeth. He served his time at a Jewish reform school and was released into the custody of a neighborhood pal, George Raft. The future Hollywood leading man steered his ward away from the ballet school his mother had enrolled him in and toward the

Rosenbloom allowed mobster pal Mickey Cohen to slap his name on a nightclub on Beverly Boulevard. The club featured such hot and up-and-coming acts as Jerry Lewis and Dean Martin, Jackie Gleason, Danny Thomas and Phil Silvers. Unfortunately, the signmaker at the successor club on Wilshire Boulevard, shown here, misspelled Rosenbloom's nickname. Courtesy of Marc Wanamaker/Bison Archives.

ring, where Raft felt Rosenbloom's skills might be more profitably applied.

From the beginning, Rosenbloom was a pugnacious youth who punched anyone who called him a ballerina. He was an eccentric fighter who got into shape by "dancing and prancing" in the gym. He was a defensive boxer—hard to hit. Offensively, his openhanded cuffs were delivered in startling bunches with playful footwork that confused his opponents and wore them down.

He also soon discovered he could make people laugh with his parody of a punch-drunk fighter.

On June 25, 1930, at age 25, he won an American version of the light heavyweight title from Jimmy Slattery in 15 bloody rounds. In 1932 he won the world title with a 15-round decision over Lou Scozza. Two years later Slapsie lost the title to Bob Olin in Madison Square Garden.

But his time in the limelight had brought him some glamorous friends, and he would soon find a new career in the movies. Actress Carole Lombard asked him to teach her how to box, saying she wanted to clip her future husband, Clark Gable, when she felt he deserved it.

In exchange, she put him in her 1937 movie *Nothing Sacred*, a Ben Hecht–scripted comedy about a conniving newspaper reporter that became a hit. Rosenbloom was terrific, and signed a contract with Jack Warner. Warner quickly sent him to Max Reinhardt's acting school to study diction. There he met Marlon Brando.

"He talked exactly like me," Rosenbloom quipped. "I learned to talk real good and went back to Warner . . . who three weeks later fired me because he said it wasn't the real me."

Washed up as a fighter but marked for life by the game with his flattened nose and cauliflower ears, Rosenbloom hung up his gloves for good in 1939 and returned to acting.

In the early 1940s, when his first and only marriage ended, he moved into the Hollywood Plaza Hotel on Vine Street, where he became a kind of living landmark for the next 30 years. A true New Yorker to the end, he never learned to drive. His friends would pick him up at the hotel and chauffeur him around from racetrack to racetrack.

Horses and the track were his great love—and ultimate downfall. Over three decades he made more than 100 movies, always playing a

Over three decades he made more than 100 movies, always playing a boxer or a comic tough guy, usually a B-movie-variety gangster, saying "dese," "dem" and "dose."

At the 1939 opening of their movie "Babes in Arms," Mickey Rooney and Judy Garland congratulate Rosenbloom and his new wife. Courtesy of *Herald Examiner* Collection: LA Public Library.

boxer or a comic tough guy, usually a B-movie-variety gangster, saying "dese," "dem" and "dose." All the money from those roles, however, went to cover gambling debts or was simply given away.

But even when he lost, he had his best friend, Gladys Parker, the *L.A. Examiner*'s cartoonist and creator of the comic strip "Mopsy," to bail him out of trouble.

Another favorite diversion was softball. Slapsie started a league on a ball field where the Beverly Center now stands, dubbed it "Rosenbloom's Ragamuffins," and attracted Hollywood friends such as Jerry Lewis, who played first base. (An offshoot of the league endures to this day, with games played Sunday mornings at West Hollywood Park.)

And his gambler's instincts sometimes paid off, as in 1946, when he lent his name to a pal, the dapper mobster Mickey Cohen, who wanted to increase his show business holdings.

Smack in the middle of a Jewish neighborhood, only blocks away from another of his investments—the Band Box nightclub—Cohen threw open the doors to Slapsie Maxie's at 7165 Beverly Blvd. Cohen's name never appeared on the deed; the club was managed by comedian Ben Blue and promoter Sammy Lewis.

Cohen put up more money to bring two struggling unknown performers, Jerry Lewis and Dean Martin, from Atlantic City to headline at the club. It didn't take long for Lewis and Martin to pack the club and become the hottest comedy team in America. When they weren't hassling and heckling young female patrons, Martin crooned ballads.

The club also featured a svelte and youthful Jackie Gleason, along with other showmen, including Danny Thomas, Joe E. Lewis, Phil Silvers and Peter Lind Hayes. Drinks were 40 cents and there was a cover charge of 25 cents, "to keep the riff-raff out."

Of course, the main attraction was always Rosenbloom and his impersonation of Little Lord Fauntleroy, one of his many acts. But within a year, when payroll checks began to bounce and the Spike Jones Band walked out, even Rosenbloom took his act to other clubs, including Hollywood's old Florentine Gardens, where he and fighter-turned-actor Max Baer left the crowd in stitches.

After the original Slapsie Maxie's went belly-up, businessman Charles Devore, who owned a chain of expensive men's clothing stores, purchased the club's name from bankruptcy court and reopened the nightspot in a new location on Wilshire Boulevard. But the new place didn't fare much better than its predecessor, and closed in 1949.

Rosenbloom's career continued in films, and his Broadway debut became his signature role—the gambler Big Julie—in the stage version of *Guys and Dolls*. In 1956, in the TV series "Joe Palooka," Rosenbloom played Clyde, Palooka's assistant.

But the spotlight dimmed on his show business career during the late 1950s. Desperate to stage a comeback, Rosenbloom set up a phony holdup in 1961 to get his name into the papers. He said a man had tried to kill him by firing a shotgun through his door and then disappeared. The newspapers reported it, but the studios never called.

The champ got one more round of applause, in 1972, when he was inducted into the Boxing Hall of Fame. It isn't clear, though, whether he took note of the event, as his final years were dominated by another souvenir of his years in the ring, pugilistic dementia. It made a particularly sad end for a man who had earned so many laughs portraying a punch-drunk fighter. Slapsie died in 1976 at age 71.

A Real Rocky Story

For more than half a century, it was a musty pugilistic monument—preserved in liniment and sweat—where generations of Los Angeles prizefighters learned the lessons of "the sweet science."

The Main Street Gym, on the edge of Skid Row, was the rattiest workout venue in the city, but it was also the most famous. "World Rated Boxers Train Here Daily" read a sign at the entrance, and that was no idle boast. Rocky Marciano, Floyd Patterson, Jack Dempsey, Muhammad Ali (then Cassius Clay), Joe Frazier, Jim Jeffries and Sugar Ray Robinson had all trained there.

From 1960 to 1977 the gym was run by Howie Steindler, a guy right out of central casting. He had decades of experience in the fight game and talked like a character in a Damon Runyon story. The old man was gruff, profane and deeply enamored of the boxing world. "Maybe it's my sense of humor that keeps me coming back, but I like this business," he said after a half-century in it. In the *Rocky* movies, the trainer played by Burgess Meredith was modeled after Steindler.

Steindler had a dream he never let go of: He wanted to manage a world champion, or at least a challenger. In 1977 his dream came true, when a fighter he trained at the Main Street Gym, featherweight Danny "Little Red" Lopez, won a world championship title against David Kotey in Ghana.

The Main Street Gym opened in 1933 at 321 S. Main Street as the successor to a nearby venture, the Spring Street Newsboy's Gym. It was a grimy little place where the bells bonged every three minutes and the dirty wooden floors creaked. Nonetheless, it drew the greats, along with the not-so-greats who didn't know a left hook from a fishhook. In 1951 it burned down while the night watchman slept, and the enterprise was moved across the street to 318½, atop the old Adolphus Theater.

Howie Steindler was an amateur featherweight fighter in New York who started training other boxers when he was 17. In 1942 he drifted to Los Angeles and worked as a crane operator at the shipyards. Later, as a prop man for RKO Studios, he met George Hansford, a former featherweight professional, and trained him for a successful comeback.

Steindler took over Main Street Gym around 1960 and ran the place like a drill sergeant in a boot camp. He had help from two savvy sidekicks, Arthur "Duke" Holloway and Rip Rosenburrow. Feisty, crusty and often sarcastic, Steindler cultivated a tough-guy persona but was known as a soft touch for anyone with a hard luck story.

With the Union Rescue Mission down the street from the gym, there

Howie Steindler in 1961

was plenty of hard luck around. Steindler kept a billy club hanging on the wall in case of trouble. Occasionally a bum would find his way up the stairs, and Steindler or one of his assistants would eject him with a few harsh words—except on rainy days.

His sidekick Holloway, a big man with a big cigar and a derby, nurtured some of the greatest, including Joe Louis, whom he trained back into shape after the champ was discharged from the service after World War II.

Black heavyweight champion Jack Johnson hung out at the gym in his later years, prior to his death in 1946, flashing his gold-toothed smile at the young toughs. Cocky heavyweights would coax the 60-year-old man into the ring. He would strip to the waist and put on his 16-ounce gloves, but he never

In the *Rocky* movies, the trainer played by Burgess Meredith was modeled after Steindler.

threw a punch. With his gloves, he just picked off every punch thrown at him.

Young boys routinely peered through a crack in the gym door, straining for a glimpse of their heroes, while others paid a dime or two for admission to watch sparring matches and champs readying for a fight at nearby venues like the Olympic Auditorium, Hollywood Legion Stadium or Wrigley Field.

In his time, Steindler trained more than 100 fighters and devoted his life to an enterprise that, many years, barely broke even. In late 1976 it all paid off when Lopez won the title fight. Steindler, by then 72, indulged in a flashy Cadillac to celebrate his victory. But four months later, Steindler's world would end.

On March 9, 1977, he locked up the gym, walked down the dirty marble staircase and got into his new Cadillac for the last time. On the street near his Encino house, he was jumped by unidentified assailants. They beat him, smothered him by pushing his face into the car's seat cushion, robbed him and threw him onto the floor in the back. They then abandoned the car with him in it on the Ventura Freeway, near the Laurel Canyon Boulevard off-ramp in Studio City. The slaying devastated L.A.'s boxing world.

Theories of what had triggered the crime were numerous. Steindler had reportedly become "difficult to deal

Sugar Ray Robinson, then a boxing tutor at age 48, fends off an attack by Ernie Lopez at the Main Street Gym in 1970. Lopez was preparing for a world welterweight title.

with" after Lopez won his world title, and there was talk of a contract hit by mobsters. On the day before his death, Steindler had tried to contact Sen. Alex P. Garcia (D-Los Angeles), a member of the state athletic commission, to discuss problems he was having.

For a while, LAPD detectives followed the leads of an eyewitness who had seen Steindler, on the street beside his car, get roughed up by two men on the night of his death. But police couldn't find suspects who matched the witness' descriptions. They were still looking into it 10 years later, but the case was never solved.

The Main Street Gym survived until 1984 and was featured in the first three *Rocky* movies, as well as *The Main Event* and other films. Its ambience was perfect for Hollywood, with life-size cutouts of champions and posters of boxers Joe Louis and Max Schmeling lining the peeling walls. A sign read: "Please do not bring children under 8 years old in the gym. We don't want anyone smarter than us in here."

Steindler's daughter, Carol, a lifelong boxing fan, assumed control of the gym toward the end, until it was demolished for a parking lot. She then managed another Main Street Gym, behind the Olympic Auditorium at 18th Street and Grand Avenue, until that too was torn down, closing a colorful chapter in boxing history.

A Rags-to-Riches Drama Unravels

He turned a backwater coastal town into a major center for legitimate theater, and became fabulously wealthy along the way. But his own rags-to-riches saga had a tragic third act—and nothing in his bag of tricks could bring back the applause.

Oliver Morosco came to Los Angeles in 1899, with $40 in his pocket, and became one of the greatest theatrical impresarios of this century. Magnificent theaters sprang up with his name on them; actors' and writers' careers were launched, and long-running Broadway hits like *Abie's Irish Rose*, *Peg O' My Heart* and *Bird of Paradise* were christened with his Midas touch.

But about 25 years into his good fortune, Lady Luck deserted him. After he fell in love with a young actress and divorced his first wife, he embarked on a downward spiral of lawsuits, financial disaster and ill health that left him without a penny to his name.

Born Oliver Mitchell in Utah in 1875, he had not seemed blessed at the outset. His father deserted the family. His mother took him and his older brother to San Francisco, where he joined a troupe of acrobats at age six. While performing on the iron railing of a restaurant, the spirited lad caught the eye of a wealthy theater impresario, Walter Morosco, who owned the Royal Russian Circus and San Francisco's Grand Opera House.

The elder Morosco took the fatherless boy under his wing. Young Oliver regarded him as a foster father and adopted his name. He went to work in the box office of the Grand Opera House and was quickly promoted—to part-time manager, press agent and treasurer.

Early on, he discovered a lucrative sideline: making high-interest loans to actors who borrowed against their weekly salaries.

Much later in life, when he was in desperate financial straits, Morosco would turn to his early training as a source of strength and hope.

"I began as an acrobat—I can still turn handsprings and do back somersaults—and I hope to do such feats financially as well," he said in a 1934 newspaper interview after he had filed for bankruptcy. "All I ask is one more chance to land on Old Man Hard Luck, and put him down forever."

But it seemed Morosco had gotten his share of chances earlier on in life—and he had run with them.

Young Oliver came to L.A. at age 24 with his new wife, Annie, their baby and his mother-in-law. Legend

Oliver Morosco and his wife, Genevieve, in 1936

has it that he owned only $40 in cash, but he also had the financial backing of his mentor, the elder Morosco, which enabled him to take over the ailing Burbank Theater on downtown's Main Street. The theater was no prize; it had been dubbed the "hoodoo house" for the bad luck it seemed to bring down on all who worked there. But Oliver Morosco dispelled the hoodoo forever.

He saw L.A. as a wide-open frontier. Theater in those times was sewn up by the Theatrical Syndicate in New York; its producers sent their traveling productions to Los Angeles and reaped profits in a young town eager for diversions.

Morosco decided that plays should originate in Los Angeles.

Between 1905 and 1922 he launched 84 new productions here. At the Burbank, he developed a stable of artists that at its peak included 500 actors, directors, writers and stagehands. He turned the house manager's role into something more like today's artistic director, giving the manager an active part in developing and staging plays according to his own vision.

For the first time, Morosco offered L.A. audiences new plays that drew on California history and the Western experience, such as *Under the Bear Flag*, *Rose of the Rancho* and *The Judge and the Jury*. And if the productions also contained wild tales of outlaw love, who could complain?

"The Best Players in the Best Plays in America for the Money," the Burbank advertised. As the film industry developed, it became known as a "stairway to the stars," launching actors such as Eddie Cantor, Charles Ruggles, Bebe Daniels, Charlotte Greenwood, Lewis Stone and Warner Baxter, the original Cisco Kid.

Morosco wanted more theaters. He sought out Dave and Moe Hamburger, who were building their namesake department store at Broadway and 8th Street in 1906. He convinced them that putting a theater next to their store would attract more customers to the area. They agreed, and Morosco's new 1,650-seat Majestic Theater sprang up, with an adjacent office tower in which he devoted an entire floor to a school for drama.

Business boomed, and in 1913 he opened the 1,450-seat Morosco Theater at Broadway and 7th. It cost $500,000 and was hailed as the finest theater in the country. Morosco added the Belasco theaters to his chain, becoming the biggest

> "I began as an acrobat—I can still turn handsprings and do back somersaults—and I hope to do such feats financially as well," he said in a 1934 newspaper interview after he had filed for bankruptcy.

manager of staged theater on the West Coast.

He was also one of the richest men in the game. His 1912 origination of *Peg O' My Heart*, starring Laurette Taylor, was a smash hit, inspiring a waltz, a cigar and a sundae named for its leading lady. When it went east, it ran for two years, with more than 600 performances. Some reports said Morosco netted millions in profits from that play alone.

Another play originated by Morosco in Los Angeles was *Abie's Irish Rose*, a comedy about the marriage of a Jew to a gentile. It went on to become the longest-running hit in Broadway history—but Morosco didn't share in those profits, having parted ways with the author in a legal battle.

Still, he was hailed as the "Oracle of Broadway"—New York's Broadway—and he built another Morosco theater on that city's West 45th Street.

But by 1919 his personal life had begun to unravel. His wife Annie had been with him for 21 years when she learned of his affair with Selma Paley, a former stage star who was then supervising wardrobe and scenery for all of Morosco's theaters. Annie sued for divorce, also alleging that Morosco had beaten and injured her on at least two occasions.

"His matrimonial affairs were dragged through the divorce courts most sensationally," wrote a newspaper columnist in 1934. Morosco married Paley when he was free, but his luck began to turn. A writer who claimed that one of his early hits, *Bird of Paradise*, had been stolen from a script she sent him, was awarded $500,000 by a jury who agreed with her. The first Mrs. Morosco had testified that she saw her husband using the plaintiff's script while he developed the hit production.

Morosco suffered more losses in a stock swindle. Meanwhile, nickel movies had become the new sensation, drawing 35 million people a week. With evangelists like Aimee Semple McPherson enjoying great success in L.A., Morosco attempted to stage "musical miracles" that added religious fervor to the bill, but they didn't catch on.

In 1926 Morosco declared bankruptcy, leaving many bitter creditors holding the bag for huge amounts. It didn't bode well for his future. Paley divorced him. Three more marriages, and two more divorces, were to follow.

Over the next 19 years, Morosco tried his hand at new productions and even writing, but nothing clicked. He began to suffer heart attacks, and once collapsed on the street. A stranger called an ambulance. In 1945, at the age of 70, he was struck by a streetcar on Hollywood Boulevard and died of his injuries. His fortune had vanished—he had just 13 cents in his pocket.

Had one of his plays ended that way, there wouldn't have been a dry eye in the house.

The Comedian Who Survived As a Sandwich

Patrons of Canter's Deli still come across his name, attached to a deli sandwich proffered to insomniacs with cast-iron stomachs. But few know that comedian Billy Gray was once linked to much more than chopped liver. Just steps away from where they sit, Gray ran a thriving, colorful nightclub—the Band Box—that was a mecca for Angelenos who liked their comedy blue and their company lively.

Billy Gray

In the 1940s, when Los Angeles' burgeoning Jewish population began leaving Boyle Heights, with its 30 synagogues and streets lined with barrels of pickled herring, Fairfax Avenue became the city's Jewish heart. Its status was confirmed when Canter's Deli followed its patrons west in 1948. The 24-hour restaurant set up shop across the street and down the block from the Band Box, a flashy comedy club that had attracted celebrities to Fairfax since the mid-1930s.

For three decades, the Band Box was where racy comedians kept audiences laughing. "Slapsie" Maxie Rosenbloom, Buddy Hackett, Polly Bergen, Alan King, Billy Barty, Don Rickles and Jackie Gleason all appeared there.

When Gleason began hosting a variety show for the short-lived DuMont Television Network, he tried out such now legendary characters as the boozy playboy Reggie Van Gleason III, Joe the Bartender and the Poor Soul on the raucous regulars at the Band Box.

Though it was owned over the years by various entrepreneurs, including comedian Lou Costello and labor enforcer Max Gold, the best-remembered Band Box proprietor was stand-up comedian Billy Gray.

Gray, born William Victor Giventer in New York in 1904, moved to Omaha, Nebraska, where he graduated from Creighton University. While studying to be a lawyer, he won a dance contest and decided to take up show business.

As a hoofer and comic, Gray worked the Los Angeles nightclub circuit before settling at the Band

For three decades, the Band Box was where racy comedians kept audiences laughing. "Slapsie" Maxie Rosenbloom, Buddy Hackett, Polly Bergen, Alan King, Billy Barty, Don Rickles and Jackie Gleason all appeared there.

Box in 1936. That year, an incensed patron slugged Gray, triggering a brawl that spread through the crowd. Actress Eleanor Whitney was carried out in hysterics, while Barbara Stanwyck and Robert Taylor watched the melee from a safe corner.

In 1937 Gray married the 17-year-old daughter of a prominent dairy executive. His in-laws offered him a partnership in the family business, but when that didn't work out, they asked him how much money it would take to buy him out of the match. That worked.

The marriage was annulled, and Gray, who would go on to marry three more times, walked away a richer man. He used part of his matrimonial windfall to buy the Band Box, officially changing its name to "Billy Gray's Band Box."

When Gray wasn't warming up Las Vegas audiences for big headliners or providing the voice of the baby on the Eddie Cantor radio show, he was the main attraction at his new 210-seat club six nights a week. Among the celebrities frequently found in his audiences were Robert Mitchum, John Ireland, Veronica Lake, Groucho Marx, Jack

In the 1940s, the Band Box was a popular hangout for the glamorous crowd that included movie actress Dorothy Lamour, right front. Courtesy of Marc Wanamaker/Bison Archives.

Benny, Betty Grable, Harry James, Sonny Tufts, Claire Trevor and Cesar Romero.

Another regular was a celebrity of a different sort—debonair mobster Mickey Cohen. In fact, after hours, the club was the venue for Cohen's nightly meetings with his henchmen. He also used the Band Box as his mail drop, receiving letters there under the name "Mr. O'Brien." (The FBI, Cohen reportedly figured, would never suspect him of using an Irish alias.) His two bulldogs, Toughy and Mickey Jr., came in for special attention from the club's cook, Jimmy, who prepared steak dinners for the pooches.

Cohen thought so highly of the Band Box that he forbade his associates to commit any act of violence there, because it would jeopardize Gray's liquor license.

On payday, the club's staff received a unique fringe benefit: At closing time, a bookmaker friend of Gray's would snap open his trunk full of hot items, which he fenced to the waiters at bargain rates.

Saints 'n' Sinners, a men's charity club, took over the Band Box one night each week for 20 years. The stag dinner meetings were emceed by Gray's attorney, Jerry Weber, who later did a bit of jail time for soliciting a bribe.

Gray ran into legal trouble of his own over a satiric review—"My Fairfax Lady"—produced by comedy writer and lyricist Sid Kuller, who penned lyrics for its keynote songs, including "The Street Where You Eat":

I have often walked on the street before.
But I never knew that borscht had been a beet before.
Indigestion comes, so I carry Tums
Knowing I'm on the street where you eat.

The show enjoyed a five-year run at the Band Box, from 1956 to 1961. But when Gray made a record album from it, he was sued by lyricist Alan Jay Lerner and composer Frederick Loewe because he'd never obtained clearances to their song "The Street Where You Live." Gray was forced to pull the record off the market.

Meanwhile, Gray was maintaining a busy career in front of Hollywood's movie cameras, with minor roles in at least 23 pictures, including *Two*

Cohen thought so highly of the Band Box that he forbade his associates to commit any act of violence there, because it would jeopardize Gray's liquor license.

---

for the Seesaw and *Some Like It Hot.*

In 1961, after a string of setbacks, Gray took his act on the road. Shortly after he temporarily closed the club's doors, the FBI—then pursuing a tax evasion case against Cohen—reopened them and seized all the club's records. The feds had finally stumbled onto Cohen's Irish nom de guerre, but no evidence turned up.

In subsequent years, Gray's career suffered from the public's changing tastes in comedy, his own ill health and his sorrow over the death of his 13-year-old son in a car accident.

The club closed for good in 1967, becoming a bank parking lot. But it took the new owners longer than expected to erect the bank, because for several months before the club closed, the waiters would steal a few bricks on their way home from work.

As Gray's health worsened, exacerbated by heavy drinking, his fortunes continued to decline. He was virtually forgotten when he died in 1978, 73 years old and on welfare.

But his name lives on at Canter's—still open around the clock, and still serving Billy Gray's Band Box Special: an open-face chopped liver, minced onion and chopped egg sandwich for $7.25.

The Father Of All Tommys

In the early part of this century, when many Los Angeles restaurateurs catered to the population's hankering for sophistication, one entrepreneur found remarkable success by doing just the opposite.

He set up a no-frills chili joint and called it Ptomaine Tommy at a time when food poisoning was no joke. Angelenos laughed anyway, and for decades they flocked to his hole in the wall, where patrons who could afford no better ate the humble, but addictive, fare alongside luminaries who definitely could.

Angeltown's most famous chili parlor began in Lincoln Heights on North Broadway in 1913, when law student Tommy DeForest spent $75 to open a six-stool lunch wagon. His enterprise proved so profitable that he abandoned his law studies at a time when he needed a living more than a degree.

In 1919, after serving a hitch in the Army in World War I, he opened a little eatery at 2620 N. Broadway. Ten years later, Tommy's moved two blocks south to 2418 N. Broadway, in a predominantly Italian-American neighborhood. The joint had a tiny U-shaped counter with a few booths and sawdust sprinkled on the floor.

Tommy's beans and hot sauce quickly caught the fancy of the sporting crowd and the pâté de foie gras set who wanted to go slumming. Over four decades, Tommy's customers ranged from Mae West, Mary Pickford and Dorothy Lamour to Bob Cummings, Robert Preston and the youths from nearby Lincoln High School.

Pictures of famous people hung on the walls, but fame alone was not always enough to qualify for such an honor. Tommy had an inflexible rule: "No matter how famous someone is, if he doesn't eat the grub in the joint, he doesn't hang."

Tommy was not the only entrepreneur in the family. His cousin, Lee DeForest, invented the vacuum tube. Tommy's claim to fame was the "chili size," a hamburger adorned with chili and "flowers" (onions).

In August 1958, Tommy was forced to close his restaurant because of financial difficulties. He died one week later. Family and friends say his death was from a broken heart caused by the loss of his restaurant.

At burger joints and diners all over L.A., Tommy's legacy endures. There will always be a chili size. But it will never taste quite like Tommy's—he took his secret red sauce recipe to his grave.

And though a chain of "Tommy's" chili-burger joints (and their knock-offs) has sprouted all over the city, they bear no connection to the entrepreneur whom true old-timers remember as having started it all.

Tommy DeForest and his wife join the white-uniformed staff of their restaurant in the early 1930s. Courtesy of Tom Romano.

Tommy's beans and hot sauce quickly caught the fancy of the sporting crowd and the pâté de foie gras set who wanted to go slumming. Over four decades, Tommy's customers ranged from Mae West, Mary Pickford and Dorothy Lamour to Bob Cummings, Robert Preston and the youths from nearby Lincoln High School.

Acknowledgments

In researching and writing these stories, I have benefited from the generous assistance, insights and knowledge of scores of people—scholars, librarians, journalists, artists, community activists, friends and colleagues.

Five individuals to whom I owe a debt of gratitude deserve special mention: Patt Morrison, writer-editor and talk show host, for teaching me how to take a piece of history, mold it into my own thoughts and words, then spin and weave it into a tale; Tim Rutten, *Los Angeles Times* city-county bureau chief, for his brilliant editing and unstinting encouragement and support; Gloria Ricci Lothrop, who holds the W.P. Whitsett chair in California history at Cal State Northridge, for sharing her great wealth of knowledge and supplying me with endless story ideas; Marc Wanamaker, historian and writer, for allowing me to pick his brain, always generous with his time and expertise, not to mention written material and photographs; and my close friend Burt Folkart, a retired *Times* writer whose friendship remains constant and invaluable, supplying me with editorial advice and writing tips day and night.

This book would not have been possible without the help of my bosses, Leo Wolinsky, Roxanne Arnold and Bill Boyarsky, who have been my incentive and my motivators. I also owe a special debt of gratitude to Contributing Writer Amy Dawes and Times Book Development Manager Carla Lazzareschi. My grateful thanks also to my husband, Jim Rasmussen, my champion, my friend, who offered advice, opinions and transportation to many of these historical spots. His interest and encouragement has helped me over many rough spots as I rooted myself ever more deeply into the past.

My deep appreciation to the many readers, colleagues and informed and resourceful individuals who have contributed greatly to my stories: Isaac Artenstein, Joyce Baker, Charley Barr, Mary Barrow, Dr. Charles A. Bearchell, Helen Benedikter, Suellen Cheng, Albert Cline, Ed Cress, Siegfried Demke, Tony DiMarco, Leon Dixon, Fredrick Dockweiler, Raymond Docter, Donald Duke, Ashley Dunn, Bill Estrada, Seymour Fabrick, Margaret Farnum, Greg Fischer, Sue Forgie, Harold Greenberg, Patrick H. Griffin, Earl Gustkey, Scott Harris, Arnett Hartsfield, Steve Harvey, Jim Hayes, Gary Hertzberg, Nieson Himmel, Bob Holly, Stone Ishimaru, Ruth Issac, Charles Knill, Verne Langdon, Milt Larsen, Joan Lavine, John Lucero, Eric Malnic, Joan McAllister, Rev. Patrick J. McPolin, Toyo Miyatake, Charles H. Mont, John W. Myers, Paul Michael Newman, Gary Nordell, Mary Olsen, Steve Pastis, Bob Pool, Ray Ramirez, David Reichert, Ronald Rindge, Val Rodriguez, Gail Ryan, Joseph Ryan, Elaine St. Johns, Stephen Sass, Rosemary Silvey, Rich Simon, Bill Southworth, Jeff Stanton, Rudy Tellez, Marty Tregnan, John Underwood, Juliana Waycus, Msgr. Francis Weber, Willie Wilkerson, Doris Wong, Dr. Murray Zimmerman and Larry Zuckerman.

Librarians, archivists, curators, museum administrators and friends and acquaintances in the history field ferreted out specific information and photographs. Among them were: Michael Salmon and Shirley Ito, Amateur Athletic Foundation; Robbin Goddard and the *Times* Photo Department for photographic printing for this project; George Kirkman, Santa Monica Museum of Flying; Richard Kalk and Birget Aviles, Los Angeles Police Department Historical Society; Miles Kreuger, The Institute of the American Musical, Inc.; Carolyn Kozo Cole and Glen Creason, L.A. City Library; Virginia Elwood-Akers, librarian, Cal State Northridge; Carolyn Garner, Pasadena City Library; Dace Taube, USC Regional History Center; Tom Sitton and Tom Cahoon, Los Angeles Natural History Museum, Seaver Center for Western History Research; Mayme A. Clayton, Western States Black Research and Educational Center; Tom Tomlinson, USC Law School; Japanese Cultural Center; Southern California Historical Society; Southwest Museum; L.A. Conservancy; Huntington Library; and Bureau of Indian Affairs, Riverside.

I also want to give credit to the *L.A. Times* librarians: Jacquelyn Cenacveira, Peg Eby-Jager, Julia Franco, William Holmes, Peter Johnson, Janet Lundblad, Robin Mayper, Maloy Moore, Cary Schneider, Paul Singleton, Steve Tice and Scott Wilson. And photo librarians: David Cappoli, Ed Natividad, Marcia Nuñez-Valenzuela, Suzanne Oatey, Gay Raszkiewicz, Chris Rice, Mildred Simpson, John Tryell and Laura Ugalde.

And my apologies to contributors I have omitted.

Index